Kevin Cooney

Blue skies
AND
stormy days

The further memoirs of a sailing man

Mereo Books

2nd Floor, 6-8 Dyer Street, Cirencester, Gloucestershire, GL7 2PF. An imprint of
Memoirs Books. www.mereobooks.com and www.memoirsbooks.co.uk

Blue skies and stormy days

ISBN: 978-1-86151-820-0

First published in Great Britain in 2022

by Mereo Books, an imprint of Memoirs Books.

The address for Memoirs Books can be found at www.mereobooks.com

Mereo Books Ltd. Reg. No. 12157152

Typeset in 9/15pt Century Schoolbook by Wiltshire Associates.

Printed and bound in Great Britain

Contents

Introduction
Dedication
Acknowledgements

Introduction

One day while I was sorting out various diary entries and logs of sailing trips and putting them in order, I realised that many of the stories were in danger of being lost unless I put them together. I then decided to write this record of sailing trips and related events as I saw them.

My various crews over the years may have seen some of these happenings differently, but I hope we are all still friends and that they value their experiences sailing with me and have mostly happy memories. I certainly do, and I hope that reading my version of events will reawaken memories of some of the drama, pleasure and enjoyment of those times, and perhaps make them smile or even chuckle to themselves as they remember the parts they played in the story.

Dedication

To the person who has stood by me through good times and bad, backed me up in all things and been my rock for over 50 years – my wonderful wife Ann.

Acknowledgements

I would like to thank the crew on two of my Atlantic crossings: Laurie Mullaney, who joined me on a trip from Bermuda to the Azores in *Forever in Blue Jeans* in 2001 and in *Blue Genie* for the ARC in 2002, and Terry Lovett, who also joined *Blue Genie* for the 2002 ARC, and produced a comprehensive diary of the trip.

CHAPTER 1

The call of the Caribbean

❦

Sailing in the Caribbean is living the dream for a boat lover, and to sail back to the cold waters of the English Channel is a less appealing challenge. The only reason I was considering it in 2001 was the prospect of a new boat, and then making another trip back in it to paradise – or that's what I was telling myself.

I'd sailed across in 1999 with my wife Ann in our 42ft. ketch, *Forever in Blue Jeans*, and we were now preparing the boat for the return trip to the UK from Antigua via Bermuda and the Azores to Plymouth. Our plan was to spend winters sailing in the Caribbean and fly back to the UK for the summer, and on our last trip back I'd decided to change the boat for a new Moody 47, which was more spacious than our Halberg 42 ketch.

I loved the Caribbean. We had had several friends join us for some winter sailing as we sailed up and down the Island chain down to Grenada, where we had left the boat for the

1

summer hurricane season, and up as far as the Virgin Islands. The trip back was departing from Jolley Harbour, Antigua, on 10th May 2001. As part of ARC Europe, the boats ranged from a Crealock 34 to a Hylas 54 and there were 31 boats in the fleet. The social activities and safety briefings were most enjoyable, and the camaraderie among the crews made the trip. The rally was due to be joined by another group of boats in Bermuda that set out from St. Augustine in Florida.

The start line wasn't too bad as there were a lot fewer boats than for the start of the ARC and everyone seemed to know what they were doing. We were soon clear and sailing in the 12-knot easterly breeze and looking forward to six or seven days at sea.

A pod of bottle-nosed dolphins welcomed us back into the Atlantic, diving in and out of the bow wave. They love interacting with yachts, and as Antigua disappeared into the afternoon heat haze astern their clicking noises as they dived in and out of the bow wave seemed to be saying 'welcome back to sea',

The first day's run was 128 miles, and we were soon into the seagoing routine of four-hour watches in daytime and three-hour watches at night. For the first few days the wind was light and variable. There were squalls around which could be seen approaching and most would miss us. Occasionally we would be caught and drenched with torrential rain, but they rarely lasted and we were soon sailing or motor-sailing in the light and variable northerly wind.

During the last 24 hours, as we approached Bermuda, the wind backed round to the west and increased to 20-25 knots, so we were beating into it. It was squally and very wet with poor visibility as our destination appeared out of the murk about eight miles away. As we entered Town Cut, leading into

St. George's Harbour, we crossed the finish line. It was 15:38 on 17th May 2001, and the trip had lasted just over seven days.

The last time I'd been in Bermuda was in 1967 on a ship called *Albany* on which I was an Engineer Officer. I was captivated by the island and the characters I met there and I promised Ann that one day I would take her, not realising that It would be 34 years later and in our own boat,

We had to dock on the customs berth, but the reps from World Cruising met us and gave us a hand to tie up and told us what to do regarding immigration etc. In Bermuda there were very strict firearms regulations and customs insisted that all guns, including flare pistols, had to be handed in. I had a Pains Wessex flare pistol and boxes of red green and white flares. Some of the weaponry the American boats handed in was interesting!

Car hire is not available in Bermuda, but it was possible to hire scooters and Ann and I went to the hire shop. I went off for a practice before picking her up, not having ridden a scooter before, but I could ride a bike so it couldn't that difficult, could it? I found that if I went slowly and only turned left it wasn't too bad with Ann on the back, and if we needed to turn right I would stop, Ann would get off and when clear I would push the scooter round the corner and she would climb back on.

The marina was surrounded by cliffs, and the road in and out was very steep and winding. Ann used to walk up to the top and wait for me on the main road. I would then ride the scooter up the winding track to the top and she would climb on, or that was the plan.

The first time I tried it, going round the bend I misjudged the amount of throttle on the scooter, shot across the road and rammed it into the cliff. As I sat there feeling foolish I could hear Ann screaming with laughter. It must have looked comical, but luckily I was un-injured and the scooter undamaged. I was worried that I might have bent the front wheel, but everything seemed OK.

Being moored bows on to the dock, it was tricky getting on and off the boat. The supermarkets supplied brown paper bags for groceries, but the handles were always breaking. On one occasion the handles on my bag snapped without warning, depositing all the contents into the harbour. I managed to retrieve most of the items, but all the tins of food went straight to the bottom. Luckily I had a Sea Searcher magnet on board. It must have looked strange as I fished out the lost items. I was able to save all the tins, the only problem being that all the labels had come off in the water, so it was impossible to know the contents, and mealtimes became a bit of a guessing game!

When I visited in the sixties a favourite watering hole was the Hog Penny Pub, and with Bermuda being an island in the middle of the Atlantic all sorts of interesting characters congregated there and many hours were spent yarning well into the night. It didn't seem to have the same atmosphere this time around. I suppose now we were among the 'interesting characters', having sailed there in our little boats.

Laurie Mullaney, one of our sailing buddies, joined the ship for the leg of the trip from Bermuda to the Azores. We'd sailed in company with Laurie, his wife Jackie and their daughter Katherine in their boat *Northern Lights* on several trips to northern France, the Channel Islands and Brittany; he was an accomplished yachtsman and their daughter Katherine was also excellent crew.

The seven days in Bermuda seemed to fly past and all too soon it was time to leave. There was a message that the crews could now pick up any firearms that had been handed in to customs from the Marina Restaurant. It was a slapdash affair

4

with the weapons left in a heap on the floor for their owners to collect. There was no security, which was surprising after the fuss Customs had made over handing them in.

We said goodbye to Bermuda at midday on 23rd May. There were more boats doing this leg of the trip, and a contingent from Florida had joined the rally, but as usual, within a few hours there were none to be seen.

On this leg of the trip Ann was rally radio controller. Each day at noon all of the yachts would radio their latitude and longitude, which Ann would then log.

Our rig for downwind sailing was twin headsails; this was two Genoas on one luff tape, with two poles. This rig was great for short handed downwind sailing, as to reduce speed the Genoas could be rolled up together to reduce sail area as the wind increased. I also fitted two "lazy" sheets so that if the wind changed direction the leeward lazy sheet could be used to pull the windward sail across so that the two sails would lie together, acting as one for upwind sailing. With just one pole set to windward and both sails deployed it was possible to use this set up almost to a beam reach.

On 25th – 26th May our heading was 120 and the wind was gusting N or NW 20 to 25 knots, Ann was due to take the watch at midnight and we decided to take down the pole as the wind was unreliable and the sea was very lumpy. As Ann took over there was a sudden wind shift which resulted in a vicious gybe as the main boom and the mizzen boom crashed across. The sheet fittings on both the main and mizzen parted company with their booms. I re-set the Jib to retain control and then set about lassoing the main boom, which was wildly swinging from side to side as the boat rolled in the ever-increasing seas. As soon as the booms were safely lashed down we were able to roll up the mizzen and mainsail and continue sailing with just the Jib to await the dawn and assess the damage and attempt repairs. It was fortunate that the jib and mizzen both had in-mast reefing, so it was relatively easy to roll them up once the booms were made safe.

I then sent Laurie below to get some sleep and Ann took over the watch. As soon as it was light, after rummaging in the spares locker, I found some fittings that I was able to use to re-attach the main and mizzen sheets to the booms. During the drama the jib luff had partly pulled out of the luff track, but it was a simple task to let the sail down a few feet and slide it back in, as the wind had now moderated and by mid-morning was down to around 10 knots.

For the next few hours the wind was light to moderate and to keep up a reasonable daily average we used the engine, which also kept the batteries charged. The water maker was 220v and it was necessary to run the generator whilst making water.

On the morning of 26th May smoke was seen billowing from the locker that housed the generator. I immediately shut it down, but the smoke continued, so I grabbed a fire extinguisher and opened the locker. There were flames and smoke coming from the generator housing. One of the rally boats, a 40ft ketch, was about a mile away on our starboard quarter and having seen the smoke it called on the radio asking if we required assistance. We asked them to stand by while I sorted out the problem. With the generator shut down the smoke and flames subsided and I could see that it was the electrical wiring that had overheated and caught fire. Luckily the fire had been contained in the generator locker, and I soon had it under control.

I investigated and discovered that the insulation on one of the heavy cables had chafed on a generator engine support, causing it to short out and catch fire. The result was that the generator was out of commission for the rest of this leg of the trip. With the generator out of commission I couldn't run the water maker, but I had sufficient water for the rest of the trip in the tanks.

On 27th May at 1930 It was my watch and I was just having a cup of tea as we motor-sailed in a flukey force 3-4 when the boat came to a grinding halt and heeled over. It felt as though we had run aground, but we were in the middle of the Atlantic. The boat juddered and came upright and I then saw an enormous tree trunk disappearing astern! I checked the boat from stem to stern and there was no apparent damage, so we were soon pottering along in the light winds. This is an ongoing problem that yachts on ocean passages have, as there are a lot of things floating about in the oceans to bump into.

There were several days of light winds and the odd ship passed fairly close – I think they just came to have a look at us. The wind started to pick up on 27th May, and with all sail set we started to make good progress. From the early hours of the 28th, with twin headsails set and main furled, we enjoyed a 30-hour downwind run until the following day, when the wind backed from SW to W, decreased and became variable. I decided to start the engine to keep up our daily average, but it just went "clunk" and refused to start. This could be a big problem, as at that moment the engine was the main source of electric power; the wind generator, although fairly efficient, would not cope with our daily needs. I changed the engine battery for one of the house batteries and luckily the engine burst into life.

We were now in seagoing mode, having spent a few days at sea, and I was able to replace the burnt-out cables on the generator. Luckily I had spare heavy cabling in the spares locker and it was a relief after re-wiring when the generator started and was producing power almost as if nothing had happened. This was a good result as the water maker was mains power only, and although we had enough water in the tanks for the trip it was reassuring to have the extra capacity.

The wind was now steadily increasing and we were sailing with jib and mizzen, the main being snugly stowed. Fuel needed to be transferred from the on-deck jerry cans, and to make this easier I had a submersible pump connected to a length of plastic pipe. It was a simple task to drop the pump into the jerry can and put the end of the pipe into the fuel tank, then switch on the pump. This was much easier than struggling with the jerry can trying to pour the fuel into the tank and invariably spilling diesel all over the deck. The generator was operated for an hour in the morning and an hour in the evening for battery charging and water making.

Laurie decided to do a quiz each day on the SSB radio. He would announce the quiz and then ask a question, and any ship answering would shout the boat's name and the answer. At times it became quite lively as people tried to be the first to answer! The quiz was very popular and the crews on other boats in the fleet looked forward each afternoon to the questions. Laurie made an excellent Quizmaster and other boats used to listen in. He was also excellent crew, and having him on board made tasks like sail changes so much easier than when it was just Ann and I.

In these latitudes the magnetic variation was 16 W and being used to the 4 or 5 degrees around UK waters, some of the headings seemed a long way off.

As May turned to June and we approached the Azores the daily routine and watch system, three hours on and three hours off at night and four on and four off during the day, worked very well. We took it in turns to cook. I have always made a point of having three meals a day whilst at sea, and all three of us were reasonable cooks so we didn't go hungry.

On the 4th June I heard Laurie and Ann laughing and shouting on deck, and rushed up to see what the commotion was about, The sight that greeted me was an enormous whale alongside the boat. It was only about 30ft off the beam and seemed quite happy to swim alongside. After a few minutes it disappeared, only to surface on the other side. We were all rushing about to find our cameras, but then it dived and was gone. We identified it as a fin whale, the second largest in the ocean after the blue whale, and from its size it was probably a fully-grown male. Dolphins often kept us company, but this was the first time we had been escorted by a whale.

The finish line on the island of Horta was finally crossed at 11:44 on 7th June. It had been an interesting trip, The World Cruising team were there to meet us and advise us regarding customs and immigration. Laurie had to leave the ship almost immediately, as his daughter had arranged his flight home from another of the Azores islands and he was pushed to catch the flight. This was a pity, as most of the other boat crews had grown to like Laurie mainly due to the afternoon quizzes, and several were disappointed that he'd left so soon.

There are nine major Azores Islands in three main groups, and visits were organised to some of these places. We spent six days in Horta and on 13th June embarked on the 10-hour trip to Graciosa and then to Sao Jorge, anchoring in Vila das Velas. From Velas we sailed to Pico. Various trips were organised, and one of the most memorable was a trip to the whaling museum. Whaling is no longer practised by the Azorean people, but it was difficult not to admire the courage of the whalers going out in their tiny boats to harpoon these leviathans.

From Pico it was a gentle 26-hour sail in light and variable winds to Ponta Delgada. There seemed to be a lot of boats around us. The winds were SW and although light we managed to sail most of the way. The in-mast reefing was very stiff; I have found this to happen sometimes. If the sail is going to stick, it usually sticks in the mast. Some people worry that it may not roll up, but I have never had this happen.

On arrival in Ponta Delgado we anchored, and then moved the boat to the end of C Dock. *Misty Lady* managed to ram us, bending one of the stanchions. The damage wasn't too bad and I didn't make a fuss, as the skipper was embarrassed enough!

The five days in Ponta Delgada were spent doing minor repairs. I freed off the mainsail in mast reefing. The halyard was too tight, but I soon had it running free.

The boatyard that did most of the repairs was called Mid Atlantic Yacht Services, MAYS, and they were under a lot of pressure with the sudden influx of the ARC fleet. They were constantly being called by yachts needing assistance and the conversations became quite heated as the MAYS radio operator told callers to be patient!

Ann and I had become good friends with the crew of *Ocean Drive*, an Oyster 45. It was customary to write your boat's name on the harbour wall, and some of the crews were quite artistic and did interesting badges with boats' names. Ann and I were so busy getting the boat shipshape for the 10-day ocean passage to Plymouth that we didn't have time to do one. The young couple crewing on *Ocean Drive* offered to do one for us, and it was far better than Ann or I could have done and featured a pair of blue jeans on a washing line!

We had an electrical problem on *Blue Jeans*, with the switching between charging systems, and I was mystified as to the reason. I was thinking that I would have to postpone leaving until I could get an electrician to sort it out. The skipper on *Ocean Drive* was into boat electrics and offered to come aboard and have a look. He brought his meter and soon discovered the fault. The diverter switch for switching between systems was faulty, which had probably happened when we had the generator fire. I by-passed the switch and connected the wires dirct and was relieved to find everything worked OK.

Forever in Blue Jeans on the dock in the UK Marina.

Forever in Blue Jeans sailing downwind with twin headsails set, heading for that endless horizon.

At 12 noon on 23rd June we crossed the start line, looking forward to the 10-day passage to Plymouth. Some of the fleet were heading for Gibraltar and the Mediterranean. We'd said our goodbyes to the many friends we'd made on the trip so far, which was sad as we were never to see most of them again. On this leg of the trip Ann and I were back to just the two of us. This was no problem, as by now we could handle the boat in any conditions.

I am always thoughtful, and at the beginning of any sea passage I always wonder what adventures lie ahead. *Blue Jeans* was a well-found yacht with thousands of miles under her keel, but there is always the unexpected.

After the first few hours the winds became light and variable and we motor-sailed for a time as we got into the seagoing routine of three and four-hour watches. In spite of the calm conditions the first day's run worked out to be a respectable 128 miles. The wind remained light and unpredictable, going from NE to SW and then variable and settling down to SW 3-4 on the afternoon of 25th June.

In the early hours of the 26th, the engine decided to die on us. I think we may have picked up some dirty diesel. The wind was now a steady SW4 and *Blue Jeans* was creaming along at a respectable 6 knots with all sails set. Ann was on watch and I'd decided to bleed the fuel system, which was fairly easy despite the boat being heeled over. I cleaned out the fuel pipes as best I could and lo and behold, I pressed the starter and after a couple of turns the engine burst into life.

As the evening wore on the wind increased and backed slightly, putting us on a run. I decided it was time to set the twins and with them set and a reefed main and mizzen, we settled down for the night. The wind steadily increased as the night wore on. I stowed the main and reduced the headsails and with twins set and the mizzen, we settled into a comfortable downwind run towards Plymouth.

Early in the morning the wind started to ease, so I let the twins out fully. *Blue Jeans* loved this rig and was soon flying along at over 7 knots.

I consider that this downwind twin headsail rig is ideal for a small crew. It can be rolled to reduce area as the wind increases, and if the wind shifts the windward sail can be pulled across so that both sails can lie together. I always rig a lazy sheet on each sail to enable the windward sail to be pulled across to lie against the downwind sail.

During the evening of the 26th the wind started to back, gradually coming round to the south. I pulled the windward sail across as we settled onto a reach with the wind on starboard beam, and we settled down with reefed main, mizzen and the twins both on port side. This lasted a couple of hours until the wind veered SW, when the twins were redeployed and the main rolled away. With 20 knots of wind dead astern we were in for a very rolly night and the same the following day.

The wind started to moderate early on 29th, but the seas were still big. The wind backed slightly and I gybed the pole to give the twins a better angle to the wind and set the mizzen, which cut down the rolling in the 12-knot breeze.

I'd been running the generator for several hours a day and took advantage of the calmer conditions to top up the fuel tanks. The generator had a separate fuel tank that was in the cockpit locker. The locker used to house the holding tank for the aft toilet, but I replaced that tank with a 5-gallon diesel tank. The main fuel tank on the Rassy is in the keel and the lift pump on the generator wasn't powerful enough.

On 30th June the wind became light and variable and it was

necessary to start the engine. We had a sea mist during the night as we approached good old England, so thank goodness for radar, although no ships came close.

As Lizard Point hove into view through the early morning mist I realised that this was the last trip I would be doing in *Forever in Blue Jeans*, as our new boat, yet to be named, awaited us in Moody's Marina. *Blue Jeans* had served us well during two Atlantic crossings. She always looked good with her flush decks and I always felt proud of her and was a bit sad to be saying goodbye. We'd bought her in '95 with the dream of doing the ARC in '99. We crossed the finish line at 1230 on the 1st July, the trip from the Azores having taken us 10 days. On the 4th July, after filling tanks at Clovelly Bay, we set out for Swanwick Marina. I was looking forward to seeing the new boat.

Victor, the Moody broker, escorted us to the boat. When we looked at the outside the first thing I noticed was that the spray hood (dodger) was in a poor state, having been left folded down, and was full of water, though I intended to change it anyway for a larger one. On entering the boat we saw that instead of the layout we had ordered it was the standard layout, and Ann was furious. We had asked for the two port side armchairs to be changed to a long settee that could be used as a bunk with lee cloths, as we intended to do ocean passages and the two saloon berths were ideal for this purpose.

We went into the office and saw David Moody, who agreed that it was wrong and promised to change it. The problem was that the material was no longer available from the supplier, but Ann managed to find some with another upholsterer that had some in stock. Eventually the layout was changed to our satisfaction.

I contacted an upholsterer to make a new spray hood. I wanted it higher to make the main hatch more accessible, and I had a small step made so I could see over the top. It gave me great pleasure to dump the Moody-supplied hood in the skip.

I requested that all the deck fittings should be supplied by Cooney. I had supplied Marine Projects, who manufactured Moody yachts, on and off over the years and I didn't want a competitor's product on my boat. I supplied the latest design of davits and eventually she was everything I had dreamed of. I noticed that when the engine was running the oil pressure was low. I mentioned this to Moody's and they said it was probably the gauge and not to worry!

I'd put *Blue Jeans* onto Moody brokerage, so I knew approximately what she was worth. There were several enquiries and people wanting to view, so we cleaned her up and got her sparkling. The teak deck I cleaned with oxalic acid, which brought out that beautiful teak shine. It was a conventional deck and one or two of the teak plugs had worn away, exposing the screw heads. I re-plugged where necessary and when I had finished it looked like a new deck.

I had an offer from a Mr Sims and after paying a deposit, subject to survey, he instructed a surveyor, who said the hull was showing the onset of osmosis, and told all sorts of horror stories, but Mr Sims instructed him to continue the survey. I decided to appoint my own surveyor to advise me, and he said it wasn't too bad and the boat was in remarkably good condition. When I mentioned this to Sims, he was annoyed and threatened to pull out of the deal. The price to repair the hull, which would need the grinding back of the gel coat and repair with epoxy, was £11,000, and I offered to either get the repair done or reduce the price by the same amount. Eventually the deal was done.

Ann and I were doing sea trials in the Moody, which we finally named *Blue Genie*. The maiden voyage was a trip round to Poole, where we tied up in Dolphin Quay Marina. On 2nd June our friends Stan and Maureen Chalker joined us for a few days, and we sailed over to East Cowes and berthed on E pontoon. We then sailed over to Haslar Marina, stayed overnight and then made our way back to Moody's at Swanwick. The boat sailed remarkably well, and with the in-mast reefing main, self-tacking staysail and furling Jib she was a joy to handle, ideal for short-handed sailing

On 11th September we took the boat to Ocean Quay Marina to use it as accommodation for the Southampton Boat Show. As we were tying up at Ocean Quay we were told of the shocking news from the USA that terrorists had flown aeroplanes into the twin towers, killing thousands of people.

Blue Genie was ideal as accommodation, and even after paying mooring fees it was a lot cheaper than a hotel. We had several groups of people from Cooney's and they seemed to like the idea of staying on a yacht.

After the show we returned to Swanwick to continue preparations for the trip to the Canaries and onwards across the Atlantic.

CHAPTER 2

Atlantic crossing

A lot of effort was needed to prepare *Blue Genie* for the Atlantic crossing. Although it was a new boat, there was a lot to do. I wanted lee cloths fitting to the bunks, as having spent many nights at sea in various yachts I considered this essential. I designed a small stainless mast to accommodate the aerials for GPS, Inmarsat C, and Raytheon GPS with computer interface.

I considered SSB Radio to be vital for communication, so one of the back stays had insulators fitted and became the aerial. A cradle was fitted to the pushpit to house the life raft, and I changed the guardrail wires for plastic-covered wire and fitted gangway stanchions and side boarding ladders. I purchased a carbon fibre passerelle for boarding the boat when moored stern to the dock. I obtained a wind generator from a company in Trinidad that had a high power output; the wind generators available in the UK seemed to claim output far in excess of what they actually produced.

I contacted Dolphin Sails and ordered a twin headsail rig, two identical headsails sewn onto one luff tape, similar to the system I had fitted on *Blue Jeans.* In my opinion this is the best system for a long downwind passage. The Moody was a much faster design than the Rassy and although there would be four of us crewing the boat I considered it essential to have an easily handled rig for a passage of several weeks, and the passage down to the Canaries would be just Ann and me.

There follows the first of many edited extracts from my diary.

30ᵗʰ July 2002

Preparations complete, we cast off berth E43 in Swanwick and started on our next big adventure. It was a cool summer morning with a slight early morning mist and the promise of a hot day ahead. The forecast was NE 4-5 and we were looking forward to a brisk sail down to Alderney and the Channel Islands. The forecast wind didn't materialise; it turned out to be light and variable, so we motor-sailed most of the way to Braye harbour, arriving at 1800 and mooring up on Buoy 52.

With so much to look forward to, we spent only a couple of days in Alderney before sailing down to St Peter Port in Guernsey, anchoring in Havalet Bay. We moved into the marina when there was sufficient water over the sill for last-minute preparations. I gave the generator a 50-hour service, topped up water tanks, checked electrolyte levels in the batteries and serviced the main engine.

Whilst there Ann had a phone call from our daughter Teri. Our grandson Christian came on the line and said, "Mummy's got a baby in her tummy and it's 12 weeks old!" We were surprised but very happy for Teri, and appreciated her novel way of announcing that she was pregnant again!

We eventually cast off from the fuelling berth and headed for northern Spain on the 13ᵗʰ. It was August motoring in calm sea and sunshine, with the wind light and variable for the next few hours, Motoring along the French coast in bright sunshine, we almost started enjoying ourselves. Small brightly coloured fishing boats seemed keen to keep out of our way, although we altered course for some of their larger cousins,

The night was a joy, with a magnificent canopy of stars. At sea, with no light pollution, the stars always seem so much closer.

In the early hours of the 14ᵗʰ wreaths of mist started to surround us and by 0600 we were in thick fog and were keeping a radar watch. Radar is invaluable in these conditions, but there are lots of small fishing boats that don't show an echo so it's a worrying time, and with only two of us on board it's difficult to keep a look out. When the fog is so dense that you can't even see the bow of the boat, it's down to the radar!

Plotting the course of radar echoes around us, we needed to alter course a couple of times, but at 0900 the mist started to clear and soon we were motoring along in bright sunshine once again. With Ushant just a smudge on the horizon to port, we set course across Biscay, headed for La Coruña.

Several times I have crossed Biscay and always headed well out to sea rather than take the coastal route round the Brittany coast, but on this occasion I wanted to get down to northern Spain and call in at La Coruña, and then round to Vigo. The wind was very flukey, light and variable, mainly SE but it would suddenly swing round to SW. However it was barely strong enough to fill the sails, so we were motor-sailing or motoring most of the way.

The mornings would start with early morning mist,

which would then become fog, but by mid-morning we would be pottering along in bright sunshine. The odd ship on the horizon and a few fishing boats were the only excitement. I was concerned at the amount of diesel we were using, although I had enough for the trip.

On the night of 15th August the wind settled down to a steady NNE 3 and with all sail set we settled down to some pleasant downwind sailing. In the early hours of the 16th we saw the Punta de la Estaca de Bares light through the early morning mist, and as the mist cleared we followed the coast round to La Coruña, eventually picking up a mooring buoy at 1530. It had taken us less than four days, which was a fast passage considering the unstable weather.

La Coruña, formerly known to the English as Corunna, is a port city popular with British yachtsmen. It's known for its Roman lighthouse, the Tower of Hercules, which has sweeping coastal views. In the medieval old town is the arcaded Plaza del Maria Pita. In this square is the Estatua de Maria Pita, a statue of a 16th century woman who warned the town of an invasion by Sir Francis Drake. At the northern end of the crescent-shaped city beach called the Playa de Orzan there are. many "must see" attractions. We spent four days in Corunna, enjoying the city with its many restaurants and bars and filling tanks and doing all the maintenance tasks that seem never-ending on a yacht.

Eventually we cast off at 9:45 on the 20th for the eight-hour trip round to Camarinas. There was little wind, but as we rounded Islas Sisargas, it began to increase to a variable 3, mostly on the nose. As we arrived it had settled down to an SE force 4, and there was a slight swell as the anchor rattled down among the fishing boats.

On 22nd August at 0700 we motored out of the Ria and as

the wind settled down to NW 3 we had a leisurely sail under mainsail and yankee round to Bayona. As we dropped anchor at 1830 the oil alarm sounded on the main engine. The next morning we moved to a marina berth to check out the oil system. Everything seemed OK, but I changed the engine oil and filter, and although the pressure appeared low when I re-started the engine everything seemed to run satisfactorily. The oil pressure had seemed low ever since I had taken delivery of *Blue Genie*, but Moodys' said it was all right and probably the gauge was under reading!

I fuelled up in Bayona and met up with Derek, the owner of the Oyster 65 *Silent Wings*. I first met Derek in Antigua when Ann and I crewed with Dennis Knights and Janet on their Oyster 435 *Shilling* in the first Oyster Caribbean Rally. Dennis is an excellent racing skipper and *Shilling,* although one of the oldest boats in the fleet, won a lot of the races. In the evenings we would meet up at the Tot Club. Mike Rose, the founder of the club, organised most of the rally and the club was held at whichever island or bay the boats anchored. Sometimes it was on one of the rally boats.

The next port of call was Lexios, about 60 miles down the coast but across the border in Portugal. The wind was now in the north and we had a downwind run with poled-out jib, yankee and main, arriving at 1830. We anchored in the harbour, but to go ashore we dinghied over to the marina. The staff objected to us using their marina to moor our dinghy to go ashore, so we only stayed one night and left on 29th August, heading for Cascais, about 150 miles down the coast.

The wind seemed settled in the NE but was light and variable, so we motor-sailed with yankee and main for most of the trip, I ran the generator from time to time to power the water maker, a very efficient unit, but it needed a 220v power supply. It was a beautiful clear night with the shore lights of Portugal to port with a huge moon, a myriad stars and the Milky Way above and dolphins diving through the bow wave. A constant watch was needed to dodge the many fishing boats, but they seemed as anxious to miss us as we were to miss them.

In the early hours of the 30th the dreaded fog enveloped us, but within a few hours we were approaching Cascais marina in bright sunshine and were berthed around 1100. Cascais is to the west of Lisbon and was to be our departure point for the Canaries. I intended to go via Porto Santo, a small island to the west of Madeira. I'd heard that the Marina at Madeira was very small and apparently unwelcoming to yachts, whereas the one at Porto Santo was larger, and when we stopped off there in 1999 the facilities were excellent.

At 0930 on 7th September Portugal disappeared astern the wind was on the nose, and no matter what heading or sail combination we tried, all we could do was motor-sail in the general direction of the Canaries. The wind was SW3-4 and on the morning of the 8th I decided to give Porto Santo a miss head and directly to Lanzarote. The wind started to pick up and for a few hours we were creaming along with 20 knots of wind from the SW.

A few ships were spotted, but none came closer than about two miles. The wind was flukey; it would settle for a few hours and good progress would be made, but then it would die down and change direction. The sails were up and down and in and out and it was quite frustrating, the engine being used to keep up a decent daily average.

We eventually tied up on the fuelling dock on 11th September, and after topping up tanks we moved to a berth.

I was concerned about the low oil pressure and changed the oil and filter, but it was still very low. I disconnected the pipes and turned the engine over to see if there was a blockage in the pipe. To my amazement there was no oil coming out of the inlet pipe, but there was oil coming out of the outlet pipe. I then realised what the problem was; the oil filter had been connected the wrong way round. I swapped the pipes over, ran the engine and now had high oil pressure. I was so happy – one of my major concerns was now resolved.

We left Lanzarote on 25th October and motor-sailed the short distance to Puerto del Rosario, anchoring in 5.4m on the island of Fuerteventura. The next day we motored down the island and anchored off Moro Jable town. Ann and I thought we would take the dinghy over to the beach and go for a swim. As we approached, we realised it was a naturist beach. When we pulled the dinghy up the beach, a man came over and jabbered something to us. A few moments later a Land Rover drove up and a lifeguard came over, also Jabbering and gesticulating, then a few other people came over. Some had some English and we gathered that dinghies were not allowed on this particular beach. Some of the men gave us a hand to re-launch the dinghy, all of them stark naked! We returned to *Blue Genie* and had a swim off the boat.

The next day we motored across to Las Palmas and tied up on the fuel berth - this is customary, to fill tanks and then be allotted a berth. Las Palmas Marina is enormous, and has to accommodate the 200+ ARC fleet each year.

Ann's brother Ron and wife Kate came out for a few days sailing, and we sailed down the east coast and around the point where there is an enormous wind farm on the Dunes de Maspalomas, ideally placed in the wind acceleration zone at the south of the island. We visited Pasito Blanco and Puerto

Rico and decided to head back to Las Palmas after staying a couple of days in Puerto de Mogan.

The wind down the east coast is generally northerly, so we expected to have to motor into it at some stage of the proceedings. We were enjoying a leisurely motor-sail in the light NW breeze with the Maspalomas lighthouse abeam and as we approached the wind acceleration zone the wind had started to increase and the swell to build up when the engine decided to die on us. Although the wind was only about 15 knots (F4), the direction was rapidly changing. No sooner were we sailing in a suitable direction than it would change 90 degrees. I had to get the engine going again!

When we took delivery of the boat I saw advertised in a yachting magazine a type of in-line filter that worked by magnetism, and was hailed as the latest device to ensure clean, bug-free fuel. I had one fitted, hoping that the fuel quality would be improved.

As Ann tacked back and forth in the wind, which was now becoming squally, fighting to keep us off what was a lee shore, I was down below trying to sort out the fuel system. It was over 30 degrees C below decks and working on a hot engine increased the discomfort.

I was concerned for Ron and Kate, who sat in the cockpit unable to do anything to help, probably worried about catching their flight home the next day. If all else failed I could have dropped anchor off Mogan, Puerto Rico or one of the ports on that coast and taken them ashore in the dinghy, from where they could pick up a taxi to take them to the airport.

I suspected that the engine pick-up pipe had a blockage, and eventually connected the engine fuel line to the generator pick-up. Thankfully the engine then started. It had taken almost four hours to sort out the problem, and my clothes were drenched with sweat. Ann was exhausted, so we decided to go into Pasito Blanco and tie up in the marina. Ron and Kate were able to hire a taxi to the airport the next day.

I was able to find a mechanic in the marina to check over the fuel system, and he decided that the magnetic in-line filter was the problem, as it was attracting the swarf and filings that had been left in the tank during manufacture. I took out the filter, and sure enough it was full of swarf. I then connected everything back up and the engine started and ran OK. As a precaution I rigged up a fuel pipe from the engine fuel line to the generator fuel line with a diverter valve to enable me to switch to the generator fuel line from the engine fuel line in an emergency.

After waving Ron and Kate goodbye we decided to make our way back to Las Palmas, as we were looking forward to the arrival of our crew, Laurie and Terry, who were joining us for the Atlantic crossing. The wind was light and variable, but as we motored along the south coast of the island with Maspalomas abeam the engine decided to stop. This was in the same position where it had stopped last time, abeam the Maspalomas light house!

Luckily I was prepared. I switched the fuel pipe as described, and had the engine going again after about 15 minutes. We were back on Pedro's fuel berth in Las Palmas at around 1500.

The boat was supplied as standard with three 110 amp-hour lead acid batteries, which were supposed to be 'marine' type. The problem with batteries on a boat is that due to the often violent motion, they need to be securely fastened. I had added an additional battery of the same type as the original ones fitted and improved the fixings, The ARC inspectors were fairly strict on the secure fitting of batteries. I was concerned that some of the batteries weren't 100%, so I decided to install four new ones. It is not recommended to replace part of a battery bank as the duff batteries would pull them all down to the same level.

I bought four new Vetus sealed marine batteries that had similar dimensions to the originals and fitted them into the battery locker. Batteries are very heavy, and it was a struggle to remove the old ones from the boat and install the new. I used a shopping trolley to take the old batteries to the garbage dump, where there was a separate area for engine oil, batteries etc, and left them stacked against one of the skips. Within minutes I saw a man with a meter checking them out and within half an hour they had disappeared! I have found this quite often when dumping redundant equipment. I suppose one man's rubbish can be another man's treasure!

I enjoyed the lectures that the ARC team delivered, although I had heard most of them before, when we did the ARC in 1999 in *Blue Jeans*, but it was good to refresh our memories and I'm sure Laurie and Terry found them instructive.

The social events were great fun, but the start date was looming and the boat was stuffed with provisions. The problem I'd found on previous trips was that the enormous branch of bananas is great until a few days into the voyage, when they all go rotten at the same time, and it's the same with a lot of fresh fruit and veg. On *Blue Genie* we had a small freezer and with forward planning we didn't waste much at all. We stuffed it with fresh meat and some frozen items. We also had a plentiful supply of tinned food – we loved Fray Bentos steak and kidney pies and had a stack of them.

This was one of the things I liked about the Moody. A lot of the other boats had poor stowage space, and some of them had to use the forward head for stowage, rendering it unusable.

The night before departure day Stokey Woodall gave the final lecture, the main theme being that once you leave here you are on your own, you have to sort yourselves out.

The start was due to be around 12.30 on 24th November, but due to some funny weather down the bottom of the island there was an indefinite postponement. Yachts all around us were leaving for the start, but I held back until nearer the start time to avoid the chaos of 200 boats clamouring to be first over the line. We eventually motored out and set the twins and main in a 6-knot breeze and steadily passed many other boats heading down to the acceleration zone at the bottom of the island, where the wind started to pick up and the seas were becoming very rough.

As the wind increased to 25 knots, we could see boats ahead heeled over. As the evening approached we noticed a lot of navigation lights coming towards us, and it turned out that some of the starters, with all sails set, had hit the acceleration zone and sustained damage and were returning to Las Palmas to effect repairs. After slogging our way round the bottom of the island we were soon clear and running with twins and main set, and soon there were very few of the ARC boats visible around us.

The wind built up to 35 knots and we needed to reef. I tried to start the engine but it was dead. The seas were 10 to 15 feet, so we were in for a hard night. All round the horizon were black squalls. We tried to miss them if possible but were sometimes caught out where the wind would change direction 90 deg. and scream through the rigging, dumping torrential rain on our heads as the watch huddled under the spray dodger. Then the squall would pass and often the wind would then be variable for a time until it settled into the NE and we would be running once again with twins and main set.

In the early hours of the morning the spinnaker pole came adrift, crashing down to the deck across the foredeck hatch. Luckily there was no damage and it was re-set after a bit of a struggle.

The watch system I set up was four hours on **0600** to 1800 and three hours on 1800 to **0600**, with a free day every fourth day. Whoever was on the free day was duty cook. It worked very well with everyone on call in cases of safety of the ship, reefing, sail changes etc.

It seemed strange having crew; usually on passage either Ann or I would be on watch so at sea we were never able to sleep together. We would lie there listening to every groan and creak of the boat until we fell into a fitful sleep.

The boat was in her element, at times logging over **9** knots. Terry and Laurie were trying to beat each other's speed. The wind started to veer easterly and it was decided to gybe the pole, Laurie leapt into action and we were soon sailing more smoothly. We'd been at sea for four days and everything was working well. Terry, who before the trip couldn't cook, had asked Sue, his wife, to teach him the basics of cookery and we all took it in turns. I have always operated a watch system so everyone knows where they stand and it minimises arguments. Luckily, with Laurie and Terry both experienced yachtsmen, there were no problems. We'd all known each other for many years and sailed in company several times.

Terry's efforts when on cooking duty never ceased to amaze me. We all tried to outdo each other when our turn came, so we ate remarkably well for a crew on a little boat in an enormous ocean!

On the SSB radio net it was reported that another Moody 47, *Trust Me*, had returned to Las Palmas with continuing rudder bearing problems. We had not experienced any problems and as we were a long way from anywhere and had to, as Stokey had explained before we left, "sort ourselves out".

Day 5, Friday November 29th

While sailing with the twins and surfing down huge waves, with the wind over 30 knots at times, we spotted a pod of pilot whales. On Terry's watch we logged 11.2 knots but averaging over 10 knots. On watch at 0200 I had to call all hands on deck to reduce sail for fear of blowing out clews! We now decided to alter course towards St Lucia – only 2380 miles to go! The luxury of having a crew of four made life a lot easier than on our last ARC and the daily averages were easier to maintain.

Day 6, Saturday November 30th

Ann and I were turned in together and could hear the wind generator becoming louder and louder. We realised that the wind must be increasing. Normally as we were sailing downwind the wind generator didn't do much as the boat speed reduced the wind speed over the generator blades. I rushed up on deck. The wind was over 30 knots, and by the light of the early morning watery sun the seascape was spectacular, with heaving crests with deep holes into which Blue Genie was plunging, white water hissing down the topsides as we surfed down into watery valleys. Laurie and Terry, with beaming faces, were loving the excitement and exhilaration, but we were going far too fast, and were in danger of pitch poling (when the bow digs in and the boat somersaults). We needed to slow down, so we rolled the twins and reefed the main even further.

Day 7, Saturday November 30th

We heard the dreadful news that a man had been lost overboard from a UK-registered yacht, Toutazimut, a Formosa 51. The yacht was being sailed by two brothers. One unfortunately went overboard and although still attached to his lifeline, he died whilst in the water. Yachts in the vicinity were closing their position to assist. This dreadful news emphasises the importance of the strict safety rules and lectures that the ARC organisers insist upon. The chatter on the ARC radio net was very subdued and didn't last long.

Day 8, Sunday 1st December

The wind was moderating slightly, but we have still been able to average 7 to 8 knots boat speed, about 190 miles per day. The seas were huge and I insisted that everyone should wear their harness and life jacket and remain clipped on and if possible stay in the cockpit.

We received a Pan Pan call from Zara aboard yacht F2 to say their rudder had snapped off and they had no steerage way in the heavy swell. I ask them their position and realised they were about 59 miles astern of us. I asked if they were taking on water, which they weren't. It would take us about 12 hours or more for us to turn around and motor into the weather to reach them and there were several boats upwind of them and nearer to their position. Muskrat radioed to say they were three miles behind F2 and would attend. I spoke to Victoria Vision on SSB radio, who was also behind F2 and also confirmed she would attend the scene.

F2 was crewed by Pete and Zara and their enormous dog Ellie. This was to be their great adventure, and they had only about nine months' sailing experience. There was a lot of chatter on the radio on how to rig a jury rudder, but in the middle of the Atlantic with the huge swell and rough conditions it's not so easy. F2 was about 350 miles from the Cape Verde Islands and couldn't motor into heavy weather without a rudder.

Muskrat advised F2 to stream a sea anchor and drogues to reduce rolling and make things as comfortable as possible overnight. The barque Tenacious (a barque is a three-masted sailing ship) was also making for the scene. I didn't think the crew of F2 had the experience or stamina to steer their boat under jury rudder the remaining 1700 miles to St. Lucia in this weather. Meanwhile we ploughed on under reefed sails in the stormy conditions. We were fascinated by shoals of flying fish, which leapt from the water and seemingly glided over the tops of the waves for many metres, We often found them on deck where they had collided with the sails. If possible we threw them back in, but by the time we had found them they were often already dead.

The wind would moderate for a time and we would unroll some more jib and mainsail, but it would then pick up and we would have to tighten everything back in again. The wind was from an easterly direction veering from ENE to ESE and back again. Gybing the pole was a chore and Laurie seemed keen to volunteer, so we let him do it!

Crossing the line, 2002 ARC. With a happy crew,
Terry, Laurie, Ann and Kevin.

Blue Genie on the dock in English Harbour, Antigua

Day 9, 2nd December

The miles were disappearing astern and we were achieving daily runs of over 190 nm surfing down the waves sometimes at over 15 knots! The news from F2 was encouraging. The Tenacious was standing by and they had a workshop on board. They had contacted Legend Yachts in the USA and had drawings faxed to them and were in the process of making F2 a new rudder. That was good news but I didn't know how they intended to fit it in those conditions. We still had 25-30 knots of wind and heavy swell.

Day 10, December 3rd

At last the wind was showing signs of moderating. The day dawned with puffy white trade wind clouds, brilliant sunshine and a slightly reduced swell. I decided to roll up the mainsail and rig the twins with the pole to starboard and the port twin fixed to the end of the main boom, hoping that we could now enjoy a nice trade wind run for a day or two, but no such luck! By late afternoon the wind was such that we were once again sailing with poled-out twins and a full mainsail set. The wind was now down to 20 knots and the motion of the boat steadier, making life aboard much more comfortable, so it was now much easier to get around. There was no shortage of water and the crew were taking regular showers. I would run the water maker each day when I did the daily generator run. It produced about 25 gallons an hour. The news from F2 was positive; the construction of the new rudder in the Tenacious workshop was well under way and it was hoped that it would soon be fitted.

Day 11 - December 4th

The wind was now decreasing further and our daily run was only 159 miles, this was good for F2 and the fitting of the new rudder. It was eventually fitted and Ann spoke to Pete who confirmed that the new rudder was fitted and worked. This was an enormous achievement by the crew of Tenacious and Pete and Zara. Pete confirmed that the new rudder was working and they were now once again heading for St. Lucia but taking it easy with Yacht Muskrat standing by.

Day 12 - December 5th

The wind is a steady 20-25 knots but conditions are now squally and the swell is building up, The reception on the SSB is poor so there was no roll call today. The noon day's run was 179 miles, better than yesterday. Terry was duty cook and we had hoped for Liver, mash and onion gravy for supper. Unfortunately the label had fallen off the meat in the freezer and it turned out to be ostrich, but it tasted fine and was enjoyed by all. The squalls are a nuisance, there are too many to try and miss, when they hit the wind backs about 30 degrees and tons of water are dumped on us in a very short time, we keep re-setting sail to no avail.

We are making very good progress with good daily mileages and have only just over 1000 miles to go. As we make more southing and the wind settles to a 10-15 knot breeze with puff ball clouds and the temperature increasing, the boat is looking after herself. The SSB radio reception is still poor although with the Iridium Satellite phone we are able to communicate. It seems a bit peculiar sailing in mid-Atlantic with Terry happily chatting to his wife Sue on the phone. The piles of fresh fruit and veg that everyone bought at the beginning of the trip is now past its best and has sadly been consigned to Davy Jones locker. Terry, trying to save the carrots, spent hours trying to scrub off the black mould, but sadly they had to join their mouldy colleagues in the deep!

Day 14 - Saturday December 7th

We were making good progress downwind, often with gusts of 35 knots; with twins set and mainsail it was important to watch the wind direction constantly. Last night a squall hit and Laurie had a nasty accidental gybe which broke the preventer and the boat surfed out of control. It was all hands on deck for a time as we struggled to regain control. There was no damage done except to the preventer.

We had not seen any ships for about six days when suddenly an enormous refrigeration ship appeared out of the murk and altered course, probably to have a look at us! We called them up on the VHF, but the watch officer wasn't very communicative.

Day 15 – Sunday December 8th

The time was rolling by, with only a few more days to go. There was an air of excitement as we looked forward to our arrival. Terry and Laurie were looking forward to seeing their wives, who should be waiting for us. If they wanted to they could all stay on board, but Terry and Laurie were moving into a hotel for a few days, having had enough of the sea and the discomfort of a long sea passage.

Although we were looking forward to arriving, there was also sadness that the trip was coming to an end. I used to feel this on big ships; the routine and the friendship one has with shipmates is indescribable and knowing it's coming to an end is always sad, although new adventures await.

A message was received from ARC office at 2200 to say that F2 had lost their Jury rudder and were taking on water. Muskrat was standing by, but F2 was not thought to be in imminent danger, although there was a danger she might have to be abandoned.

Sue and Jackie, our trusty crews' wives, had already arrived in St. Lucia and Terry rang Sue at the hotel, apparently their flight had been delayed over six hours due to a bomb scare, so they didn't arrive until after midnight.

Day 16 – Monday December 9th

I was handing over to Laurie at midnight when sails started flapping and the boat gybed and hove to. I thought the confusion was caused by a wind shift, but then realised that the autohelm self steering wasn't working. Laurie hauled the boat back on course and I went down to investigate. Ann was in the aft bunk, so I had to get her out of bed and lift the bunk to investigate the steering quadrant. It turned out that the spigot holding the hydraulic ram to it had sheared off, so all we could do was hand steer.

We all had a cup of tea and a crew meeting to decide how to hand steer for the remaining 500 or so miles, and decided that we would take it in turns for one hour with three hours off. This would mean far more work for the crew, so the Autohelm would be sorely missed. Terry took over from Laurie just in time to be caught in an enormous squall that soaked him through.

Ann took over from Terry at 0330. I was rummaging in the

spares locker looking for a way to jury rig the Autohelm, and found a 12mm bolt and a short length of pipe. With a bit of sawing and filing I was able to make a new spigot to connect the Autohelm.

To connect my newly manufactured parts at dawn we "laid a hull" with Laurie holding the wheel hard over and Terry trimming the sails while I struggled to reconnect the Autohelm to the steering quadrant, with Ann holding my legs as I was head first in the locker under the bunk. My main worry was that Laurie would lose control of the wheel and my hands would get mashed by the steering quadrant!

Eventually I had everything bolted up securely and rewired. We thought our problems were over, but the problem now was that the Autohelm wouldn't steer the boat when we switched it on – the ram went to full extent and didn't respond to the course dictated by the compass. We tried all manner of theories as to why this was happening, and in the end I decided to ring Autohelm in the UK on the satellite phone. I estimated that with the time difference in the UK we were within office hours, so there should be someone there. It only rang for a few times before being picked up, I explained that I needed to speak to an engineer, as I had a problem with an Autohelm. She told me to hold on, and then a Dalek-like voice came on explaining that I was in a queue and someone would be with me shortly. Inane music then started. It seemed bizarre. Here we were in the middle of the Atlantic, miles from anywhere, and I was in a queue listening to annoying music! The wind was NE 20-25 knots and we were beating into it, so it was hard work for the helmsman and the boat was being swept by the odd rogue wave.

The music stopped and another girl came on the line. I explained that I needed to speak to an engineer, and she told me to hold on. I had visions of more inane music, so before she could put me on hold again I said "Look I'm in the middle of the bloody Atlantic, don't put me on hold in a bloody queue, I need to speak to an engineer now!"

At last an electronics guy came on. I explained the problem, and he said the two main wires, a red one and a black, were the wrong way round and to connect them black to red and red to black. He explained that when the boat builders installed these autopilots the wiring often got switched around. I was very wary of switching the wires, but if that was the expert's solution I decided to do it and re-wired the unit. I switched the Autohelm on again and was amazed – it was working perfectly.

Sadly we had a message from the ARC office to say that Pete Sara and Ellie had been taken off F2 at 1500 yesterday and the boat scuttled. We all felt sad for them, but then Pete came on SSB radio to say that after eight days it was a huge relief. They were now aboard Laurie Gray 2, a Dix65 with muskrat still in attendance.

Day 17 – Tuesday December 10th

Only 350 miles to go! It looked like arrival at Rodney Bay around 0800 on Thursday. It was another bright and sunny day with a deep blue Atlantic sea. We were now running downwind with the windward twin poled out and the leeward lazy sheet through the end of the boom and the main stowed. Our heading was now straight for St Lucia, the wind astern, with little rolling. The autopilot was still behaving.

Day 18 – December 11th

This would probably be our last day at sea and although we were looking forward to arriving, I was sad that the trip was almost over. Over the last few days we had had some classic trade wind sailing on some watches, averaging 12 to 12.5 knots. The high points had outnumbered the low points, the main low points being the misfortunes that had befallen other vessels. The dreadful news from Toutazimut and the loss of F2 did put a damper on things.

I expected our ETA to be about 0600 the following day. We had not seen another boat for days, but there was now a yacht on our port quarter about six miles away. It was probably Escapade, an Island Packet 42, but she was not responding to our VHF calls and probably had her VHF switched off. As we saw the loom of Martinique appear over the horizon on our starboard bow we could see the lights of one or two yachts with headings similar to ours. I told the crew to get showered and spruced up ready for arrival.

As we approached Pigeon Island, dawn was breaking and we were all on deck in excited expectation of arrival, Terry and Laurie looking forward to seeing their wives. Saraband, a Swan 45, was to port of us and they decided to race us to the finish line. They had a large crew and were carrying full sail. We had started stowing everything ready for docking and needless to say they beat us to the finish, by about two minutes.

As we cross the line the ARC photographer zoomed round us in his Zodiac and got some good action shots as we crossed the finish line close-hauled. We had been 17 days and 22 hours at sea. It was great to see Sue and Jackie waving to us from the end of the pontoon. They'd been up since 0430. We were all on an amazing high as the ropes went ashore and we were welcomed in to a rum punch and a basket of fruit, courtesy of the St. Lucia Tourist Board.

Blue Genie, anchored in northern Spain on our way to the Canaries

Blue Genie approaching St. Lucia

It had been a remarkable trip, and though for Ann and me it was a bit of an anti-climax, the boat had handled superbly and we had made a good passage time. It was a great success having the extra crew. We had known Laurie and Terry for years and knew they were extremely capable yachtsmen with years of experience as skippers of their own boats.

You always take a chance with crew. If there are tensions when miles out at sea it can blight the trip, but luckily everything went OK. The watch system worked and we all took our turn cooking with each of us trying to outdo the last cook's efforts.

On arrival Laurie and Terry went to stay in the hotel with their wives, while Ann and I stayed on for the prize giving – not that we had won anything, but it was nice to support those that had. We flew back to the UK just before Christmas.

I flew back out to the Caribbean on January 12th and set about the numerous tasks that needed doing to keep the boat in tip-top condition, mainly maintenance and minor repairs. Ann stayed behind to await our daughter Teri's happy event, and our grandson, Taylor, was born on February 3rd 2003. The boat was hauled out for a bottom pressure wash and anti-fouling, and while she was ashore I stayed on a friend's Beneteau 50. The boat was re-launched around the 10th Feb and Ann flew back out a few days later.

On 26th Feb we were fuelled up and all set to leave Rodney Bay and point our bow north for Antigua, picking up a mooring in Falmouth Harbour. On 4th March we headed for Montserrat and anchored in Little Bay. We left the next morning for the short sail to Nevis, anchoring at Charlestown. We then visited Basseterre, St Kitts, Simpson Bay, St Martin and then Gustavia, St Barts and then back to Jolley Harbour, Antigua.

Our good friends Don and George joined us in Jolley Harbour, arriving on 19th March. We sailed to Charlestown and Pinney Beach, Nevis, and then back to Jolley Harbour and English Harbour, Antigua. I had decided to take the boat down to Grenada as it was out of the hurricane belt and it was possible to get insurance cover for 'named storms'; the alternative was to take the boat down to Trinidad.

On 13th April 2003 we cleared the fuel berth at Jolley Harbour at about 0800, heading for Guadeloupe. There was little wind, so it was a gentle motor-sail down to Deshais, where we anchored at 1500. We left the next afternoon heading for St David's, Grenada, where we intended to leave the boat for the summer. We anchored in the bay at 1130 on 16th April.

It was January 2004 before we returned to St David's. The boat had survived the lay-up fairly well and everything seemed to be working. Our intention was to sail the boat back up to St Lucia and then on to Antigua. Alan and Max Watts joined us for the trip, arriving on 25th January. Alan and Max were experienced sailors and had their own 42ft boat.

We left Prickly Bay on 26th January, motor-sailing into the ENE force 4 breeze and heading for Carriacou. The pilot books recommend that it is wise not to sail over the 'Kick em Jenny' volcano to the north of Grenada, but we did so with no problems, dropping anchor in Tyrrel bay at 1520. We took a taxi to the customs and immigration in Hillsboro to avoid running the gauntlet of the boat boys on the dinghy dock in Hillsboro. We ate ashore in the yacht club, which wasn't too bad.

The next day we motored over to Sandy Island, a small tropical sand bar lying in Hillsboro Bay, with palm trees and a coral reef, and we all went ashore in the dinghy. Alan was suffering with sunburn, not being used to the Caribbean sun, and was wearing socks to protect his feet! He'd decided to go snorkelling and we soon lost sight of him, eventually seeing him on the deck of *Blue Genie*.

From Hillsboro to Union Island is only a couple of hours and we picked up a mooring buoy in Clifton harbour on the afternoon of 28th January. I wanted to take Alan and Max to Lambi's Bar. Lambi was a larger-than-life character who ran a restaurant, offering a buffet meal, eat as much as you like for a fixed price, with a steel band. They specialised in limbo dancing, and he had several beautiful daughters who limbo'd almost impossibly low. It was a great night!

Next was Saline Bay, Mayreux, where we snorkelled among the turtles, and then on to the Tobago Cays. From Tobago Cays to Mustique once again the wind was on the nose, but with reefed main, staysail and yankee we tacked and were on a buoy in Mustique three hours later. We spent the night in Basil's Bar, and no, there were no celebrities there!

The next morning, after a swim off the back of the boat, we upped anchor and sailed with main and yankee the short distance to Admiralty Bay, Bequia. On 3rd February we moved round to Princess Elizabeth Bay, where we went ashore and did the taxi tour to the pottery and the hawksbill turtle sanctuary. The turtle sanctuary do some excellent work rescuing baby turtles; the local fishermen bring any that they find stranded in the rocks or being attacked by frigate birds.

Next came the short sail up to Walllilabo, St Vincent. This is a regular overnight stop for yachts on their way to or from the Grenadines. The boat boys can appear quite aggressive, wanting to help boats anchor and then take lines ashore to fasten to palm trees. They will quote a price to tie the boat up to include untying the next morning, but in the morning they are nowhere to be seen and you have to pay someone else to untie you. Also they will offer to tie you to a mooring buoy for a price, but as soon as it gets dark the owner of the buoy appears, demanding payment with the threat of casting you adrift!

Wallilaboo was where *Pirates of the Caribbean* was filmed, and the harbour was still like the film set. Alan was very interested in in this, being a fan of the film, and it was good to go ashore and wander and imagine Captain Jack Sparrow ashore and the *Black Pearl* lying at anchor.

On 5th February we said goodbye to Wallilaboo and headed back to St. Lucia. The weather was foul with winds up to 32 knots with poor visibility and rain squalls. As we approached Marigot Bay we saw an upturned dinghy adrift, so I put out a Pan Pan radio call warning with the chart coordinates to inform boats in the area. As the weather was so awful we decided to pick up a buoy in Marigot Bay and continue to Rodney Bay the next day.

The weather had moderated by the next morning and we motor-sailed with main and yankee in the flukey wind up to Rodney Bay. The *Queen Mary 2* was anchored off Castries as we sailed by with their jolly boats puttering back and forth taking people ashore. Berth A 104 was available and we were tied up by about 12:40. It was time for Alan and Max to leave for the airport. It had been a good trip and it was good to have competent, experienced crew.

Our plan was to sail up to the Virgin Islands for the season, a trip of about 350 miles. On 14th February we left the marina and motored to the fuel dock. They were very busy and after messing about dodging the fishing boats jockeying for position I decided to anchor in the bay and have another attempt early the next morning.

On the 15th we upped anchor and lay off the fuel dock, where an assortment of boats were alongside the dock having been there overnight. They had all left by about **0800** and we were alongside and fuelled up before **0900**.

A reefed main and yankee gave us 7-8 knot beam reach in the 23-knot ENE wind. I decided to make the most of the conditions and head straight for Tortola, as the wind seemed set fair and there was very little shipping. 181 miles were logged in the first 24 hours, but during the morning of the 16th the wind started to moderate, so we motor-sailed for about eight hours until the wind picked up, giving us a brisk sail up to Tortola.

To clear customs in the BVIs, the ruling is that you are not allowed to pick up a mooring; you have to anchor, otherwise you are deemed to have landed without customs clearance. It seems strange that anchoring is OK but mooring is not!

Paperwork done, we moved round to Sopers Hole and on the 19th to Jost van Dyke, where Foxy's bar is always a good run ashore. In 1997 we had chartered a 40ft Beneteau for New Year with our friends Graham, Cesira and Joyce and spent New Year in Great Harbour.

On 20th February we left Jost and sailed over to Cane Garden Bay, picking up a mooring. The northerly swell made it a bit rolly and we watched the surfers surfing up to the beach. During the night the northerly swell increased, and the boat was rolling onto her beam ends. Everything was moving around and it was difficult to move around the boat, and impossible to sleep. At first light we left the mooring and headed for Virgin Gorda, picking up a buoy in Leverick Bay at 1015.

We sailed around to different islands, ending up back at Nanny Cay, Tortola, to await our friends Dawn and Richard, who were joining us for a couple of weeks. They arrived on the

28th. We had never sailed with them before, although Richard had sailed previously on a large catamaran. We did a short sail to Norman Island and had dinner in the *Willy T,* a trading schooner that had been converted to a restaurant. It was turbulent with fairly high winds, and with all of the dinghies tied alongside the ship it was tricky clambering over them to reach the boarding platform. I should have insisted on all of us wearing buoyancy aids, although no one else on the ship seemed to have them. The meal was OK and the music and general atmosphere, although rowdy, were pleasing

The weather, although fine, was very windy with gusts of up to 30 knots. We sailed from Norman Island to Sopers Hole with reefed main and staysail, a short trip, but there were no mooring buoys so we carried on to Jost van Dyke, stayed the night and visited Foxy's Bar. Next morning we did a short beat to Sopers Hole. Dawn and Richard were loving the short day sails to the different Islands, especially the snorkelling on the Cooper Island Reef. The wind was a relentless 20 to 30 knots, but moored in the lee of the Island it was fairly calm.

Virgin Gorda is beautiful and so is Gorda Sound, a large sheltered bay with Moskito Island lying at the entrance. A few years ago whilst chartering we'd anchored and gone ashore for a meal in the restaurant, and we took a wander around now it was deserted, taking Dawn and Richard ashore. The restaurant was abandoned, but the bar still had full bottles on the shelves and tables laid and looked as though it was waiting for customers. The chalets still had bedding and everywhere was neat and tidy. We wandered around wondering what had happened to cause the island to be deserted.

The path round to the beach was bordered by small solar-powered lights, so we felt as though we were trespassing, but all of the beaches in the BVIs are open to the public. On the beach, the bar looked forlorn. We paddled and were amazed at the fish swimming so close in. The Island seemed an idyllic spot for a small, peaceful resort and it was sad to see it deserted.

All too soon it was time to head back to Nanny Cay to say goodbye to our crew. The Baths off the End of Virgin Gorda are a popular snorkelling spot, so we picked up a mooring and took the dinghy to the dinghy mooring buoys, where we spent a pleasant hour splashing about among the rocks and the myriad of brightly coloured fish.

It was sad to see our friends leave, but we had Graham and Cesira due to join us a few days later. They arrived on 20th March and we left Nanny Cay and motor-sailed up to Virgin Gorda, anchoring off the Bitter End for the night, and then once again to anchor off Moskito Island. Our new crew were amazed at the island being abandoned, as the last time we'd visited we'd all gone ashore for a meal. I was fascinated by the Island and I'd heard that it was for sale, the price being $7m, which didn't seem too bad!

On 23rd we moved to the dock at Leverick Bay to fuel up, we planned to sail down to Antigua, and on 25th March we said goodbye to Virgin Gorda and headed for Nevis. The wind was a steady 15 to 20 knots and with reefed main, staysail and yankee we had a brisk 6-7 knot sail, anchoring of Pinney Beach around 0900 on the 26th. Going ashore in the dinghy to check in with customs etc, the dock was seen to have lost some of its planks and sharp nails were sticking out, threatening to puncture the dinghy, but we found an area with a better edge.

It was interesting to visit the Nelson Museum. Nelson met his wife Fanny Nisbet in 1781 while commander of the frigate *Boreas*. Her father was a senior judge on the island. They married in 1787 and she fell ill in 1805 after Nelson's death at

Trafalgar and never fully recovered, dying in 1815.

A 12-15 knot ENE breeze took us the 40-mile sail to Antigua. The wind was steady and moderated as we approached the Island, and we were tied up on C dock in Jolly harbour at 1515. I'd been looking forward to visiting the Tot Club, which I Joined in 2000. The club carries on the tradition of the Royal Navy tot of rum, which was stopped in the 60s when it was considered dangerous for sailors to be operating technical machinery under the influence of alcohol! We anchored in Falmouth, just a short walk to English Harbour. The Tot Club meetings were in the Copper & Lumber Hotel. Graham and Cesira were not usually rum drinkers, but they enjoyed the tot. I always found it amusing that after the tot suddenly everyone was talking in loud voices!

Next was a short motor-sail to Green Island, where we anchored and snorkelled. Afterwards we returned to English Harbour and had another night at the Tot Club. As it was my birthday I declared a mismuster. which involved me in asking all the members to join me for another tot.

We were tied stern to the dock in English Harbour, which was most convenient as Graham and Cesira were leaving the ship and Alan and Karen were joining us. Alan walked on to the boat on the afternoon of 3rd April, having left Karen in one of the dockside bars enjoying a gin and tonic, so we all went to join her. As Alan is a keen snorkeller, we left English Harbour on 5th April and motored the short distance to Green Island, where the snorkelling is exceptional. We stayed until the 7th and then sailed and motor-sailed round to Falmouth and had dinner in the Yacht Club.

The bus service in Antigua is remarkable. For two EC dollars (at that time the exchange rate was $4EC to £1) you can go almost anywhere, and we decided to take the bus to

Radcliffe Quay, a duty-free area selling jewellery etc. Alan and Karen seemed engrossed in a large tray of rings in one of the big jewellery outlets, and then announced that they had just got engaged! Ann and I were so happy for them and to celebrate we had a bottle of champagne.

Next port of call was Deep Bay, with its idyllic half-moon shaped beach, gin-clear water and the wreck of the *Andes*, a schooner sunk over 100 years ago. The wreck is an ideal snorkelling site, being shallow with part of the bow of the ship out of the water.

At the end of the bay was a large hotel which had a dress code of collared shirts and trousers for male diners. Alan and I were wearing shorts, but we managed to get served. On returning to the dinghy we had a nice surprise – someone had left several bags of garbage in it, probably thinking it funny!!

Next morning we dinghied over to the wreck of the *Andes*. The hull is intact and is home to a myriad brightly coloured fish. The snorkelling is superb and dinghies can be tied up to the bow of the wreck.

On 10th April it was time to head back to Jolley. Alan and Karen were leaving and there were maintenance jobs to do before the trip back down to Grenada and our summer hurricane berth. The trip to Prickly Bay, Grenada is about 350 miles, and I planned to set off from Jolly Harbour and then Island-hop down to St Lucia and then sail non-stop to Grenada.

The first hop was a 40-mile beam reach south to Deshais on the NW coast of Guadeloupe. We left Falmouth at 07:45 on 19th April under main and yankee. The wind was easterly 20- 28 knots and as it increased we needed to reef the yankee as we approached the island. It was a good brisk sail, and the anchor splashed at about 1430.

Isle Des Saints was a short trip and we anchored off Isle Cabrit for the night before heading down to Roseau, Dominica, where we picked up a buoy off the Anchorage Hotel. From Roseau to Anse Mitan, Martinique, It is only a short trip to St Lucia from Martinique and we were on berth 56 in the Marina midday on 26th April. I decided to service the engine before the trip to Grenada, although It had only done 549 hours from new.

We were on the fuel dock on the morning of the 1st May, and after filling tanks we cast off for the 150-mile passage to Prickly Bay. The wind was ESE for most of the trip, gusting up to 30 knots, but with reefed main and yankee we were making a good 7 knots as we sailed down the Windward Islands Chain, St Lucia, St Vincent and the Grenadines, Carriacou and Grenada, dropping the hook at 09:45 on 2nd May. The boat was scheduled to be lifted out and laid up ashore at Spice Island Marine Services in the north-west corner of Prickly Bay. This was a large secure boatyard with most marine trades available.

With all of the canvas removed and the water maker full of chemicals to protect the membranes, she was ready to be hauled out, and we moved into Cool Runnings, a small apartment block overlooking the boatyard. We'd had a good season with several couples joining us. From leaving St David's on 26th January we had sailed 1327 miles, had four lots of friends sailing with us and visited numerous Islands. As we headed away from *Blue Genie* in the taxi, we wondered what the next season had in store for us.

CHAPTER 3

Hurricane

Returning to the UK in May was all part of our plan to spend winters sailing in the sun and the summer at home in the UK, and soon it was as if we'd never been away. Ann and I went back into the office to find that the company were employing a lot of agency workers and the profit margins were down. This was in part due to customers messing us about. A lot of the old-school managers and supervisors had left or retired and the new intake thought boatbuilding could be managed like mass production in the motor trade. "Just in time" supply didn't work, designs changed frequently, and quite often parts supplied bore no relation to the drawings on file at customers' design offices. Often a line manager or supervisor would ask for a part to be changed slightly to better fit the boat, and this happened frequently. This became obvious if they tried to buy the part from elsewhere, although they would often send one of our products to be copied. For "just in time" to work we would have to keep large stocks of customers' products, even if we were given schedules of requirements for forward planning because of last-minute design changes it didn't work.

To start with we sacked all of the agency workers and then increased the number of employees on piecework. This seemed to work, and profit margins started to increase. We had been supplying all the major boatbuilders with a range of oval-topped cleats, hinges and various other standard parts. The orders started to dry up, and I discovered that a large Italian company had copied all of our designs and included them in their brochure. I was annoyed, but I couldn't do anything about it. One of my customers must have given them our parts to copy. This went on a lot in this industry but I couldn't understand why a customer would pay more for a competitor's product!

I was looking forward to the next Caribbean season, although the UK weather was OK and it was nice catching up with friends and having barbecues with the swimming pool in daily use. I was collecting the necessary spares for *Blue Genie* and planning the next season. I had a berth booked at Manuel Reef Marina in Tortola for the next season and planned to sail the boat up there in November.

At the beginning of September there was news of a storm in the Caribbean approaching Grenada. I wasn't particularly worried, as Grenada was out of the hurricane belt, or so I had been led to believe. It developed into Hurricane Ivan. I walked into our office on 8th September and our office lady Julia asked, "Have you heard the news? A hurricane has hit Grenada, and the whole island is devastated."

"It can't be, Grenada's outside the hurricane belt," I replied.

She dialled up some news footage on her computer, and I could hardly believe the scenes being shown. St. George's, the capital, was wrecked and the damage appeared to be over the entire island. Ann and I were shocked and fearful for the fate of *Blue Genie*, so we tried contacting the marina, but all communications were out. Our friends Hans and Hazel were staying in Grenada and we tried to contact them, and they sent us photographs of our boat.

Sailing in the BVIs after Alan and Karen's wedding, boat on autopilot with us all sitting on deck.

Blue Genie under sail.

Kevin and Ann on the bow of *Blue Genie*.

Disaster – boats wrecked in Grenada during Hurricane Ivan, *Blue Genie* 2nd from left with dinghy hanging from 1 Davit. The dinghy disappeared along with countless other items of equipment.

The whole line of boats had fallen over, like a line of dominoes. *Blue Genie* was lying on her side, the mast broken at the spreaders, the dinghy hanging erratically from one davit. The whole marina was like a bomb site. A lot of the people had lost everything. The island's emergency operations centre was destroyed and there was widespread looting. The island government imposed a curfew. Apparently the boatyard was littered with equipment that had fallen from the damaged yachts, but within a day or two it had disappeared. It was reported that soldiers were sent from Trinidad to assist in restoring order.

On 9th September, crews from two Royal Navy ships cleared the flooded airport and emergency flights started to get through. I was anxious to fly out and see the damage to *Blue Genie* for myself, so as soon as a flight was available Ann and I flew out. We had booked into True Blue Bay Hotel, which was fairly close to Prickly Bay and had a restaurant. The curfew hadn't yet been fully lifted, but we could do all that was necessary during daylight hours.

We checked into reception and were shown to our apartment. The girl showed us how the hot water controls worked in the bathroom, and that evening I decided to take a shower, but no matter where I turned the control there was no hot water. Later I looked up at the roof of the apartment and realised that the cistern was missing from the roof. Still, we were lucky – some apartments no longer had roofs!

During the night it started to rain and water was dripping into the apartment. As the rain increased the drip turned into a deluge, though luckily it was missing the bed. I didn't want to complain, as the hotel were doing their best under dreadful circumstances, but next morning I mentioned it to reception and the guy said that he would get a tarpaulin fitted to the roof, which they did, so at least we weren't being rained on.

On board *Blue Genie* we had two De Blasi folding bikes that had survived the storm, and these were invaluable for getting around. The boat looked sad and forlorn, but the hull appeared intact, the main damage being to the rig. I spoke to the insurance company and they appointed a surveyor, but he couldn't do anything until the boat was lifted upright, and there was a lot of clearing up to do before that could be done.

We weren't there when the boats were lifted, but the horror stories of masts being sawn off at deck level and the crude manner the boats were treated were reported to us, and we wondered what to expect the next time we flew out.

The surveyors, appointed by the Insurance company

Caribbean Marine Surveyors, ascertained that the hull was intact but there was some water damage below decks. Goodacre Marine from Port Solent were appointed by the insurers, and they shipped out a 40 ft container fitted out as a workshop with woodworking equipment and tools. I wondered whether I should have insisted that the boat be shipped back to the UK. Some of the other owners did this, but I decided that if the boat could be repaired where she was she would be back in operation quicker.

Just after the storm the dinghy had been hanging from one davit, and it was also there when the boat was lifted upright. I noticed it wasn't there when we flew out and went to the office and asked where they were storing the dinghies removed from the boats. The girl gave me a blank stare and said "What dinghies?" The dinghies had apparently gone to the same place as all the other kit that had disappeared into thin air!

The work done by Goodacres was excellent. The interior of the yacht looked like new, but the new mast was a problem. The company supplying the mast and rigging was Turbulence Ltd, and they had to obtain the mast from Kemp Masts. The original rig had been produced by Kemp in the UK, but Turbulence could only buy from Kemp Masts USA. The whole situation was to me haphazard, to say the least.

I obtained drawings of the rig from Moody's in the UK. The 47 was a new design, *Blue Genie* was boat No. 8 and when I looked at the rig Turbulence were about to supply, to my horror it appeared nothing like the original. It was about 2m shorter and the distance from deck level to the keel was also different. With keel-stepped masts the distance from the deck to the keel is crucial. On investigation I realised that the mast specification they were about to supply was for a 1980s Moody 47. Turbulence were adamant that they were correct and I had to produce drawings from the designer to prove that they were wrong.

The summer of 2005 was very stressful, but everything eventually came together, with the boat looking like her old self. There was much new equipment that had replaced items lost in the storm and its aftermath that needed to be checked out. The insurance company had done a deal with Budget Marine Chandlers, large chandlery, to give a 20% discount. We had a nice new dinghy and various other items that had been lost or stolen, and anything we required we could obtain at a discount.

The boat was launched in November 2005, and we were excited to take her out for sea trials.

On November 22nd 2005, we had moved the boat off the dock and anchored, and now we were ready to sail off into the sunset. The anchor was lifted and at 1120 we set off up island heading for Carriacou. At 1210 I noticed the battery warning light was on, and on investigation I found that he fan belt had fallen off. The engine was stopped and we tacked back to Prickly, dropping anchor at 1250. I fitted a new belt and on 25th I went for another check-out sail. The engine behaved itself and we tacked back and forth testing sails and rig; all seemed OK, so we returned to Prickly and anchored. I decided to move to a quieter location, and as the anchor came up it picked up an enormous lump of coral, we moved to the other side of the bay, where we were able to dislodge it and re-anchor. This is a problem in the Caribbean. Most of the bays where yachts anchor are now devoid of coral which has been dragged up by yacht anchors.

We moved the boat onto the dock at True Blue Bay, the Horizon yacht charter's dock, but they had space and agreed to look after the boat until we returned in February,

28th November 2005: A few days were spent checking everything out and then it was time to fly back for Christmas. The boat was back together with all of the repairs done, but I could see that there would probably be underlying problems for the foreseeable future.

Alan and Karen's engagement in Antigua when they had been visiting us in 2004 was about to culminate in marriage. They were looking forward to having the ceremony at the Peter Island resort in the British Virgin Islands and then board *Blue Genie* for their honeymoon cruise. We needed to sail Blue Genie up from her berth at True Blue Bay, Grenada, to Peter Island, 500 miles to the north, for the wedding on 18th March.

We joined the ship on 9th February and left the dock on the 11th, looking forward to the BVIs and meeting up with our friends, but the engine immediately started giving problems. It wouldn't achieve full revs and the drive belt was slipping, so we sailed into St George's and anchored to try and fix the problem. I gave the engine a service and on the 12th we set off once again. At 1200 we were abeam Ronde Island, the wind was NE 25 gusting 35 knots, and under reefed main and genoa we tacked up to Tyrell Bay, Carriacou, then from Carriacou to Clifton Harbour Union Island. I'd had a new generator fitted in Grenada, and the insurance company seemed happy to pay for it. It had done 65 hours, so I decided to give it a first service.

Next came Bequia and then an overnight sail up to Rodney Bay St. Lucia, arriving at 0630 on the morning of 19th February. St. Lucia is a tropical rain forest island and the mosquitos are sometimes unbearable. Ann suffers more than me, I rarely get bitten and if I do the bites aren't too debilitating. The worst time is about 6 pm, and when you're walking on the beach the sand flies attack your ankles if you're unwary. A lot of the beach bars supply repellent sprays for their customers.

We spent a week in St Lucia while I was trying to fix the engine problems. It was overheating and smoking, so I changed the impeller on the sea water pump and fitted a new drive belt (no. 3).

At 0630 on the 29th, with tanks filled and everything working, we set off for Antigua, and as we rounded Pigeon Island with a 24-knot wind on the beam we were looking forward to a brisk 150-mile sail up to Falmouth. After about six hours the wind decided to mess us about, becoming light and variable for a time, and then gusted up to 30 knots before dying completely. There were squalls during he night that would strike without warning, drenching the boat and the watch keeper. Visibility was down to about a mile, but there were few ships around. On one occasion we saw a small ship with another huge radar echo fairly close. There seemed to be a lot of activity between the two with flashing lights, and I realised it was a tug towing an enormous barge or oil rig. The distance between the two was about half a mile, and we altered course so as not to go between them.

We could see the squalls on the radar. The wind would back and increase to about 35 knots as they struck. As we approached Falmouth the wind settled, and for the last six hours we had a brisk and uneventful sail, picking up a buoy in Falmouth harbour at about midday.

John and Andy came over to visit; we first met John and his Swedish boyfriend Anders when we did the 99' ARC. He'd now split from Anders and was with his new partner, Andy. They were now living on John's Ocean 60 schooner and were working on the superyachts in Falmouth and English harbours.

On 9th March in flat calm, we set off for Tortola. The wind picked up and soon we had a N/NE 15-knot breeze. As the day turned into night the moon and stars shone so bright it was almost like daytime. Approaching Tortola, as we sailed between Dead Chest and Deadman's Bay, I looked at the entrance to the resort. We planned to stay a few days on their dock during the wedding, but the down side was the cost. The price to lay alongside their dock was 150 US dollars per night! But it's not every day that your best friends get married.

We went into Nanny Cay for a few days and then moved over to Peter Island on the 13th March 2006. Ann and I started getting the boat ready for the happy couple. They were due to arrive on the island ferry about 10pm. We saw the ferry arrive and were relieved to see a tired Alan And Karen disembarking. They had been travelling for over 20 hours. After checking in at the hotel they were whisked away to the beach bar for a meal, but we'd already had dinner so we agreed to see them later. We hitched a lift on one of the many buggies (golf carts) that were used for transporting people around.

Their room was a chalet fairly close to the dock. The Peter Island staff seemed a bit resentful of Ann and me for some reason; the resort had a beautiful half-moon-shaped beach and they were trying to keep non-residents away. We were just about OK as we were with Alan and Karen. They could identify residents by the yellow hotel towels, and anyone with a different colour towel was asked to leave. Luckily our boat towels were the same colour as the hotel's.

I was running the generator for charging and the master switch burnt out, so I plugged into the Peter Island shore power, but that didn't work either. The Peter Island electrician came on board and took the master switch apart and said he could obtain spares. I was having to run the main engine for charging, and I didn't want our mechanical problems with the boat to cast a shadow over the events. The electrician didn't really know what he was doing and left us with the switch gear in bits, and then avoided us.

The four of us took the ferry into Road Town Tortola to arrange flowers and meet up with the minister who was doing the wedding ceremony, Alan needed to buy a new shirt as he'd forgotten to pack his wedding shirt.

It was a happy time as the wedding day approached. On the day I "dressed ship" (put the flags out) so the boat looked impressive and I was proud of her – shame the electrics were shot. Karen looked lovely in her wedding dress and Alan looked smart in his cream suit. Ann and I dressed up for the occasion and after the ceremony the photos were done on the beach. I'd arranged for the photographer from Yacht Shots, who did the wedding photos, and he agreed to take some photos of the boat sailing with us all on board when we left the island.

After the wedding ceremony we returned to *Blue Genie* for some champagne, and invited a couple from a yacht that was lying alongside to join us. The champagne flowed and we had a jolly time. There was a buffet meal in the hotel restaurant in the evening to round off the celebrations, and we looked forward to sailing away the next morning.

I tried to contact the Peter Island electrician for news of our electrical spares, but he was nowhere to be seen and wasn't answering his mobile phone. He'd left the Mastervolt switchgear in bits, so I re-assembled everything to make it safe, but was left the engine alternator as the only means of charging!

The resort had ice lockers positioned around the chalets and we filled the now defunct freezer with ice cubes. Bags of ice could be bought from most dockside shops, so that wasn't a problem. When I went to the office to pay for our dockage they wanted to charge for the time the electrician had spent leaving our electrics unsafe and in a mess. I was furious and told them what I thought of their services, but in the circumstances I didn't want to make too much of a fuss.

As Peter Island disappeared astern and we headed up to Virgin Gorda, the Yacht Shots photographer was zooming around taking photos, I set the autopilot and with main, staysail and yankee set we all sat on deck as he took the photos.

We picked up a buoy in Leverick Bay and the next day moved to the Bitter End, the final island outpost before the Caribbean meets the open Atlantic. The enormous coral reef that protects the bay from the Atlantic, Eustacia Sound, has several snorkelling areas and I took Alan in the dinghy to a site that I had visited previously. Amid the coral were the timbers of an aged wreck with the remains of a couple of cannons festooned with coral.

We left the Bitter End and anchored off Moskito island. The snorkelling isn't as dramatic as the Bitter End reef, but the coral wasn't too bad. We all went ashore, but now there were notices warning people off, although the Island was still uninhabited, so we didn't stay very long.

On leaving Gorda Sound we picked up a mooring at the Baths for some more snorkelling and then motored to Cooper Island. The coral at Cooper is beautiful and as we snorkelled we could see scuba divers beneath us. On leaving Cooper we visited Marina Cay and for our last night together picked up a mooring on Norman Island for a visit to the Willy T restaurant. We all had rotis, a Caribbean dish that is like a pancake filled with chicken and potatoes, very filling. We also had quite a few drinks. From there we went to Road Town, Tortola, where we picked up a buoy off Penns' Landing Marina. Karen had an upset tummy, and we didn't know whether it was the Willy T roti or the copious amounts of rum we had drunk! It was a bit shallow where we were and we started touching bottom, and although it was sand I decided to move to our berth at Manuel Reef Marina.

After the hurricane our insurers, the Navigators and General, paid out without question and couldn't have been more helpful. However we decided not to renew with them as they were not prepared to offer named storm cover, and as we intended to remain in the Caribbean we changed to Pantaenius Yacht Insurers. Named storm cover was possible with them and they would cover boats in Tortola providing they were prepared to their instructions. The boats needed to be ashore at Nanny Cay Marina, mast removed, all covers and canvas removed and the boats shored up with the supports chained together and anchored to the ground with special ground anchors. This was fairly expensive, and the marina insisted that no one was allowed on the boats once they were laid up. We decided to do this rather than have the bother of moving the boat down to Trinidad or some other place beyond the hurricane belt.

So *Blue Genie* was laid up at Nanny Cay Marina in Tortola for the hurricane season. I had been watching the weather closely and fortunately the season's hurricanes had missed the Virgin Islands.

On our next visit to the Caribbean we decided to stay for a few day in Antigua and visit the Tot Club and catch up with the English harbour crowd. I'd given Instructions to Nanny Cay to re-launch and re-rig the boat and place it on a berth ready for our arrival. Alan and Karen were joining us for a week's sailing and we were looking forward to being on the boat again.

In Antigua I had a phone call from the manager of Nanny

Cay Marina to inform me that the boat had suffered some water damage and he had put it on a marina berth but wanted us to move it as soon as we arrived. We were a bit worried after the problems we'd had in Grenada, but the manager told us he had run the engine and everything was working OK.

As soon as we arrived we went to see the guy and he said "It's very bad," but assured us that the boat was OK, When we went to the boat she looked OK from the outside but when we went aboard it was heartbreaking, All of the beautiful Joinery that had been re surfaced or replaced by Goodacres was now stained, and there was a tidemark around the inside of the boat about 9" above the floor. The smell was awful. I realised what had happened. When the crew from Nanny Cay had moved the boat ashore they had placed all the fenders in the aft lockers and hadn't fastened the lockers down, so when it rained the lockers leaked into the boat.

The marina manager came to the boat and told us we had to go to as he needed the berth for a rally which was due to start, and the Marina would be full with no available berths!

On checking the boat I found the engine alternator wasn't working, and the starter motor worked only intermittently. The fresh water pump, shower pump and refrigeration were not working, the radar cable was corroded and the radar not responding, and the water maker pump was inoperative. All of the 240 circuit was suspect. All of the pumps below floor level were not working and the floor itself needed replacing.

I went to see the Manager and he told me again that we had to leave as the boat was operational and they needed the berth. I told him the boat was not safe to move, and he said he'd checked it out and it was. In the end I told him to move the boat to somewhere else in the marina to free up the berth, but I wasn't prepared to take a boat out to sea in that state.

I contacted Pantaenius insurance and they agreed to send a surveyor to inspect the boat in the meantime I had Alan and Karen coming out for some sailing! I couldn't let them down and they were due to arrive in a few days. I decided to see if a charter boat was available and went to see Horizon Yacht Charters, who operate out of Nanny Cay. They had a Bavaria 42 available, It wasn't as plush as *Blue Genie* or as big, but the accommodation was adequate. Ann and I cleaned the boat up, I checked the oil levels that Nanny Cay claimed to have changed and found the gearbox to be full of water!

The surveyor who came was very thorough and implied that the company would pay for repairs, but it was a shock to then receive a letter from the insurers to say that as the water ingress had happened over a long period the boat was not covered; they said the boat should have had regular checks. The problem was that I had wanted to arrange for the Marina to do regular checks, but I was told that once boats have been laid up no one is allowed to board them.

The marina denied any responsibility, and nobody would talk to me. It was one of the worst times I had endured during the whole of my sailing years. That was the moment I decided to ship the boat back to the UK and put it up for sale on brokerage.

The charter boat, *Dawn Raider*, was booked from the 12th April, I wondered what Alan and Karen would make of it, as they were due to arrive with no idea there was a problem.

I was using a hire car to get around, so I was able to pick them up from the airport. They were a bit disappointed that they were not sailing on *Blue Genie*, but when I took them on board they realised that the charter was the best solution.

The Bavaria 42 was a superb sailing machine and handled beautifully. We did a short sail over to Cooper Island to put her through her paces. We had booked into the Cooper Island restaurant for the evening, but there were no moorings, and as the holding is no good for anchoring we called them on the radio to cancel and headed over to Marina Cay to spend an evening in the Pussers Rum Bar and sample their "Pain Killers" (rum cocktails), picking up a mooring buoy at 1530.

Next morning we motor-sailed up to Virgin Gorda, past Spanish Town and into Gorda Sound, mooring up in Leverick Bay around mid day. On 15th April we went alongside to fill up with fuel and water, as not having a water maker I needed to ensure that we didn't run out!

Next we planned to visit Anegada, a low-lying coral island that is not visible from a yacht until you're a couple of miles away. It has a large offshore reef rich in marine life and dotted with shipwrecks, Yachts stray from the buoyed channel at their peril!!

We entered the anchorage and found there were no moorings available, The bay is fairly shallow and the Bavaria with 9ft draught was 2ft deeper than the Moody. After several attempts to anchor, occasionally touching bottom, we decided to head back to Virgin Gorda mooring at Bitter End. Bitter End is a 'good run ashore' with several bars, a pub and a large yacht club/restaurant. Not many people were using the outdoor gym, but it was nice to explore the area.

On this trip we hadn't done much snorkelling, so we decided to stop off at the Baths on our way to Trellis Bay. We left Bitter End at 1000 on the 16th and anchored at the baths at 1130, where we snorkelled for a couple of hours before upping anchor and heading for Trellis Bay. Trellis is not that popular with charter boats and is home to a lot of 'live-aboards', but there are some great bars and a well-stocked supermarket. We dinghied ashore to try one of the bars. They were serving very strong rum punches, and Alan got so plastered he fell out of the dinghy!

After Trellis we headed for Cooper Island, planning to arrive early, hopefully before all of the mooring buoys were taken. We arrived about 0930 and luckily a buoy was available. The coral reef at Cooper was Alan's favourite snorkelling spot. We spent the day there and had dinner in the restaurant.

On 18th April it was time to return to Nanny Cay and hand *Dawn Raider* back to the charter company. The boats were handed back on the fuel berth in order for the charter company to fill all tanks ready for the next charter and to ensure charterers pay for the fuel and water used. The boat was then taken round to the Horizon dock.

Unfortunately it was time to say adios to our crew. The trip had been a success despite the problems with *Blue Genie*, I had organised the shipping back to UK with Seven Star Yacht Transport and a spell in Goodacre's boat yard for Barry Goodacre once again to work his magic on the woodwork.

CHAPTER 4

Business bothers

Back in the UK everything was going well, and our new house was nearing completion. We were now in **2006** and businesses were going into recession, although we had got used to this happening every 7-10 years over the last **30** years or so. The UK economy had for several years been experiencing steady growth, although manufacturing generally was sluggish, and the UK unemployment rates were similar to the rest of the EU.

We moved into Acre House on 6th October **2006**. it had taken over a year to build and was slightly larger than Chapter House next door, which I had sold to my son James.

On Friday 13th October, Fairline summoned James and Andrew, our Operations Director, and told them that they were moving all of their stainless steel supplies to other suppliers unless we reduced all of our prices by 25%, there were several other demands, but it was obvious that they were sacking us. We could survive by reducing the workforce and cutting back, but it came as a shock as we had always gone out of our way to supply them on time.

The bad news wasn't over. That evening there was a knock on the door. It was Richard with the dreadful news that Don, one of my closest friends, had been killed in a motor bike accident the day before. My business problems suddenly seemed trivial compared to the horror and grief that Don's wife George and daughter Emma must be suffering.

The loss of the Fairline work made a big difference, and 2007 became the first year that the company had made a loss since 1980.

Back in Tortola, the boat was loaded on 11th May 2007. Sevenstar Yacht Transport BV were a very efficient company and made the process as painless as possible. I had arranged for the boat to be delivered to Premier Marina in Port Solent where GBR (Goodacre) were based for the refurbishment. I had full confidence in GBR after the excellent service they had given me down in Grenada. It arrived together with 42 other yachts on the MV *Slotergracht* on 21st. May. I planned to put the boat with Moody Brokerage ashore at their Swanwick Marina, each year in September, during the Southampton Boat Show. Moody's hold a "Used Boat Show" and have minibuses running people back and forth to the show. I thought this would be a good opportunity to sell the boat, as she was in excellent condition with everything working and although she had done many miles the engine hours were very low.

Although there were a few viewings at the September Used Boat Show, no one was prepared to make an offer in the difficult economic conditions. This wasn't a great problem, it was just costing me marina fees while the boat was laid up ashore.

Meanwhile under the Tony Blair Labour Government the UK economy was going from bad to worse, and in June 2007 Blair was succeeded by Gordon Brown, but the economy continued to decline. Cooney Marine was back in profit after our problems in 2006, but I could see problems coming up. I decided that the company needed to tighten up in preparation for the looming recession. One of the managers seemed to be causing dissent in the factory and problems with customers, though my attitude that 'the customer is always right' even when they are wrong had always stood us in good stead. It was difficult to get rid of anybody, especially with employment tribunals that were loaded against employers, so it was necessary have a 'compromise agreement' and pay them off. It had become very difficult for employers to sack people. After this man had gone several former employees contacted us asking for their jobs back and customers rang to say "Thank goodness you've got rid of him".

Finally I had an offer on the boat. I was asking £260,000, and the offer was 250,000 euros, approx £200,000. I turned it down. Moody's were selling off two 47s for the same asking price and the broker said I should have no problem achieving this.

I had no interest in sailing *Blue Genie* now she was for sale and decided to awaken my interest in gardening. Acre House as the name implies, has a very large garden, and I planned to grow vegetables in the raised beds. In my diary I wrote:

28th August 2008

Yesterday I had a greenhouse delivered, it arrived at about 0900 and there were many parts to assemble. The instructions were quite poor and some of the components were missing. The photographs and diagrams were not much help. I suppose it will take quite a few days to finish off.

I don't know why I wanted a greenhouse in the first place, I'm probably making a rod for my own back.

I am hoping to sell the boat soon but the way things are going with the economy it is a struggle and I am beginning to think I should have accepted the offer made recently even though it was quite low. I don't think I shall buy another boat although Ann keeps looking on the internet at small monohulls. I think she has gone off the Idea of a catamaran.

Our friends Dawn and Richard have invited us down to the south of France for a few days. I quite like the idea of a house in France. I would like to spend a lot more time there and an apartment can be obtained quite cheaply. I quite fancy the French way of life and I think I could master enough of the language to get by.

We have company this weekend, Alan and Karen and tomorrow, Saturday I shall do a barbecue, that is the easiest meal for me to do and for Sunday I have a brace of pheasants in the freezer. It is a nice evening, very mild although overcast, and we are sitting out on the patio. I can hear children's laughter, I think they probably have a swimming pool party going on.

At the moment we are watching the progress of Ann's dad's trains on ebay. Ann said they had no value and I should put them in the skip, I said it would be a shame to throw them away so why not put them on ebay. We are up to 84 quid so far. Well! Surprise surprise, in the last few seconds of bidding they went up to £312.

Ann's Dad's model railway had been packed away after he died and Ann wanted to clear out a load of unwanted bits and pieces. She was going to throw it all away until I suggested that we sell it on ebay.

Alan and Karen came for the weekend and on Saturday night we had a barbecue and on Sunday we had the pheasants, so it was a good weekend. On the Sunday we all went to Huntingdon Garden Centre. I bought some pictures for the pool building, but wouldn't have time to hang them before going to France.

At work, the Nissin pipe bender was out of action on 1½" dia tube and spares were proving difficult to obtain. James and I flew out to Japan when we bought the machine, but we were having to obtain spares through their German agent and they seemed to have no sense of urgency. On the 2nd September we were flying out to France and staying with Dawn and Richard at Le Lavandou campsite.

3rd September 2008

Yesterday we went to Hyères and believe it or not ended up at the marina. Dawn has been feeling a bit rough all day with chest pains and pains in her arms, and we all know what that sounds like. Ann and I prepared dinner and Dawn turned in early. The rest of us were steadily drinking when the power went off. Richard found a lamp and we took a candle back to our caravan.

At 0700 we heard Richard's car – he'd taken Dawn to the local hospital. We had a message from Richard that she was undergoing tests for a suspected blood clot.

It's about midday and I do not know what's going to happen. D&R are at the hospital, Ann is at the pool and I am reading my book.

Dawn was OK, the doctor said it was an infection of the pericardium, whatever that means. Ann and I did dinner and Dawn turned in early – she looked a lot better already.

7ᵗʰ September

Today Dawn and Richard took us out to lunch to Auberge De La Male, a family-run restaurant that is always full and very good. They were treating us as a present for our 40ᵗʰ wedding anniversary, which is on 14th. We will be in Paris on 14ᵗʰ, I'd decided that we didn't want a big party to celebrate and that we would go away, just the two of us.

Tomorrow we fly back to England. The weather has been wonderful in France and I wonder what to expect back home. The Southampton Boat Show starts Friday, we will be away until Wednesday although I will probably go to the show some time next week.

A long weekend in Paris on the train was planned, and we left the car at Huntingdon Station, planning to travel first-class all the way to Paris. We got as far as St. Pancras only to be told that the Channel Tunnel was closed due to a fire.

We decided to go to Dover in the hope of getting on a ferry. On arrival at Dover there was absolute chaos. The Eurostar representative told us that a bus would take us from the station to the ferry terminal, but in the end we took a taxi.

I managed to book a Sea France ferry due to leave at 1730, but on investigation it turned out that we would get into Calais at 2030 and the last train for Paris left at 2000. We decided to cancel the trip and spend the weekend in London. A hotel was found for Friday night, but it was very expensive. Ann then managed to find another for Saturday, Sunday and Monday. On Saturday we had a day on the river. On Monday evening we went to see the show *Hairspray*, which was very good. I missed the Southampton show, the first I had missed for many years.

18th September

Apparently we are doing quite well at Southampton, although the visitor numbers are lower than last year. James is in the office today but will be back in Southampton tomorrow.

Teri's dog had a hysterectomy yesterday and also had her tail shortened. The dog is expected to make a full recovery, but I don't know how long it will take. It was necessary to shorten the tail because it kept being injured and was bleeding over the furniture. I was under the impression that it was illegal to shorten dog's tails, but apparently it is allowed for health reasons.

Another Friday, another weekend. I don't know how this month is doing, it has been very hard to achieve required production levels. A lot of the Jobs are now quite tight on price so if anything goes wrong it soon makes a loss.

The year to date is overall making a profit, but I think it will be tight, however after last year that will be a good result. The loss of the Fairline work made a big difference to the company but it seems that we are pulling through. Last year was the first year that we have made a loss since we started and it was good that the company had a healthy bank balance to carry us through.

Blue Genie is not selling. I think that with the credit crunch it could be some time before she is sold. It is a pity that Ann has gone off sailing and won't go anywhere near the boat, so we haven't done any sailing for over a year.

I thought we could charter a boat this winter but that Idea seems to have gone cold.

Tomorrow I will have another attempt to build the greenhouse. Richard has offered to help me fit the glass, although the base needs doing first.

I am disappointed with the garden this year, all my brassicas have been eaten by caterpillars.

22nd September

Yesterday Ann and I had a swim in the morning and missed breakfast. Our daughter Teri came over at about 12. The dog seemed a bit sorry for herself she was wearing an enormous collar to stop it tormenting the stitches on its tummy and the end of its tail. We were doing dinner for 9 people. Teri took Christian to play a football match in Raunds and while they were gone Ann and I prepared dinner.

I pulled some carrots from the garden, they are the only surviving vegetables apart from a few tomatoes and some onions.

We eventually ate at 1630 and after we sat outside, some of the kids went for a swim and some played football in the garden.

September was a very busy month and everyone was working very hard to ensure targets were met. To improve morale I have bought cakes for everyone and will give them out for afternoon break.

Over the last few weeks we had been negotiating with Premier Marina at Swanwick with regard to taking over their fabrication department. They had some interesting plant and machinery that should give us extra capacity and some highly skilled fabricators. Their order book was strong, which was surprising...

Fairline announced 90 redundancies due to the downturn in orders. it seems that since taking their marketing away from B.A. Peters and sacking us they have lost a lot of business. Luckily we do very little for them now.

October should be a good month as it is a 23-day month. I had another offer on Blue Genie, 150,000 euros, I don't think they are serious and it probably will not sell until next season. The new tooling for the Nissin bender arrived but was tight, we did however get it working

6th October

I heard this morning that our offer for Swanwick Marine Fabrication had been accepted, I am in Swanwick at the moment checking over the boat.

I am staying at the Spinnaker, which is a pub opposite the marina. Andy Sims is coming down tomorrow morning for a meeting with the directors of Premier Marinas. With the doom and gloom in the financial markets I think it is a brave move to be making, but I am looking forward to the new challenges that this takeover represents.

I am looking forward to the announcement in the press, which should send a positive message to our customers and competitors. It should also cause a buzz of excitement among the Cooney workforce.

I noticed on the boat that one of the window leaks had reappeared so I have been to the chandlery to get some Creeping Crack cure. It is a real pain in the arse finding leaks on a boat. The leak is usually quite a way from the damp patch inside the boat.

The meeting should have taken place at 0930 on 7th October and I was expecting Andy to arrive at the Spinnaker at 0800 for a breakfast meeting to go over the proposals, but I had a phone call from him at 0800 to say he was stuck in traffic on the A34. I had checked out of the Spinnaker and eventually met him in the car park at 0940 where we had a hurried meeting to discuss options before our postponed meeting with Swanwick Marina's directors. The meeting went very well and everything that we queried was settled and agreed.

Today is the anniversary of Fairline giving us the sack, it is also the anniversary of finding out that Don had been killed the day before. A lot has happened in two years. We have a sound customer base and are in profit in spite of Fairline.

We have agreed terms on the Swanwick takeover and it is being seen as a very positive move by Cooney people and customers alike. But whenever we have positive things happening there is always something or someone that clouds the situation.

There were two employees that were negative in their attitude and affecting the morale of others. This was causing a lot of problems, especially among the apprentices and more impressionable younger workers. A few years ago it would have been possible to sack them, but now it had become almost impossible to get rid of anyone, no matter how useless they were.

CHAPTER 5

Sailing through troubled waters

✖

As winter **2008/9** approached *Blue Genie* wasn't selling and I knew she probably wouldn't sell now until next year. I had received silly offers, but I was not prepared to give her away. Usually after a recession the sale of used boats picks up due to the fact that not so many new ones have been produced. The negative stories in the press were not doing industry much good and it would probably remain like that until the new year.

At work the order book was now holding up very well, although several of our customers were laying men off.

23rd October 2008

This year seems to have flown past so far, the months seem to go quicker and quicker. There are a lot of positive things happening, James has sold his house and the business seems to be doing well in spite of the recession and all the crap that Gordon Brown has got us into.

We've had to suspend an employee for stirring up trouble in the factory. I am hoping we will have grounds to sack him. He was a chargehand and one of his duties was handing out Job cards and progressing the work, checking times etc. He was stirring the men up by comparing people's earnings, which was expressly forbidden under the conditions of his employment contract.

When the contract was brought to his attention the response was "I didn't sign that, I'm dyslexic and can't read." Even though his job was issuing Job cards he was claiming to be disabled due to his dyslexia. Eventually it was decided to pay him off and not have the stress and disruption of a tribunal.

We are up against it in the Factory, we are 4 polishers short. After we found that they were illegal immigrants they left!

James is handling the production and making it happen. There always seems to be a problem just around the corner ready to knock production, but James usually overcomes it.

29th October

Went down to the boat yesterday to put a heater on board. When I arrived she was on a trailer being moved. I managed to climb aboard and rigged up a de-humidifier and heater. I then went to the brokerage office to discuss the offer on the boat and decided to accept it. It's a bit lower than I expected, but now I just want to be rid of it.

The trip back from Swanwick was pretty awful with a blizzard reducing visibility to a few yards.

Another month draws to an end and we have the usual chaos. There is always something to go wrong. Some of the rails for Sunseeker would not fit on the truck, so they will have to go on Monday.

Last night six of us went to a medieval night at Coombe Abbey organised by Andrew Sims with his BMF hat on. Most people dressed up but a few didn't, which was a shame, Andrew managed to get Sunseeker and Princess there, but Sealine and Fairline chose not to support the event. Andrew stayed over and had meetings with both customers and some suppliers this morning. Pete Gregory of Sunseeker is here at the moment being shown around. Quite a coup really to get a high profile executive from Sunseeker here. I don't know what the final figure for the month will be but I am hoping for a profit.

James and Louise had decided to move from their home at Chapter House. Louise had decided that she didn't like the house and they had purchased a house in School Lane which was in the same village. As they were sorting out their old house we had a table delivered, having sold the old one on eBay. It was solid oak and very heavy, and James came round to help me to fix the legs.

The couple buying Chapter House came round and introduced themselves and we discussed the house.

We had a lot of packing material from the table which we loaded into the truck and took round to James's new house. He had a bonfire going, so we were able to burn our rubbish. It was a beautiful day, Teri's kids came round and they found a pram dinghy, all of the kids, set to, cleaning the dinghy and then launched it in the pond. Elliot took charge and was rowing the others around.

On Sunday Teri and her friend Tracy came over with her son James (14 months) and after lunch we all went for a dip in the pool.

On 11th November I went down to the Bank and on the way back stopped in the centre for a coffee. At 11 o'clock everything stopped and there was two minutes' silence. I found it quite moving, hundreds of people all standing silently to pay their respects.

I needed to take the centre of the new table back to the shop as the finish was poor. It appeared to have been packed before the lacquer had solidified. They changed it without question.

I had a conference call with Pete Bradshaw and Andy Sims, who were both in Swanwick. I compromised on a few clauses in the agreement, as did Pete, and I was hoping things could now go forward. I received a copy of the lease and sent it to Tollers, solicitors.

13th November 08

We still have issues with the Swanwick Marina's Business Purchase Agreement, as I am not happy with some of the clauses and am waiting for a new draft from solicitors. I have not heard anything regarding the sale of Blue Genie. I'd hoped to hear by now, if I could get the boat sold I could look for something else in the Caribbean a bit smaller and less of an investment.

I have asked several friends if they would like to join us in chartering, but as soon as they realise the cost they find they can't make it, although they seem to be perfectly happy to come sailing if it's free. James and family have now moved in with us and everything seems to be going OK, the boys are quite well behaved and it's nice having the company. The house will feel empty when they leave, probably around the 24th.

We are working with Oyster Marine design department on a large davit and their design people are with us.

24ᵗʰ November

METS is now a distant memory. The trip over went to plan and stand set up was finished by about 1500 Monday. The hotel was adequate, Andy Sims was staying in a different hotel to Ian Walker and me.

On the first day of the exhibition there seemed to be a positive feel for the general situation. The Prime Minister, Gordon Brown, seems to be hopelessly out of his depth and is getting the country into record levels of debt to finance his previous incompetence. We are working very hard to keep things together and I wonder what the situation will be in 2009.

The acquisition of Swanwick Fabrication is going ahead and this week should see most things sorted.

On 25ᵗʰ November I had a meeting at Tollers to discuss the Swanwick acquisition. The soonest we could complete would be 1st January 2009, but they wanted to complete on 1ˢᵗ December and were not happy with the situation.

We were suffering from absenteeism and had five production staff off, so we were struggling to reach our production target. James as usual was working very hard and seemed optimistic. We were very weak on purchasing, and goods inward materials were being rejected and returned to suppliers with no paperwork, so the system was in chaos. No one wanted to accept responsibility, and they were always ready to blame someone else.

I think we were at the lowest point for a long time. The Government had almost bankrupted the country and as usual for a Labour regime they were borrowing record amounts to bale themselves out and true to form were increasing taxes on higher earnings and various other spiteful measures to punish wealth creators.

Order cover was a bit thin and it looked as though Fairline would not pay us. Ann was keen to pull out of the Swanwick deal, but I thought that would be a mistake.

Despite the absenteeism, we managed to reach our target turnover in November.

3rd December 2008

Still no payment from Fairline. We have now taken court action and should get judgement on 22nd December. I am optimistic that they will eventually pay, but it is a great shame as we need all the customers we can get.

We had a meeting to discuss the level of work, as things are looking a bit grim. We have just about enough for December but January is looking a bit thin. The Swanwick deal is going ahead and that may help both companies with the new capacity.

John Mitchell, the Swanwick manager, came over today and we had a good meeting, I am visiting them next week and we will announce the takeover to the workforce to take effect on 2nd January.

Yoshi is here to work on the Nissin tube bender. Since our problems in the summer we need help to ensure that it doesn't happen again.

8th December

The month is going quite well, we are almost on target, but being a short month I can foresee a loss. January is still a bit short of work, although Andy Sims is working hard to pull in as much as possible.

Tomorrow Ann and I are going to Swanwick with Andrew

– James was hoping to come but is too busy on production. We eventually did a deal with Fairline, agreeing to take the account over three months. The first payment was last Friday. I just hope they last long enough to pay it off in full.

The figures for November surprisingly show a reasonable profit. This month is always a loss month but we are attempting to minimise it by buying only what is absolutely necessary. I think January will be very tight as work schedules seem quite low.

25th December 2008

Christmas morning I went down and got Ann a cup of tea. The grandchildren were all up and playing with their presents. Ann and I then exchanged presents and cards. One of my presents was a miniature suit of armour, about 12" high. Ann showered and then went downstairs, and I showered and dressed. I headed downstairs and stared in disbelief. There, standing in the middle of the hall, stood a full-size suit of armour. Ann and the kids were all laughing at the sight of me standing there speechless!

I had seen the armour in the Showhome Warehouse, a large showroom that sold bizarre items; if you wanted a full-size Dalek or a plastic dinosaur this was the place to go. They also sell off items from redundant film sets and as the name implies, redundant showhome furniture and accessories. Our house has a large hall which had tended to look empty and needed a few large items.

Christmas was uneventful. James and family didn't come to dinner but went to the Bridge Hotel and then came on to us for tea. The Bridge Christmas dinner was mediocre and the kids were a bit disappointed. Santa's outfit was ill fitting and not very good.

At New Year we held a medieval banquet, and it was quite a night. I moved the kitchen table and dining table into the hall and placed them in the form of a "T" with Ann and me at the top on two large carver chairs. I dressed as Henry the Eighth and everyone else was in costume. We did soup for the first course, ribs for the second, chicken and sausages third and cheese fourth.

We had lots of singing with everyone joining in. Ann recited a bawdy poem, Teri sang some songs and James played guitar to entertain us. Several of the guests said it was the best New Year party ever.

2009
19ᵗʰ January

The Boat Show is now over and nobody is giving out much information, although Fairline's MD claims they have sold 30 boats – I hope this is true.

On Thursday it was the Cooney Marine 40ᵗʰ anniversary party at the show, and we had an Elvis impersonator, dancing girls and Rod Stewart. The party went really well, although National Boat Shows tried to close it down. We gave away loads of drinks and a good time was had by all.

After the show a party of 35 of us went to a Chinese restaurant cum karaoke bar until 0200. James, Louise and I went back to the hotel, but a few ended up in a strip club!

Work seems a bit light and if things don't pick up we may need to cull some of the workforce. It would be a shame to have to do it when we have built up such a good team.

Went to Alan and Karen's yesterday for Sunday lunch. Teri came too and we had a pleasant time. The food was superb, and we arrived home at about 1700, just in time for the kids being returned from their respective fathers.

As the year wore on things generally were improving, new work was now coming in from Sunseeker and other customers and the Swanwick company had a good level of orders and were invoicing on a regular basis.

Saturday 24th January was the last shooting day this season, but only four guns turned up, so it was difficult to cover all the stands. It was a disappointing bag and although 78 shots were fired, only four birds were shot! I only had six shots all day but my last shot, the last shot of the day, bagged a fine cock bird.

Although there was a general improvement in business things were still a bit tight. One or two of the employees were under-performing and I was looking at ways to sort out this problem. Material costs were dropping and customers were looking for price reductions, which is all very well but they didn't want to accept price increases when costs rocketed back up again.

I was looking at various plant to increase efficiency, and was looking at a new ring roller, but I was concerned that the one I was interested in might struggle on some of the tube sizes, and I didn't want to buy a machine that wouldn't quite do the job.

On 22nd January I was at a Masonic meeting, an initiation, when suddenly one of the Grand Officers, Pat Marlow, was taken ill. An ambulance was called and we were all asked to leave the room. After 30-40 minutes we were informed that he had died. It was a shock, as although he was 80 he always seemed fit and sprightly. I didn't stay for dinner – most of us just left and went home.

The boat was not selling and with the financial climate there was not much chance of a sale before the New Year. I considered commissioning her in the spring. Ann was against it and said she never wanted to go on board again, but the boat was beginning to look neglected!

In early February we had severe weather warnings and I drove down to Swanwick for a couple of days to check that the boat was OK and visit the new company. They had had a good January and it would be interesting to see how the first quarter developed. I was hoping for a profit, as the type of work they did commanded a high price, but it depended on how the manager shaped up.

6th February 2009

For the last two days most of the country has been covered in snow. Yesterday I took James into work in the 4x4, and quite a few people had turned up. The delivery to Plymouth did not happen as the roads were blocked with snow and abandoned vehicles.

Our driver decided to leave early evening and drive through the night to make an early delivery today. Unfortunately he got stuck at Exeter and ended up in a rescue centre wrapped in a blanket. He set out this morning hoping to get to both Princess and Sunseeker.

It has been snowing heavily all morning, the schools are closed and everywhere seems quiet. Most of the people at Cooney's turned up for work, which is good as February is a short month anyway.

More work is coming in and it looks as though March will be a good month.

12ᵗʰ February 2009

The month is nearly half over already. We had everyone over on Sunday for Sunday lunch. The snow is now almost gone, although the weather is still very cold. The forecast is cold weather for the next few days.

We now have the new ring roller installed and working and I am hoping that we can do our own radiator bends and support pillars, if we can it should save us a lot of time and money. I hope the boat is all right, I shall go down to see her next week sometime.

Last night at lodge practice James did very well and was about the only one to get it right. I was surprised to see Totan there, I didn't know he was on the square (a Mason). I've not seen him for years, the last time being at the Kempo Karate club where we used to train.

16ᵗʰ February

The snow has now all but disappeared and the outside temperature is now around 7°C.

James is away for a few days and I hope Production will not suffer too much. Nick is off for one more week and Cath is chairing the production meeting. This weekend was the first that Ann and I have had on our own and we had a pheasant for Sunday lunch.

We heard yesterday that Ann's cousin Joan had died. She'd been ill for some time and was in a hospice. We will probably go to the funeral, although I only met her a couple of times.

Work is still trickling in, although we are still a bit hand to mouth. Cash flow is not too bad, although customers are paying a lot slower.

The company was having problems with sub-contractors, as the polishing quality wasn't up to the Cooney standard and we were having to re-work a lot of the parts before delivering them to customers. Our polishers worked on a piecework system whereby anything not up to standard had to be reworked, and they resented having to rework sub-contract items, although they were paid extra to do it.

Our company was doing extremely well considering the UK economy was in recession, and we were managing to stay in profit or break even. In the first three months of 2009 the UK economy shrank 1.9%, which was the biggest contraction of GDP since 1979. It was forecast that the recession, caused by the banks lending too much money, wouldn't begin to recover until the last three months of the year. We were working very hard to keep our heads above water.

As we were running a tight ship with little spare capacity, at times production was falling behind. If anyone was absent for any reason, output suffered and everyone else had to put in more effort to catch up. Nick was off on paternity leave, Chris was down at Sunseeker and we missed their input. Andy wasn't involved in production but was more on marketing, and I anxiously looked forward to the end of the month figures.

Ann and I booked a holiday for April, planning on going to Antigua for my 65th birthday and then up to Tortola to charter a boat for a week. Whilst in Tortola we were going to look for an ex-charter boat to buy. The Moorings and Sunsail sell off their fleet after about five years so it is possible to pick up a fairly recent boat at a low price.

Before the boats are put on brokerage they undergo "phase-out", where the boat is de-badged and re-fitted. After phase-out the vessels are put on brokerage, and presented as though they are about to go on charter with all bedding, towels etc. Some people buy them without viewing the actual boat, but I could never do that I feel that I must check a boat out myself before making any offer.

25ᵗʰ February

Went down to Swanwick on Monday, they didn't appear very committed and need a shake up. I went to see the broker regarding the lack of progress on the sale of Blue Genie. I was advised not to reduce the price again as this would attract silly offers, although I think I should have accepted a low offer last year, I just want to sell the boat and move on.

I went to KT last night at Huntingdon, I don't think they are as good as us in Kettering although it was a reasonable ceremony.

Still more doom and gloom in the newspapers and more and more firms going under. Steve Bird, our former designer came in to see us. The firm he now works for are going on a four-day week and are asking employees to take a 10% pay cut, redundancies are also mentioned. So far things are holding up for us but it could still all go horribly wrong!

On Thursday Ann and I drove down to Cheltenham for Ann's cousin Joan's funeral. The last time we had seen Joan was at Ann's mum's funeral. We met some more of Ann's distant relatives. It's sad that often you only meet some relatives on these occasions.

After the funeral we drove to Cardiff and stayed over in a Travel Lodge. It was typical of Travel Lodges, we only had one towel between us. The next morning we went to Sofa-Sofa to look at furniture. The suite we fancied did not feel comfortable enough for Ann but we eventually found one that we both liked.

At the moment we have a problem. Ann wants to modernise

and put modern light oak in the room and get rid of the antiques, whereas I like antiques and don't see much point in building a Georgian-style house and filling it with modern furniture.

On Saturday we went shopping for furniture, but we couldn't agree as our likes and dislikes were poles apart. We ended up in Laura Ashley, where they had some light oak French-style furniture that we both liked in the sale that finished on Sunday. The manageress of the shop agreed to open the shop early Sunday morning for us as we had a lunch appointment.

We arrived at the shop at about 10am. They were not due to open until 1030 but let us in, so we chose the furniture we wanted and left at 1100, arriving at sister's at 1215.

We plan on visiting our nephew Ian in the USA, he is studying chiropractic at the Palma Clinic and hopes to graduate in June. He will then be called Doctor.

Sales enquiries were coming in for products in bigger diameter tubes, and although we could buy 90-degree bends in most sizes there was a requirement for bends of varying radii and we decided to look at larger ring rollers. We were also experimenting with producing larger oval sections. We were manufacturing various oval tubes on our existing machines. Many of the machines we viewed wouldn't do all that was required. I was reluctant to buy a machine that would not quite do the job. The problem was obtaining a machine suitable for crushing 100mm diameter tube into oval and producing curved 100mm diameter flybridge support pillars.

10ᵗʰ March

There have been developments on the ring roller front. James *took samples of 4" dia (100mm) tube and tube to crush into oval over to Bayleigh machine tools and had a very successful trial. He bent up 4" diameter to the correct radius and was also able to make some oval tube. We have decided to buy the big machine and keep the smaller one, which will make us self sufficient in these areas. We should also qualify for a 50% grant from Business Link. The extra capacity will give us a lot more to offer customers and also give us a huge saving on sub-contract costs.*

Things are progressing quite well and although work is scarce we are ok for this month, although next month looks a bit thin on the ground. I don't know what Andy Sims is doing at the moment, he seems to spend a lot of time out and about, but I don't know what is being achieved.

I have a lot of things going on in the greenhouse. If the seeds fail I will probably buy plants, there is plenty of time, although in April I will be away for the month in the Caribbean. I have a painter starting on Monday to decorate the front room, we have ordered new curtains and furniture and will order a rug as soon as everything else has arrived.

1ˢᵗ May

The last few weeks have been quite eventful. Ann and I flew out to Antigua at the end of March and we stayed at the Falmouth Harbour Yacht Club for five days. I wanted to visit the Tot Club on my birthday and enjoyed several Tot evenings. We went from Antigua to Tortola and chartered a Beneteau 362 from Footloose Charters for ten days. The boat was quite tidy but well used, and everything worked, although on day 2 we had to call the charter company due to a dead engine battery. They sent a guy out to fix it but we lost a day messing around.

We visited most of the old haunts and before leaving Virgin Gorda we motored over to Moskito Island. This has now been sold to Richard Branson and there were signs of some development. I would love to own that island. It has such potential and I hope Branson doesn't spoil it.

Whilst in Tortola we went to look at another boat, aft cabin Beneteau 40, but it did not impress me. Chartering the 362 was a pleasant interlude but there is nothing like the freedom of sailing your own boat

After the superb accommodation on *Blue Genie* the aft cabin on the Beneteau seemed inadequate and the boat itself was uninteresting. Ex-charter boats have the advantage of low price and when offered on brokerage are usually in good condition, having been serviced and cleaned regularly. Often privately owned second hand boats of a similar age have problems with corrosion and seized sea cocks, whereas after 'phase out' on Moorings and Sunsail boats these problems are fixed and the boat is debadged and cleaned and the engine serviced. Some are better than others, so I consider it wise to inspect a boat and have a survey. If defects are discovered the broker will fix them or may reduce the price.

In May Ann had arranged to go away with her golfing buddies to Spain and I had arranged a few days' deerstalking. I travelled down to Thetford on 10th May and enjoyed the break. The early morning stalks started at 0400 and on the morning of the 12th I shot a nice roebuck. At 150 yards it was an excellent shot.

Fortunately I eventually sold the boat. We took the new owner for a test sail, and he'd paid for Moody's chief engineer to come along to check things out. Ann came with me, which was a surprise as she'd said she never wanted to step on that boat again! Luckily everything worked and we spent a pleasant afternoon sailing in the Solent.

We were working very hard to keep the company in profit; we'd slimmed down and let a few people go to tighten things up. It was quite tough, as the industry generally was shrinking and there was a lot of in-fighting between suppliers.

In June Ann and I flew to Chicago for a few days. The weather was cool and the sudden showers tended to catch us out. From there we flew to Iowa to stay with Ian and Sandra for a few days. Ian was studying at the Palma Institute of Chiropractic. Their large house easily accommodated Anne and Tony and Ann and me, and we spent a pleasant few days with them and their charming daughters. Ian graduated on the Saturday and it was nice to share the occasion with him.

Due to the economic situation generally, a lot of houses were being repossessed by the mortgage lenders and offered to the market for very low prices. I had quite a wedge of cash after the boat sale, so I decided to buy a few of these and rent them out. I have always considered property to be the best and most secure investment available, the thinking being that if the business struggled I would have an alternative income stream and I was in the process of completing on three repossessed houses.

7ᵗʰ July

We seem to be running out of work. The whole economy in the UK is in a dreadful state and we will probably need to lose some more people. It will be difficult to be in profit for the next couple of months unless business picks up. Year 2008-9 was good and we made a profit, but 2009-10 is looking bleak.

Last weekend we had a family party and catered for 18

people including children with 14 staying over on Saturday night. It's nice to see them all, but it's a lot of work. Some of the guests didn't help out and just sat around being waited on.

I am missing not having a boat, but we are considering buying another one, probably an ex-charter about 4 years old. There are a lot of cheap boats available, probably due to the credit crunch.

Tomorrow is the Marine Industry Regatta. We have two boats entered this year, but I am not going, James and Andrew are and taking some of our people and some customers.

We had a batch of orders in yesterday which will help the situation, but it is still a bit grim out there. I don't want to lose anyone as we have such a good team, but we may have to. The amount of work for August is still quite low but we have some orders for September and October. Some of the staff have agreed to take unpaid leave in August. I am hoping things will pick up from September onwards.

There is a problem with one of the houses and it now looks as though it may fall through, which would be a shame as it was quite a tidy property. The two others are progressing OK and we should complete on one this week and one next. We are having a conservatory built on Teri's house, work has now started and she is quite excited about it.

Wednesday 5th August

We completed on the first house on Friday and on Saturday I strimmed the frontage, which was overgrown. There were loads of kids around all interested in what was going on. One lad asked if he could have the balls back that he had lost over the fence, there were about five in the long grass. The children all seemed well behaved, if a little loud.

We complete on another house this week, this one needs a bit of work. The other property is becoming complicated. The mortgage company has withdrawn their offer but as it is such a a good prospect we have decided to buy it for cash.

We now have a lot more work and are ramping up production and cancelling unpaid leave. James will be back from holiday on Monday.

So far this summer the weather has been really poor, it is now pouring with rain with thunder and lightning. Earlier in the year we had quite a few hot days which required me to wear a hat whilst gardening and sometimes shorts!

Production appears to be on target this month and it will be interesting to see what James makes of it on Monday.

There are some changes taking place over the next few weeks and I am hoping that from September we will start to pull back to where we were in 2006. There are signs that the market is hardening and house prices are beginning to creep back up to pre recession levels.

A tenant has moved into one of the Corby houses and we are working on one of the Kettering houses to make it habitable. The tenant for the Corby house is a single mum with a 15-year-old and an 11-year-old.

The year seemed to be flying past, and it was probably one of the wettest summers on record. Ann and I were preparing one of the rental houses for a tenant to move in. A new front door had been fitted, Teri had shampooed all the carpets and blinds had been fitted to all of the windows. The letting agent was confident that he could find us a tenant soon.

In September, just when I thought things were improving, two fabricators handed in their notice and the health and safety person has decided that she is worth a lot more money.

A new buyer started yesterday and I think the H&S person sees themself as equal as far as salary is concerned.

Thursday 15th September 2009

The Southampton Boat Show is now on and we have people down there, although this is the first time for many years that Cooney are not exhibiting. Our agent, Golden Arrow, is exhibiting a lot of our products and we have space on their stand. August figures were much better than expected and while we keep going and making a small profit we will survive. We are doing a lot better than most of out competitors and are due to have some meetings with customers later in the Show.

Having found a tenant for the Corby house, we are negotiating the purchase of the house next door. I think the agents are trying to con me into using their mortgage service and legals, but I am hoping to make my own arrangements.

Monday 28th September

The Friday night with Sunseeker was a resounding success. I talked to several important people and they appreciated it, especially in the night club after. I managed to keep off the booze and am still dry.

The house in Corby (no 4) seems to be going OK, although the estate agent blackmailed me into using their mortgage broker and solicitor. We now have tenants for 2 houses and we have a decorator working in one of the Kettering houses and the carpets are going in on 8th. October.

Ann has won another golf trophy and is like a dog with two tails.

Monday 12th October

Last week I drove down to Exeter to the Sportsman's Gun Centre to buy a new rifle. I bought a Männlicher 30:06, having traded in two others, and I am doing an FAC variation to obtain a sound moderator.

I took Christian clay shooting on Saturday – he is quite good and hits about 75%.

Andrew and Catherine are at an Employment Tribunal today. Apparently Cath has had a really hard time so far. The EEF lawyer claimed that our case was strong, but tribunals are always biased in favour of the claimant.

2nd December

As the year draws to a close things seem to be improving generally. We are very busy and have a lot of potential business for next year.

On 13th November James was installed into the Chair of St Crispin Lodge. He did very well and learns the ritual easily, unlike me who has to work at it. I was ADC and struggled a bit, but things can only get better!

Last week I did a deal to buy our fifth house. We now have tenants in three of them and are using a letting agent, although we hope to let any further houses ourselves. Teri is handling things and as we build up our portfolio, we are hoping that she will make a nice little business of it.

CHAPTER 6

Antigua

We'd decided to do another charter in December and into the New Year, and our friends Carl and Carole Walther were flying out with us. They were staying in a resort in Antigua and we were flying up to Tortola to spend some time sailing, after which they were flying up to join us for Christmas and New Year on the boat.

We set off on 11ᵗʰ December. Carl had offered to drive down to Gatwick and they picked us up at **0330** for the three-hour trip. As we approached the M25 there were signs saying M25 CLOSED, so I suggested that we went the other way round, past Heathrow instead of the Dartford Tunnel, so we joined the M25 going in the other direction only to find that it was blocked that way as well. We then took the A10 into London, and the GPS took us through the centre of the city. I said to Ann "Look there's Big Ben" and she thought I was joking. We approached the Thames, and lo and behold the bridge was closed!

We eventually arrived at Gatwick South Terminal just in time. After boarding the plane we were surprised to see police officers and discovered that the pilot had been breathalysed and marched off the plane, Take off was two hours late, but the flight was uneventful and we landed in Antigua at about 1500 hrs. Carl and Carol then went to their resort, but Ann and I had to wait four hours for our flight to Tortola. Waiting in airports must be one of the most boring of experiences, but we eventually boarded the Liat flight which was due to land at St Martin. It was an uneventful flight and on arrival some people disembarked and others got on and off, or so I thought. The aircraft stopped taxiing and returned to the departure point after they realised that some of the passengers were on the wrong plane. After about an hour we eventually took off for Tortola, landing at about 2200 local time.

Footloose Charters' taxi was waiting for us and we jumped aboard and headed for the marina. The taxi had a clapped-out engine and kept backfiring, so going uphill we were down to walking pace. At one point I was on the verge of offering to get out and push! The taxi eventually made it to the marina at 11pm local time, just as the bar was closing. We had been travelling for over 24 hours. We walked into our hotel room with a feeling of relief that we had finally arrived.

Footloose Charters was owned by the moorings and their boats were on the moorings marina. The boat, a Beneteau 40, seemed OK, and as expected everything worked. The briefing on the boat is called "the boat show" and as well as the workings of the boat there are instructions regarding the local area regulations.

As soon as we could we cast off and sailed across to Norman Island to spend the night in "the Bight". The next morning we sailed across to Sopers Hole and went ashore in the dinghy. Its outboard had a nasty habit of cutting out for no apparent reason but would usually re-start with a few pulls of the starter cord, although I had insisted that the dinghy had a pair of oars "just in case". The next day we sailed to Jost Van Dyke and visited Foxy's restaurant and bar.

Leaving Jost we set out to sail round the north of Tortola and head for Virgin Gorda, but the wind was about 25 knots on the nose so we called into Cane Garden Bay. As the wind increased the northerly swell caused the boat to roll violently and I decided to move round to Sopers Hole again and stay overnight. It was a short sail over to Cooper Island but it was also uncomfortable in the northerly swell, so we motored over to Marina Cay. We were still having problems with the dinghy outboard, but we returned to the moorings base to pick up Carl and Carol the next day.

While at base I asked for a different dinghy as the one we had kept stopping. An engineer came and fiddled with the engine and declared it fixed.

Carl and Carol joined the ship and for a shakedown trip we set off for Cooper Island. Carl took to the boat like a duck to water, but Carol felt queasy almost straight away. I'd instructed Carl on how to work the outboard engine, so we called him "Boat Boy". The first night at Cooper Island he took Carole ashore and after a couple of hours came back to the boat on his own and told us that Carole had been ill and that they had decided to spend the first night ashore at the Beach Club. Ann and I were slightly shocked, as we'd never had crew jump ship before! I was concerned about the rest of the trip and wondered how it might progress. I needn't have worried – in the morning they came back on board and for the rest of the trip there was no problem.

For the next few days we visited Marina Cay, Virgin Gorda

and Sopers Hole and then went back to Jost Van Dyke for New Year. In Virgin Gorda I took the dinghy to the moorings support workshop, and complained about the constantly stopping outboard engine. Their fitter fiddled with it and then took the dinghy for a trip round the bay going fast and slow, zooming here and there, and declared it fixed. Carl and I jumped in to return to the boat and after about 50 yards the motor cut out. Luckily the fitter was watching and agreed to give us another dinghy. This one worked fine – the only down side was that it had no oars.

31ˢᵗ December 2009

The anchorage at Jost is becoming very crowded but we were lucky enough to find a mooring buoy. Carl and Carole are ashore, I hope she is OK and doesn't decide to stay ashore tonight. We had lunch at Foxy's and they then had their photo taken with him. I am looking forward to tonight but will be relieved when we are all back on board safe.

Carl was a keen snorkeller and Carole also enjoyed it, so for the last day we decided to return to Cooper Island. The coral and fish are remarkable and there is a dinghy mooring close to the reef.

When in the dinghy I insisted, for safety's sake, that Carl fastened the engine kill cord to his belt as a precaution. This would ensure that if he went overboard the engine would stop, He fixed it to his belt and then put the end in his pocket.

Carole wasn't a strong swimmer and wasn't comfortable in flippers (fins) so she decided to swim or snorkel without them. We all slid from the dinghy to snorkel on the reef; Carl had taken some bait to attract the fish. I soon noticed that there was a strong current and decided to return to the dinghy. I looked around but couldn't see Carl and Carole. I then noticed them in the strong current between the rocks, clinging to a small mooring buoy. I could see that they were in trouble, as Carl was whistling and frantically waving his arms around. I needed to rescue them with the dinghy, but as I looked I realised that Carl had the engine kill cord in his shorts pocket. I managed to wedge the engine cut off to enable me to start the engine, but when I pulled the starter cord it came away in my hand. A feeling of dread came over me. I couldn't start the engine and the replacement dinghy had no oars. The whistling from Carl was becoming more desperate and Carole appeared to have stopped moving, and I was in a dead dinghy and powerless. I had to do something and considered casting off the mooring and trying to float down to them, but with the strong current and wind It would have been foolhardy and could have made the situation worse.

Luckily the crew of another yacht had seen them in distress and dinghied over to rescue them. It was an American couple and they were very kind and helpful, especially with Carole. They towed our dead dinghy back to our boat. I was so relieved to have everyone back on board safe. Ann was oblivious to the drama, and was surprised to see us towed back by the Americans!

That evening in the restaurant sitting with Carl and Carole, I almost felt ill when I thought of what might have happened, and I think it must have affected them as well. The two lessons learned were: never accept a dinghy without oars and always leave a kill cord in the dinghy.

After the charter we flew down to Antigua for a few days. I took Carl and Carole to the Tot Club and Carl and I hiked the trail from Fort Berkeley to Pigeon Beach. I've always wanted to do this trail, but in the past I had had no one to do it with. We stayed at the Ocean Inn, where the only problem was the steep walk back up the hill. They did however allow us a late check out and we left at 5pm for the airport.

As Antigua Airport was a bit austere and uninteresting, we checked our bags in and then went over to the Cricket Club to wait until it was time to go through security. Often, celebrities could be seen in the Cricket Club as they waited for their flights, because the airport facilities were so poor. Amanda Holden, the TV presenter and actress, and her husband and daughter came in, and there'd been a TV programme running in the Cricket Club with Simon Cowell being interviewed. As Amanda walked past Carl stood up and said "Hello Amanda, how are you?"

She replied a little uncertainly, "Oh hello, I'm fine thank you."

Carl continued, "We've just been watching your old mate Simon Cowell on the telly." She smiled as she walked past.

The plane was delayed two hours due to snow at Gatwick and our plane was diverted to Heathrow.

2010

26th January 2010

When working out the December profit and loss I was surprised to see that we had made a small profit in December, due to it being a short month, as with Christmas bonuses etc. Dec is usually a loss month. The figures for Cooney Fabrication were disappointing and drastic action needs to be taken. I am in Southampton looking for smaller premises for them as we need to downsize and transfer the work down to Kettering, where it can be produced efficiently.

10th February

It has been decided that as the Swanwick company, Cooney Fabrication, was unprofitable, it would be wise to bring everything back to Kettering. Initially we would downsize, cutting the workforce down to two fabricators and the manager, and for the time being we would remain in the existing premises. On the first year's figures they made a loss and owe Cooney Marine a substantial amount. We are hoping to limit the damage to our cash flow and bring the good paying work up to Kettering.

We have a tenant moving into house number 5 in just over a week and it will be nice when all five properties are let. Last week I bought another gun, it is an O/U 12 bore and I bought it to shoot skeet with Christian, who lacks confidence and will only shoot with me. He has a natural ability and could be very good. At the Northampton Shooting Ground they do free tuition for juniors on Saturday mornings from 0830 until 0930. Some of the youngsters are very good and after the tuition a group of us go round the sporting course.

25th February

Weather is dreadful, snow everywhere, very cold, I think we should have stayed in the Caribbean!

Another month nearly over, and it has been quite a struggle with lower than expected orders, although the prospects for March look a lot brighter. The changes down at Cooney Fabrication are taking shape with the two poor performers taking voluntary redundancy. It will be interesting to see what the turnover is this month.

At Acre House the snow has brought down the guttering

again. I think this is a design fault and it will probably be expensive to rectify.

I am going to the shooting range this afternoon, last time I didn't do very well so I have booked an hour's tuition, hoping to improve.

Ann hasn't been able to go golfing for a few weeks but although the snow is now mostly gone, the course is waterlogged. I have now had a silencer fitted to the new rifle (the 30:06) and I hope to zero it in this Saturday.

17th March 2010

On Monday we went to a funeral down in Christchurch with Alan and Karen. Steve took his own life; he escaped from hospital and walked into the sea. He'd suffered from depression for several years and told people he just wanted to die. It was a very sad occasion. We stayed in Christchurch overnight in a nice hotel and on the way back did the tourist bit around the New Forest.

We have the figures out for February, it was a superb month for Cooney Marine international, because although the turnover was low we made a 12.5% net profit. This is due to James's running of the business, cutting back on waste and increasing productivity. Cooney Fabrication also made a slight profit, but the next couple of months will be critical.

We signed up a new tenant for house no.4 today and they want to move in on Friday, so we are now looking for another house to buy.

1st April

This month is the last month of the current financial year. It has been challenging, but overall I think we should be in profit. There have been some low points and some surprises, but with the financial situation in the country Labour have practically bankrupted the economy as they did last time they were in. Lots of small companies have gone to the wall and a few large ones as well, but we are doing well and are in a strong position. We have no overdraft or loans and a healthy cash flow.

All of our five houses now have tenants and we have now signed up for no. 6, a new build, which won't be ready until September. We are also after another repossession. Teri is managing the rental houses and I am hoping to build up a nice portfolio that she can run as a business.

It is my birthday tomorrow, I shall be 66. The years seem to be flying past. I am in very good health and have been teetotal for over 6 weeks but have a difficult weekend ahead. I would be happy not to drink at all, I sleep better, am not depressed and have a happier life, but I always crash and then wonder why.

Christian is doing well at the clay shooting. I now shoot with him, but he is better than me and if he sticks at it he could be quite good.

Karen did dinner for Ann and me for my birthday, it was very good – she went to a lot of trouble and produced a superb meal. I have now booked our January charter from Grenada and am looking forward to it.

12th May

Yesterday we finally got a new Prime Minister, but it was touch and go and we ended up with a coalition with the Lib Dems. I don't know how this will work. The Lib Dems are more left wing than Labour and I just hope they can work together.

Ann is away in Spain on a golfing holiday. I always

promise myself some fun when she is away, but all that has happened is that Sunday and Monday I drank a lot, yesterday I watched TV and tonight I am going to Ben's Chippy to pick up my dinner.

At work we have more to do than there are hours in the day and still the work pours in!

I take Christian shooting Thursday afternoons and a coaching session on Saturday mornings. He doesn't like one of the instructors and sometimes there is an unpleasant atmosphere.

This month is going very quickly and we are above target on production. There is a lot going on, morale is good and we are heading for another good month.

James is confident, although he is having problems at home, but he is always cheerful and positive. I am looking forward to last year's accounts being finalised this month.

Trying to build up our buy-to-let portfolio should have been easy, but there appear to be some unscrupulous estate agents out there. On a house that we were due to complete on, at the last minute someone else made a higher offer. It was strange the way the agent handled it. The first we heard was from our solicitor, who told us the other side would not exchange as they were considering a higher offer. I rang the agent, but no one seemed keen to speak to me. The manager said he did not know what was going on, but then let slip that he did. It was peculiar when they announced that the vendors were going for the higher offer! After paying for searches and a survey fee we stood to be £600 out of pocket and I suspected that there was something corrupt going on. To get this far and then for the deal to go bad is unusual. If the solicitor had acted a bit quicker it would have gone through. Why do I always feel let down by so called professionals?

Grant Thornton came in to do the accounts. The business was doing well and I was hoping that the worst of the recession was over.

10th June 2010

Had a phone call this morning from the estate agents to say that if we could exchange contracts tomorrow morning the house purchase could still go ahead. I rang our solicitors and they agreed to sort it out for completion next Friday. I could really do without this amount of stress and aggravation.

29th June

I am feeling depressed at he moment, the figures are in for Cooney Fabrication and there are substantial losses. The best course of action would be to close it down and bring the plant to Kettering and run it from there. It's just breaking even, but with all of the organisation and support it requires from Cooney International it hardly seems worth the effort.

The weather is glorious but the garden is looking very overgrown, the gardener doesn't like cutting lawns and it looks so scruffy. I would like to sack him but Ann is against this as he lives in the village. We now have a tenant for the latest house and they want to move in on the 1st August.

10th August

The last few weeks have flown past and we have just returned from a week in Alderney. The new gardening company started last week, but it is too early to see a difference. This company bring their own machines, mowers etc. and take away all of the prunings and grass cuttings.

It was great to be back in Alderney. We flew out with Alan and Karen, they had never flown in such a small aircraft. We stayed at the Braye Beach Hotel, formerly the Sea View, which has been refurbished and was very nicely done.

It was Alderney week and we went to several of the activities. Ann and I were drinking heavily, which spoilt it a bit, but generally it was a most enjoyable week. I thought the prices in the restaurants were high and a couple of nights we ate in the Braye chippy, which was exceptionally good. I think that if we go again Ann and I will go on our own.

We now have the figures for Cooney Fabrication and over the last three months they have made a small profit, so I have decided to keep it going a bit longer.

We now have all six houses rented out and we are due to complete on no. seven on 1st. October. Teri is running the rentals and there is only one with an agent She will be taking over this one in September.

In January we are chartering a catamaran with Alan and Karen in the Caribbean. We are all off for some training next week on handling a catamaran. I don't think I need it, having sailed with Pat Patterson on several occasions, but it will be an interesting thing to do.

I took Christian to the clay ground on Saturday morning, but there was a big competition in progress and the weather was poor, overcast with drizzling rain, so we decided not to shoot. We then visited Grimley's gun shop to pick up my game gun that had been repaired.

He had two O/Us in stock which we looked at and one of them, a Miroku, seemed to fit both Christian and me, so we decided to take it on trial. Terry Grimley then gave Christian some tuition and advice on gun mounting, so although we did not shoot we had a very pleasant and constructive morning.

Saturday evening I barbecued some steaks. Ann's was in her opinion overdone, although I thought it about right. She likes it pink in the middle, but it always seems to be either too rare or too well done!

On Sunday we were invited to a barbecue at Priors Hall. Luckily the weather stayed fine despite rain being forecast. We met some other investors and it was very pleasant. The barbecue was excellent with loads of food, but quite a few people didn't show up.

At the factory we have an underground water leak. On Thursday the water board came in with their listening rods but they couldn't find it. They ascertained where it wasn't but could not find the route into the building.

I then traced the route of the pipe using dowsing rods, a technique taught to me by Pat Patterson. I think I have found the leak but need the experts to confirm it!

3rd September 2010

Where has the summer gone? August was the coldest for several years, although the week in Alderney and the catamaran experience were enjoyable. Last Monday was a Bank Holiday, but we didn't do much. On Saturday, Dennis and Janet came over. It was great to see them, it must be 5 years since the last time and there was a lot of catching up to do.

Their boat is now in New Zealand undergoing a refit.

Our company made a loss in July, which was disappointing as I'd hoped we were past those times. The problem is that there is so much new work coming in that needs developing.

It will be interesting when the August figures are completed.

This afternoon I am taking Christian shooting. He is quite confident now but is not scoring as well as when he started. When he was shooting instinctively he did very well, but now after a lot of tuition he has become average. I think he is overthinking his technique.

My shooting has improved and I am looking forward to the game season. Our first shoot at Kirby Hall is in October.

Tomorrow we are driving down to Bridport. Nephew Philip is getting married on Saturday and we are driving back on Sunday evening.

CHAPTER 7

Charter challenges

In September 2010 the company made a good profit, although August showed another loss. The marine market appeared to be weakening and things were tightened up as much as possible. I had several schemes planned and I was optimistic for the future. Teri took Christian to Africa, as he seemed to be left out where holidays were concerned – the other two go off with their dad on trips. Teri has been saving for two years to give him the holiday of a lifetime, hence the trip to Africa.

All seven houses were now let and there were still some cheap houses around but Ann was reluctant to commit any further.

I was a bit concerned about the St Crispin ladies' night as James was Worshipful Master and it was Louise's ladies' night. She'd said she didn't want a presentation to the ladies etc, and it was billed as a charity night. I had misgivings as there was dark muttering among some of the members. The ladies' night was however a great success. Louise came and it all went well. James did the toast to the ladies and also the ladies' song, accompanying himself on the ukulele. The after-dinner entertainment in the temple was the best I have ever seen, and all the 85 people that attended said what a super night, which was good considering one of the "brethren" was ringing people trying to persuade them to boycott the event because it was not a conventional ladies' night!

James installed his successor on 12th November and it was very well done. He was word perfect and several of the elders congratulated him on a job well done, so he made me very proud.

The October figures were disappointing, the problem being that there was not enough work coming in. Things picked up in November and one of our biggest competitors was in trouble so we became inundated with work. a good problem to have. Nothing is ever easy, it's always all or nothing but the recession did seem to be coming to an end and I hoped things should improve generally over the next few years.

8th December 2010

We had a visit from Princess yesterday – they want us to take on another big slice of their stainless supply. They have agreed to give us a three-year contract worth about £2.5 million over three years!

2011

In January 2011 we looked forward to a Caribbean sailing charter. We had booked a 38ft catamaran with Horizon Yacht charters in Grenada for a three-week charter and a week in a villa. Alan and Karen were coming as crew and we were all looking forward to some winter sun.

The Virgin flight to Grenada on 6th Jan stopped off at Tobago and was an early start, so I decided that it made sense to drive down to the airport the day before and stay overnight near Gatwick to avoid panics and stress. Ann and I had previously stayed at the Copthorpe Hotel, which had adequate facilities and provided parking and transport to the airport.

The flight was uneventful, but 9 hours on an aeroplane even in Premium Economy class is tiring, and it was a weary foursome that trudged down to the charter base at True Blue Bay, Grenada.

The accommodation on the catamaran enabled each couple to have a hull with its own 'heads' (toilet), almost like having a boat each!

Boarding the boat was tricky, with a force 5 wind causing the boat to surge against its warps. We all managed it, but unfortunately Ann injured her foot stepping aboard.

Twin engines is another feature on catamarans that appeals to me. If one engine fails for any reason it's good to have a spare, although in theory if you lose an engine it should be possible to sail the boat to safety.

After briefings and provisioning and with the navigation plan worked out, the next morning we motored round to Prickly Bay to try out the anchor, which held after five attempts. I always put out chain about five times the depth and motor the anchor in with the engines going astern.

Tyrrel Bay, Carriacou, was to be our next port of call as we needed to clear customs. This time the anchor set at the second attempt. Clearing customs in Carriacou can be hard work. Most sailors clear customs in Hillsborough. A boat boy lies in wait for the unsuspecting traveller on the dinghy pontoon and offers to mind the dinghy for $10. If you don't pay, something might happen to the dinghy! Another man offers to escort you to the customs and immigration for $10. They are quite well organised and it can be threatening the first time it happens. Having suffered this several times in the past I decided to take a taxi from Tyrrell Bay to Hillsborough to clear customs and incorporate an island tour, only to find that all the restaurants were closed.

There was no let up from the wind, which had been gusting 28-35 knots since we had arrived, and our next port of call, Union Island, was dead into wind, so we motored there and decided to anchor in the lee of Frigate Island. We dinghied ashore and took a taxi into Clifton to clear customs, returning on board about 1700.

We had to call out an engineer during the battery-charging engine run. The port Engine had to be shut down when an alarm sounded, but it was only a faulty sensor and we soon had everything ready for an early start for the trip up to Bequia.

Wednesday 12ᵗʰ January 2011

Up anchor for trip to Bequia at 0730, mainsail up, decided to put first reef in and a small amount of jib. Wind was gusting 20-25 knots, but we managed to make a reasonable track sailing at about 7.5 knots, though it was very lumpy. Karen felt queasy and went for a lie down, but we took it in turns on the wheel and were making good progress.

The wind started to increase and was gusting to 35 knots, I thought about running back to Union but as we were over half way and making good progress I decided to continue.

A few miles out from Bequia, Alan went below to check on Karen. He came up and said "I don't know if it's a problem, but the floor in our hull is floating". I went to investigate and was horrified to find water sloshing around the floor of their hull. I tried the electric pump, which was also the shower pump with a diverter valve and totally inadequate as a bilge pump. I rigged the manual pump, a peculiar contraption located in the cockpit with a long large-bore pipe that could be placed in either hull and the hull pumped out from the cockpit. Meanwhile I was searching the hull from stem to stern for leaks as Alan pumped furiously attempting to reduce the water level.

Then there was a shout from Alan: "The handle's broken off the pump!" By now the water was up to the first step and the vessel was showing a pronounced list to port.

I suspected a leak at the bow, as the waves were continually breaking over the leeward bow. Alan and I started bailing out the hull with buckets, exhausting work in the 30-degree heat. Ann was on the helm and at 7 miles out of Bequia I called Horizon, gave our position and told them the problem. We were now heading straight for Admiralty Bay.

I was concerned that the mainsail was making things worse by forcing the lee hull deeper, so I took it down. Alan got Karen out of the bunk and into the cabin. She was up to her knees in water and was quite ill and very upset. We all donned life jackets.

The wind was now a steady 30 knots on the nose, and the harbour was tantalisingly close but seeming to get no nearer. I was now talking to 'African', the Horizon contact in Bequia. The wind was still gusting 30 knots and there was over a metre of water in the hull, so the boat was listing dangerously.

As we entered the bay we saw African heading towards us in a power boat. He told us to beach the boat and directed us to a small beach at the end of the bay. As Ann steered us up the beach I jumped ashore with warps to tie to palm trees. African came aboard and said, "What did you hit?"

"Nothing," I replied.

He looked all around the boat and could find no damage. An enormous diesel pump was brought on board and they proceeded to pump out the boat. The forward cabin was full of water which had then flowed aft, so it took several hours to pump out. All of Alan and Karen's electrical equipment was ruined. Luckily their berth cushion was dry but everything else in the cabin was sodden, and all bedding was sent to the laundry. African and his team inspected the hull. They could find no reason for the flooding, but suspected that the forward hatch was leaking. Alan and I spent several hours throwing buckets of water onto the hatch seals to test them, but we could not find the leak.

We refloated the boat and placed it on a mooring, then spent most of the next morning clearing up the mess and putting the ship back together before going to Coco's for lunch.

Although the weather was fine, with the wind there was no let up and it continued to blow a good 30 knots. On the Friday we took a taxi to the turtle sanctuary and Friendship Bay, planning to have lunch at the Beach Bar. This bar was quite unique, as the bar stools were suspended from the ceiling, and it was fun to have a drink while swinging to and fro. I was so disappointed when we found the bar was closed. It would have been fun for the four of us all drinking and swinging!

Put-putting around Admiralty Bay is *Daffodil*, a yellow catamaran with fuel and water tanks that can be called up on the VHF for replenishment. It is very useful and saves going alongside, which is time consuming and difficult. It needs plenty of fenders to protect topsides as often *Daffodil* tends to come alongside rather heavily.

The rest of the trip from Bequia was downwind and although the source of the leak was uncertain, I considered that as we were going downwind there shouldn't be a problem. We motor-sailed down to Mustique, where the harbourmaster tied us up to a buoy fairly close to Basil's bar, and Ann and Alan went for a swim.

The next day we hired a "Mule", similar to a golf buggy, and we went for a trip around the island. In all the bays the sea was too rough for swimming, so we ended up at the Cotton Club beach, did some shopping and had cocktails at Basil's. We decided to buy chips from Basil's to go with dinner, but unfortunately they were plastered with tomato ketchup, which made them almost inedible.

The stay on Mustique was marred by the awful weather. At all the bays we visited there was a heavy swell running, which made swimming unpleasant, and heavy showers would strike without warning.

After Mustique we headed for the Tobago Cays and had a good run with about 20 knots of wind astern, picking up a buoy about 1230. After lunch we dinghied over to Turtle Island for snorkelling. The sea was very rough, but we had a swim and a snorkel and returned to the boat, though the rough conditions made it difficult climbing back on board.

As it was so rough at the cays and unsuitable for swimming, we motored over to Mayreau, where the beach was in the lee of the island and very calm. We went snorkelling on the coral reef, which had shoals of colourful fish and beautiful coral. We finished the day with sirloin steaks on the barbecue.

21ˢᵗ January 2011

Motored over to Union Island and picked up a mooring buoy, tested it with both engines astern then went ashore for shopping. later we went ashore to Lambi's for the barbecue, but unfortunately there was no floor show.

Lambi's was a disappointment. As mentioned earlier, the evening usually ended with limbo dancing by his beautiful daughters, but there was no floor show that night, so the evening fell a bit flat.

22ⁿᵈ January

Went shopping to stock up and had lunch at the Bougainvillea restaurant. I took Alan snorkelling on the beach. The reef, which I thought was coral, was made of tons of conch shells, but there were a lot of fish. After the swim we returned to the boat and then went to the airport to clear customs.

23ʳᵈ January

Left Union at 0845 and motored over to Petit Martinique to take on fuel and water, arrived at 10 o'clock, filled tanks and then sailed to Hillsborough to clear in and got ripped off by Customs!

There was an empty mooring over at Sandy Island and after making fast Alan, Karen and I went ashore and snorkelled on the reef among the stunning coral and myriads of brightly coloured fish. Karen was duty cook and made rotis for dinner.

24th January

Cast off at 0845 with main up, running out of the anchorage in 20 knots of wind, when clear put up jib. The boat was sailing well, often over 10 knots. Arrived about 1330 and anchored off St.George's. Dinghied into town and went to see Jonathan in Island Water World to buy a winch handle to replace the one I lost overboard, then wandered around shops before returning to boat. After a swim Ann did shepherd's pie for dinner.

From St. George's we motored round to Clarke's Court bay and picked up a mooring. After a trip to the harbour office to pay for the mooring we wandered to Whisper Cove for lunch and after a lazy afternoon we returned on board for corned beef hash for dinner.

26th January

Soon it was time to leave Clarkes Court to return to Prickly Bay. Just off Tara Island the port engine stopped suddenly and I immediately suspected a rope round the prop. One of the advantages of catamarans is that they usually have two engines, so we were able to continue on our way to Prickly on starboard engine, but then decided to continue to True Blue Bay, the Horizon Charters base, where we picked up a mooring. Horizon sent over a diver to clear the prop. The culprit was an enormous length of fishing net. Spent a lazy afternoon reading and sunbathing and cleaned ship for tomorrow. We went to the Dodgy Dock and had a very expensive but very good meal.

27th January

Last day on the boat today, finished packing and cleaning then called Horizon to put the boat onto the berth (it is a requirement *that they do this). We were tied up at about 1030 and got the bags off, did a de-brief with Bernadette, and everything was OK. They then checked the port sail drive for damage, I couldn't understand why, we'd only picked up a fishing net, It wasn't our fault. They then checked the bottom for damage. Some anti-fouling paint had rubbed off when we'd beached the boat in Bequia, but that was unavoidable, in fact our actions during the hull flooding had probably saved the boat! Our $1000 deposit was returned to us.*

I phoned the caretaker from the villa, and he picked us up and took us shopping. The villa had a lot of steps, but it had a nice pool and was nice inside.

The thing that put a damper on the trip was the weather. The wind was gusting 20-24 knots most of the time and often 30 knots with sudden squalls. The hull flooding was the start of the mishaps and the fact that the sea was too rough most of the time for snorkelling didn't help. The boat was OK, but boarding from the water was difficult with the poorly designed boarding ladder.

CHAPTER 8

The *Amaranthos* years

❦

Back in the UK, business was about to get more interesting.

6th February 2011

The Princess contract has not happened yet but is still promised. James has bought a new turning centre and a manual lathe in anticipation. It seems that at the moment we get lots of promises from customers but little commitment.

14th February

At last it seems to have happened. Last week Belmar, our biggest competitor and thorn in our side for years, finally went bust. It has been on the cards for almost a year, ever since they went into a CVA (creditors voluntary agreement) last January. Everyone knew this was coming and we have been trying to get

Princess to commit to us for months. Now it's panic stations. We have a Princess buyer working in our devo. department transferring all of the open orders to us and we are frantically trying to pattern up and tool up for a massive amount of work.

There is a definite buzz and feeling of optimism in the factory. Davit sales have also picked up and other projects seem to be happening. The danger now is that our people will be poached by competitors in the area as Belmar were a big supplier to Fairline. We do very little for Fairline and it's rumoured that they are a bit rocky and don't pay promptly.

The factory is very busy with all the new work, but as usual in this situation there are cock-ups, jobs that have been done lots of times before suddenly starting to go wrong, It will eventually smooth over and perhaps we will start making money again!

15ᵗʰ March

Everyone is working very hard to get on top of the new work, all departments are busy and some are working shifts to catch up. Having inherited the Belmar backlog, this month we have an enormous hill to climb. We have a deadline this week for many items and I hope we'll be somewhere near meeting it.

Last weekend we had visitors. On Friday we went to see nephew Philip (Jinder) perform at the Stables at Wavendon, he was on the bill with Marcus Bonfartin and Lottie Mullen. Together with Ron and Kate they all came to stay at our house as they had another gig Saturday night.

As soon as they arrived they got stuck into the wine. Most of us turned in at about 0300 but the pop stars were partying until about 0430.They all stayed in bed until midday and then left at 5 pm.

Ron and Kate stayed until Sunday morning, leaving about 1130. Ann and I then went to Grantham for lunch with Anne and Tony. This was a special treat as we have been on a protein-only diet for the last month and this was our first Sunday dinner with all the trimmings for quite a while.

After the debacle of the last charter, I didn't relish doing another. The problem with charter is that the boats often leave a lot to be desired.

11th April

Ann seems to have gone off the Idea of buying a villa or condo in Florida and we are now once again looking at yachts. We'll probably fly out in June to look at boats coming off charter.

The business is doing well – we're getting on top of the influx of new work and a new contract is being negotiated. There are a few sticking points and I wouldn't be surprised to see it all blow up in our faces. We have Sealine wanting us to take on loads more work, but we are keeping our heads down at the moment. Profitability is improving and as the fabricators get more repetition they should start earning more on piecework.

23rd May

The figures are now complete for the year end. They show a mediocre performance and the year shows a break-even situation. It has been very hard, especially being flooded with Princess work, and the prices are very keen. We have not signed up the Princess contract yet as there are a few sticking points, mainly the fact that they want things too cheaply. I can understand that they want to obtain low prices, but they ran

Belmar into the ground and it is not in our or their interests for them to do the same to us.

At home over the last two weeks we have had a make-over in our main room. We have a new 3-piece suite and a new carpet. We sold the old suite on eBay together with various other bits and pieces, including my observatory and telescope.

We have now booked our trip to the BVIs to look for another boat. There are three that we are interested in, all Beneteau 393s. We fly out on 11th June .

26th May

This morning I started off with my normal exercise session, which comprises 10 minutes on the health rider, then a series of abdominals followed by 30 press-ups. I then dived into the pool, swam 30 lengths and did some aqua-aerobics. I have also been on the Ducan diet, consequently I have lost about 18lbs. In weight and I am a lot trimmer. I am now able to get into 34" waist trousers. I have done diets before but this time I am also exercising and I am off the booze, which is making a big difference to my general well-being.

I'm taking Christian clay shooting this evening. He is quite good but not brilliant and I think he needs more practice. On Saturday mornings at the shooting club there is free tuition for juniors and he seems to be improving. I am in the process of obtaining a shotgun certificate for him which will enable him to visit the range without me.

27th May

Today we are having a board meeting and I am not looking forward to it. Ann has some figures worked out showing that *with the current situation we need to cut costs and tighten up all round, whereas James and Andrew are trying for a wage increase. I am a bit apprehensive, as last time we had a meeting Ann walked out and Andrew almost resigned.*

I sometimes think it would have been better to sell up when the business was on the crest of a wave as it was seven years ago. The trouble is that when things are going well that's the last thing you think of.

The board meeting went OK and we agreed to postpone the wage increase until September.

The year was now approaching the halfway mark and we were enjoying the long spring evenings and milder weather, while the business seemed to have settled down. Alan and Karen were in the USA at a wedding, and Ann and I were off the booze and trying to get in shape swimming once or twice a day and visiting the gym. We planned to fly out to the British Virgin Islands to look at ex-charter boats for sale, and the Moorings brokerage had about 15 of the type we are interested in. We were looking for a yacht of approx. 40 ft with 6 berths and 2 heads/shower compartments.

12ᵗʰ June

Yesterday we flew out to Tortola, travelling for approx 18 hours. It was very tiring and by the time we arrived at the hotel we were both quite wound up. At Beef Island airport I got quite annoyed with the guy giving out immigration forms. He wouldn't give me two and kept giving me an immigration form and a customs form.

The hotel leaves a lot to be desired. It is quite run down and although the people are pleasant, it is stuck out in the middle

*of nowhere, a half-hour drive into Road Town, and the roads
are diabolical.*

*We are going down to the Moorings brokerage tomorrow,
they have several of the type that we are interested in for sale.
We have been for two swims today, the pool is nice and we
intend to try the restaurant tonight.*

The type of boat we favoured was the Beneteau 393, as this
boat has three cabins, a double forward of the main cabin and
two aft, with two heads, one forward and one aft. It is also
fairly roomy. It was a 393 that we chartered in 2009/10 over
Christmas and New Year with Carl and Carole Walther. The
boat sailed well and was manoeuvrable under power.

I preferred the American specification boats as they have
aircon and a spray hood (dodger), but the class does seem to
have a problem with water staining the bulkhead behind the
sink and galley.

We eventually had an offer accepted on a French
specification boat. They appeared better built and this
particular craft had air conditioning. I needed to organise
a surveyor, but at weekends on Tortola everything stops.
However I was able to spend some time on the boat. I couldn't
find much wrong with it except that the battery bank appeared
knackered.

Moorings brokerage required a 10% deposit with your offer,
and after the offer has been accepted, if you back out you lose
the deposit, unless of course the survey turns up something
major, in which case you can back out or renegotiate. Likewise
if the seller backs out he has to pay you 10%.

22nd June

Now that we have chosen the boat we will buy there's not much to do. This morning I appointed a surveyor. The only one I could find in the time was Benson from Caribbean Marine Surveyors, and it turned out to be quite an enjoyable day. The surveyor started early to get a lot done before the day heated up, Ann and I arrived about 10am. He said the boat was in very good condition but he had found several items that needed attention, corroded sea cocks etc. The haul out to check the underwater parts was scheduled for 1130. If it's done over the lunch period it's much cheaper, so we left the dock and motored round to the boat lift at Nanny Cay. There was another boat in the slings so Ann and I went for lunch, Giles the broker stayed with the boat and Benson went off to his office to check his emails.

On returning to the boat she was hanging in the slings and Benson and Giles were inspecting the hull. Benson was banging it with a rubber mallet and Giles was scraping off some of the barnacles. When a boat is surveyed in the UK the surveyor scrapes off patches of anti-fouling and tests the hull with a moisture meter. I queried this with Benson, but he said that as the boat was only going to be out of the water for a short time, the hull would not dry out enough to give an accurate reading.

The hull seemed sound, the cutlass bearing OK, but I thought the rudder bearing had a lot of play. Benson assured me this was acceptable. The boat looked enormous out of the water but apart from slight damage to the trailing edge of the keel she was sound.

She went back into the water at about 2 pm and then we did the sea trials. We motored about a bit and then put the sails up and tried her on all points of sailing while Benson went below checking that doors still fitted when close-hauled etc. We *then did engine trials, putting the revolutions up to maximum while Benson checked the engine temperature with an infra-red gauge. The engine control panel only has warning lights to indicate overheating, battery charging and oil pressure. I suppose that with charter boats everything is kept simple. A slightly high engine temperature caused concern and Benson mentioned it in his report. There was no black or white smoke and there was plenty of power available.*

Returning to the Moorings marina I was pleased with how the day had gone. The boat appeared to be in excellent condition considering it had spent the last five years in charter.

The boat has now been moved to Hodges Creek, where it will undergo 'Phase out', being de-badged and the survey items rectified. I hope to take possession in about a month.

29ᵗʰ June

One of the problems we've had is transferring money. Before we left UK we transferred $120,000 to an account to use for the boat purchase. Our offer was accepted on 16ᵗʰ June and I arranged for the deposit money to be transferred to the broker's account. On checking the account daily it appeared that the money hadn't arrived, and after about a week the bank manager rang James and said there was a problem with the forms we'd sent in. It turned out that the dumbos in Kettering branch had screwed up and there was not a problem after all with the paperwork. The money was eventually transferred ten days later.

Another problem was buying the dinghy. A deal was done with Budget Marine for a new aluminium-hulled inflatable and a new 10.8 hp outboard. If we paid cash they agreed to a 15% discount, the problem was drawing out $5,500 in cash *from various credit cards. The cash machine at Nanny Cay was next to the taxi waiting area and there were usually several drivers sitting around waiting for a fare.*

Ann and I went to the machine and both drew out $500 on our direct debit card, then tried other cards and drew out various amounts. It must have looked a bit strange especially when the next day we did exactly the same thing again, It took several days to build up the cash from various credit, debit, and other cards. In the meantime three of the cards were stopped by the bank's fraud departments and it took very tedious phone conversations to re-activate them.

Eventually we had the cash, but as it was in small denomination bills it made quite a big package, which took quite a while for the Budget Marine girl to count.

We flew down to Antigua on 28th June for a couple of days. I wanted to stay in the English Harbour area and Ann had booked us into a hostel. There was no aircon or fridge and it had a water bed. The next-door neighbour liked to play reggae music at full volume, and it sounded like someone shouting and swearing and banging a big drum. Luckily they turned it off at about midnight – it came on again at about 3am, but only for a short time.

I didn't visit the Tot club; I had intended to go, but as I am not drinking it would have been difficult. I have not had a drink since 5th February and feel better for it. Ann has been off the drink as well and has been a pleasure to live with. Now we had another boat I had something to dream about again.

Since we'd been away the business had done very well and we were being pressured to take on more work. I just hoped the bad times really were coming to an end.

Christian's shooting was a bit up and down. He was usually

far better than me but sometimes had a bad day. It seems that if the clays come thick and fast you don't have time to think and you somehow shoot instinctively, which seems easier.

The Sprinter truck's engine had blown up but luckily it was covered under warranty. It needed a new engine and we were having to hire a truck while it was off the road.

My vegetable garden was doing very well and I was freezing a lot of my produce. I managed to keep the butterflies off my brassicas so they were not eaten by caterpillars. As usual I had far too much lettuce, but the tomatoes seemed to be all plant and not much fruit. While we'd been away everything had survived, although our courgettes had turned into marrows!

We flew out to Tortola on 27th July to complete the purchase of the boat. She was lying at Hodges Creek and we were pleasantly surprised at the standard of phase-out work. The surveyor's recommendations had been followed to a high standard.

We motored the boat round to the Moorings marina to sort things out. We had intended to go off sailing for a couple of days before leaving the boat at Manuel Reef marina for winter storage, but there was a tropical storm alert and the weather was forecast to increase to hurricane strength and hit the lesser Antilles and Virgin Islands on Monday or Tuesday, which was in two days' time.

We drove round to Manuel Reef to discuss winter storage and hurricane preparation, but there was no one in the office. Talking to some of the other berth holders they recommended that we took the boat there to prepare for the worst as soon as possible. We returned to the Moorings and motored the boat round to Manuel Reef, mooring up to a slip on the north side while it was still light.

Ann in the Kayak, Virgin Gorda.

Amaranthos at anchor.

Ann on our favourite walk on Alderney, Channel Islands, with
Fort Clonque in the background.

The next morning we went into Budget Marine to buy extra
rope and fenders. Several boat skippers were doing the same.
We were asked when we were picking up the new dinghy, but
they agreed to store it for a few more days.

On Monday morning Jim Woods, the marina manager,
appeared and we signed up for the berth and monthly
maintenance.

Weather forecasts were being anxiously watched and the
storm was upgraded to Hurricane Emily. I booked us into an
hotel for a few days, as I didn't want Ann to suffer another
'bad boat experience'. Luckily the storm passed about **200**
miles to the SW of us but we still had winds up to gale force,
torrential rain and lumpy sea conditions.

It was Tortola carnival and a lot of the shops were shut.
Everywhere there were scantily clad black girls in garish
costumes – some of the girls were quite sturdy.

On Friday I went into Budget to ask them to store the dinghy until November, but as I walked into the shop the manageress said "Your dinghy is ready for you". I was not ready for it, but it had been launched and was sitting in the water with the engine running!

I returned to the boat and picked up a lifejacket, dinghy anchor, and rope for the painter. I checked the fuel level and made sure that the oars and row locks worked. I planned to motor out of the marina and see what the sea conditions were like. It was a bit lumpy but as long as I didn't go too fast it wasn't too bad and I decided to motor it round to Manuel Reef.

We needed to store the dinghy on the foredeck, so we winched it up with a spare halyard. The inner forestry needed to be disconnected to enable the dinghy to lie flat on the deck.

29th August 2011

James is on holiday and production is progressing satisfactorily, there is a lot of product going out of the door and everyone seems busy. The last couple of months we have made good profits, but in September there will be a wage review. We normally do this March/April but due to the uncertainty in the industry and the economy in general it was decided to postpone any wage decision.

The team we have at the moment is working very well, although I think we are a bit top heavy and need to increase production to carry the infrastructure.

We returned from a weekend at Ron and Kate's yesterday. Ron is recovering from bowel cancer and is doing all right. He is now 72 and unfortunately still has to work to help out his pension.

9th September

August figures turned out OK, although we haven't worked out the P&L yet. James is at Princess and I hope he is fighting our corner. Princess are our biggest customer and we are producing enormous quantities of items for them, but they are always trying to reduce prices. They ran Belmar into the ground, I don't want them to do the same to us.

So far the boat is all right. The other occupants of the marina seem to keep an eye on things generally.

It will be towards the end of November before I fly out again. I will probably go alone as Ann is scheduled for an operation on her toes in October and won't be mobile enough to travel. It would be nice if I had a mate to go with, but at the moment we don't seem to have many friends.

The Southampton Boat Show starts on the 16th and I am going on the 19th for a few days. At home we have the decorators in.

26th September

The Boat Show worked out very well. I was a bit dubious this year about hosting the showcase, but it seemed to work well. We will need to analyse costs and decide what we do in future, although London is already booked.

25th September

Ann and I took Christian to Lakenheath, where he was shooting for the Northants team. He didn't do too badly and came about third in his team. It was a lovely day, the only problem was when Barry, another grandad, brought out a tray of drinks and handed Ann and me a glass of red wine. Ann declined but I accepted, so as not to hurt his feelings. I took a sip, said how nice it was and then discreetly poured it away.

Ann has done very well staying off the booze and I have not had a drink either, and both of us are feeling a lot better for it.

11th November 2011 (11-11 11)

Tonight there is a lodge meeting, and I am looking forward to it. October figures were the best for a long time, the turnover was the highest for a few months and the net profit was over 10%, which was healthy, although I was hoping for 12%. This should be another good month but is one day shorter, so TO will be down accordingly.

At the end of this month I am flying out to Tortola to the boat, and I'm looking forward to it. I will be going alone as Ann is wheelchair bound. She should be walking normally in a week or two.

Last Saturday I was shooting at Kirby Hall. In the morning I shot rather well and bagged about 5 pheasants, but in the afternoon I didn't do so well.

22nd November

On Saturday I took Christian on his first game shoot. I let him take my peg and he shot like a hero. On one stand he shot about 6, which is unheard of at Kirby Hall. It is amusing sometimes when a pheasant flies down the line and three or four guns miss it completely.

Yesterday Ann had the last dressing removed from her foot and she is now hobbling around without crutches.

I don't know how this month is going, everyone seems to be busy. I am looking forward to the October figures. The last few months have been good but we must keep pushing and remain in profit. We are quoting on a lot of new products for next year and I hope some of it comes off.

Fairline are now trying to get back in with us. We are quoting on a lot of jobs and are already manufacturing pulpits for them.

I had decided to go out to the new boat at the end of November, but Ann was still on crutches after her foot surgery and decided not to accompany me. I arrived on board at 2300 on 30th November, after travelling for 23 hours. The boat seemed in good shape, very clean apart from a heap of filthy warps in the cockpit. I put the fridge on, made some tea and turned in.

I slept like a log until about 0600, had a shower on board and then went to see Jim, the marina manager. I then hired a Jeep and drove to Nanny Cay for breakfast.

On Sunday 4th December I used the spinnaker halyard to launch the dinghy and then spent some time fixing the name plate on the transom, not a brilliant job but I will have another go sometime.

I cobbled up some food on board and turned in early, I put both hatch boards in but didn't fix the sliding hatch. Then, hearing a noise in the cabin, I jumped out of my bunk and found an intruder in the main cabin standing at the chart table going through my electrical items. I shouted, more shocked than anything, and then launched myself at the intruder trying to grab him, but he leapt up the companionway and jumped ashore with me behind him shouting "Fxxxxxx thief!" He took of down the pontoon like an Olympic athlete. I could never have caught him and I don't know what I would have done if I had.

After he'd disappeared everything was quiet. People were staying on the other boats but no one seemed to have heard the commotion. It was only 0030, I was hyped up with adrenaline, but there was not much I could do at that time of night.

I checked to see what was missing, but as far as I could tell only my phone had gone. I brought some bedding into the main cabin and slept fitfully until about 0530, then showered and dressed and drove to Nanny Cay to email Ann to contact the phone provider to stop the phone. The email didn't work – we seemed to have a Mickey Mouse system that only works intermittently – but I was able to contact her on the pay phone and tell her what had happened.

I then returned to Manuel reef. By this time it was about 0745, Jim was in his office and I told him what had happened, I borrowed his phone and rang the police. I didn't expect them to do anything but three officers turned up. One took a statement and the others had a look round. The officer that took the statement suggested that I go to the station and make another statement and look at some 'mug shots' to try and identify the intruder.

I visited the police station, but I'd only caught a fleeting glance of his face and his back as I'd chased him down the pontoon so I couldn't identify him among the books of local criminals. I then went to the Moorings marina and hired a local phone.

Back on the Marina several boat owners came and asked about the incident, probably worried that they too might be boarded. One American guy took pleasure in explaining how he kept a machete and a flare pistol handy especially for this situation!

By the Thursday the boat was ready, and everything was in place for a short single-handed trip around the islands.

8th December 2011

The boat is about ready to go out, most things have been checked as working and the boat is in good shape. I am looking forward to casting off and I hope I can get out of the bay without mishap.

Went to the restaurant tonight and met Brian and Frank, who spend a lot of time here. Brian has a condo (apartment) at Nanny Cay. We were joined by George, the electrician who worked on Blue Genie , who now lives on a boat in the marina called Tin Hau. Amaranthos is stocked up with provisions for a couple of days. I think I will probably go to Cooper Island or Norman Island for the first trip.

9th December

Left Manuel Reef at 08:20 heading for Cooper island, wind blowing like hell on the nose, picked up a buoy on the second attempt. The boat was rolling and it was uncomfortable, so I cast off and motored over to Marina Cay.

10th December

Really rough night, dinghy is full of water and I think I will probably stay here today and move off tomorrow. I need to hoist the sails to check them out. I noticed that the Jib tack didn't have a shackle so the luff will be sloppy.

11th December

At Marina Cay, the batteries were only showing about 70% charge. I am using as little power as possible, but the charger is not very powerful.

I left Marina Cay and sailed over to Virgin Gorda, tying up about 11:20. I was concerned that the drive belt was slipping, it has a cover over the front of the engine so belt tension cannot easily be checked. I removed the cover and to my shock and horror found that the alternator pivot bolt was hanging out and the alternator was only held on by the tensioning strap. The nut was missing from the bolt. I searched the engine compartment with a torch in all the nooks and crannies but couldn't find the nut.

I replaced the bolt and tensioned the alternator, but with no nut for the bolt I was in trouble. The big problem was engine cooling water. If the alternator is not charging at least the engine will run, but if the belt comes off the cooling water pump stops and the engine will overheat and if not shut down could be seriously damaged or seize up!

12th December

I ran the engine for half an hour and checked the bolt. It had vibrated about half way out so I bashed it back in.

Tomorrow I need the engine to clear the Calhoun reef, but am hoping to be able to sail back to Sea Cows bay with minimal engine use. When Ann rings tonight I won't burden her with my problems, I hope tomorrow I will have it all sorted.
13th December

I didn't like the thought of the alternator bolt possibly vibrating out, so I looked around for a 10mm nut I could borrow. The autopilot mounting bracket was fixed with 4 bolts that looked about 10mm, so I took one of the nuts off and luckily it fitted, and I was able to use it to bolt up the alternator securely.

I put up the mainsail on the mooring and noticed that it

fouls the back stay. The jib seemed smaller than original with only one set of telltales. The main was a pig to get down, but other than that the trip back to Sea Cows Bay was uneventful and I tied up in Manuel Reef Marina with no dramas. As I came alongside several people were there to catch warps etc. Off now to hire a car.

14th December

Packing the boat up, I stowed the dinghy on deck and the outboard on the transom, Parts and power rang to say that the spare part for the alternator was in. Went to moorings to return phone and collect engine spares from Parts and Power and then on to Nanny Cay for breakfast, after which I got back on board and fitted parts to engine. Everything now seems OK on board apart from the aft shower pump, which I will not bother with until I return. I have plenty of time, I don't need to leave for the airport until 0930 tomorrow. I want to get the boat spick and span for when Ann and I return.

CHAPTER 9

Winter sun in the Virgin Islands

✖

Christmas 2011 went off OK. We had Christmas Day at Teri's and Boxing Day at our house. Teri and the grandchildren and Anne and Tony came.

We received the figures for Cooney Fabrication in Southampton. They were diabolical and I decided to drive down there. Andrew was away at the London Boat Show, so I decided to go on Wednesday and return Thursday. I had managed to stay off the booze over Christmas – we only got through about four bottles of wine!

2012

Friday 13th January

My lucky day. The Boat Show was OK and the showcase seemed to work, but we have issues with Andrew on boat shows, the showcase, Cooney Fab etc. and there will be a meeting next week.

On Wednesday we had an organised trip on a paddle steamer on the Thames with dinner on board. James and I were on the top table with Howard Pridding and Tony Morgan, the two top BMF officers. Andrew organised it so that he and the Princess buyer sat on the table with the prettiest women.

At the show I managed to obtain the spares I required for the boat. Two weeks today I will be driving down to Gatwick.

I rejected the suit of armour that Ann bought me for Christmas. The workmanship was poor and it is packed up to go back to the supplier today. It was made in Germany but the quality of workmanship was disappointing.

On January 29th, after another gruelling 23-hour trip, we landed once again in Tortola, looking forward to some winter sunshine. It's always a relief to step on board and put the stresses of the English winter behind us. Ann was now fully recovered from her foot surgery and we were optimistic for some good sailing, and on leaving the boat a couple of weeks ago most things were working. I just needed to re-launch the dinghy and sort out sails etc. I'd ordered a new set of sails from Doyle Sails but they were yet to be delivered.

Norman Island was our first destination, and it took only two hours' sailing to get back into 'boat mode'. It was a pleasant sail and in no time we were tied to a buoy in the Bight.

The restaurant at the head of the Bight had recently been rebuilt. The boutique had the usual T-shirts and souvenirs and air tanks could be filled at the dive shop.

Most of the bays and harbours in the British Virgin

Islands have a number of secure mooring buoys for visiting boats. Sadly a lot of the coral has been ploughed up by yacht anchors, but there are a few areas with colourful coral reefs, and plentiful shoals of fish.

From the Bight at Norman Island it was a short sail over to Marina Cay with 15-20 knots of wind on the beam, picking up a buoy at 1330. The buoys are quite expensive at $25 per night, but they are maintained and fairly secure.

Next, after a brisk sail across the St Francis Drake channel, we headed for Cooper Island, picking up a buoy at the Cooper Island Beach Club. It's necessary to book a table at the restaurant, which is usually very busy.

I was in the habit of locking my dinghy painter on to the dock and always did this, but at Cooper this is not allowed and if you attempt to lock your dinghy a man comes over and says it is not necessary as they may need to move dinghies to make room for an emergency boat. This is absolute nonsense, as there was always plenty of room on the dinghy dock. I wonder if they would reimburse someone who had a dinghy stolen?

From Cooper we had a leisurely sail to Virgin Gorda, past Spanish town and into Gorda sound, picking up a buoy at Leverick Bay where we went alongside to fuel and water and then anchored off Mosquito Island for lunch. Several turtles popped their heads up to see what we were doing. The reef that surrounds the island always seemed to have numerous turtles and when snorkelling they seem quite happy to join swimmers and play.

From there we motored back to Marina Cay.

13th February
Left buoy at Marina Cay and sailed via the Little Camenoe

passage to Cane Garden Bay, arriving at 1300. I hired a car for the trip to Nanny Cay Chandlery to buy spares for aft toilet. The car was a bit of a wreck but adequate for the job. Spent the rest of the day doing maintenance, and fitted a full gas cylinder. As evening approached the swell started to build up. Spent a dreadful night, the boat was rolling badly, at times on to her beam ends, and everything in the lockers was rolling about, couldn't sleep.

At first light I took the dinghy to go ashore to return the hire car key, but all the docks were being swept by waves and it was impossible to go ashore. Returned to boat and started engine. The mooring lines were in a tangle but I managed to free them off. Left Cane Garden Bay at about 0700 and motored over to Jost Van Dyke, picking up a buoy at 0830, then had a fried breakfast to celebrate! I then took the car key round to the ferry dock. I'd arranged for the ferry skipper to return the key to the car hire company.

I serviced the aft toilet and got foul-smelling water all over my feet, however it does seem to have got rid of the smell, the loo that is, not my feet! Went ashore to Foxy's for dinner, quite good.

We spent the next day at Jost VD and then motor-sailed over to Sopers Hole, but there were no moorings available so we carried on to Norman Island and picked up a buoy close to the beach.

Snorkelling just off the beach, I managed to find a small reef with beautiful coral and myriads of fish. There were still areas of coral around, usually at rocky outcrops and sometimes in the most unexpected places.

On 18th February we motored round to Benares bay, anchored in 5 metres and I took a stern warp ashore and tied up to a palm tree. This is a quiet bay with good holding and it is a good spot to unwind after enduring the long and sometimes unpleasant flights. We motored round to the Bight for lunch.

19ᵗʰ February

Checked engine oil and topped up tightened drive belt, but engine would not start. Cleaned terminals, voltage good, engine started and we motored back to Manuel Reef. Jim took line and I secured spring. Filled water tanks. 22ⁿᵈ Feb, left Manuel Reef and tacked up the Sir Francis Drake channel to Cooper Island and from there to Leverick bay, picking up mooring. At the Bitter End at 1100 on Sat 25th.

It was a good decision to sail to Anegada the next day, a brisk SW wind gave us a fast passage and before too long we could see the palm trees on Anegada's low-lying shore. Once you have identified Pomato Point to the west of the island there are three red buoys to be left to starboard and then a green buoy that is left to port, then steer 015 magnetic into the anchorage. There we picked up a mooring buoy.

As it's a coral island and not volcanic like the other Virgin Islands, it is not visible until a couple of miles off. The highest part of the Island is only about 30 ft. above sea level.

The island is surrounded by an enormous coral reef and is renowned for its lobster, and the bay is surrounded by several hotels and bars.

On the Atlantic side of the Island is Loblolly Bay. The car hire was inexpensive and the Jalopy we hired had seen better days. On the way to Loblolly bay, in central Anegada, are the ponds which are inhabited by masses of flamingoes. After lunch in the Big Bamboo we walked through to the enormous Loblolly curved beach which is surrounded by a coral reef with impressive clean, clear water. The snorkelling is breathtaking with shoals of colourful fish among the best coral in the BVIs. The beach gives the impression that there is no one else there with very few people and there are benches under grass umbrellas with hooks for hanging towels.

Cow Wreck bay is also worth a visit, also with soft sand and a beach bar.

The wind was a steady **20-25** knots at **0900** on the 28th as we cleared the Anegada channel heading for Great Harbour, Jost van Dyke. It was a cracking beam reach all the way and we were moored up by early afternoon.

After fuelling up at the fuel dock we motored round to White Bay, which is protected by a long reef with an entrance at each end. Inside the reef there is adequate depth for most of the charter boats. The coral on the reef is not very colourful, but it's worth a snorkel to see the fish.

The buoys marking the entrance are a bit faded but are plain to see. We couldn't believe our eyes as a Sunsail boat headed for the middle of the bay and straight for the reef! We shouted and waved and pointed to the buoys, but on they came, and came to a sickening stop as they hit the reef. There was nothing much they could do, as the wind was driving them further on to the reef. Panicking, they were trying to reverse with their engine, but they were well and truly stuck. The women on board were weeping and the men were revving the engine in desperation. Several yacht people went to their assistance and tried with a halyard at the masthead to heel the boat over to reduce the draught and pull the boat off. Eventually a powerful work boat appeared. It fixed a tow rope to the bow and proceeded to drag the yacht over the reef and into the bay, tying it to a mooring buoy. The boat looked OK, luckily not holed below the water line, but I dread to think what the hull and keel were like underneath.

During the afternoon we saw another boat heading for the reef. Someone in a dinghy went out to them and pointed the marker buoys out to them, so disaster was avoided.

We spent another few days round the islands, but all too soon it was time to return to Manuel Reef and pack the boat up and head for the airport. I was due out for another trip in a few weeks, on my own this time.

It was 3rd May before I had the pleasure of a stressful 24-hour series of flights to return to Tortola, and it was a relief when I eventually stepped on board.

When single-handed there is always so much to do when entering and leaving port. It's not too bad leaving, you can usually find someone prepared to untie a singled-up rope and toss it on board, and putting fenders away is not too bad with the autopilot set. I like to stow all fenders in a locker. Quite often boats can be seen under way with fenders hanging over the side, which looks so scruffy.

Picking up mooring buoys is fairly easy in the BVIs. They mostly have a pickup line attached with an eye on the end and users are supposed to put their own warp through the eye to minimise wear on the pickup line. I find it easier to fasten the pickup line to a cleat and then when the boat is safe put two lines through the eye and then release the pickup line. This method ensures that the boat is safely fastened to the buoy and the other ropes can be sorted out at leisure. The antics of some of the boats are quite comical!

Sitting in the restaurant on Norman Island it felt almost as though I'd never left. I missed Ann of course but she was due to fly out in a couple of weeks. I had a few jobs to do on board. I'd brought out some decals to stick on, but I wanted a calm day to attempt this, as I needed to make sure they were level and had no air trapped underneath.

I'd had a new track fitted to the mast which was supposed to make the mainsail go up and down more easily, as I found it hard work after the in-mast reefing on *Blue Genie.*

I pulled up the main whilst on the buoy at Norman. I think it went up easier than before but it was a struggle to get it down. I then decided to sail over to Jost Van Dyke via the Thatch Island cut, so up it went again. The sail set very well and I had a good sail across the St Francis Drake Channel. When it was time to drop the main it dropped into the cover very nicely and I picked up a buoy in Grand Harbour.

Foxy's is always a 'good run ashore' and it's sometimes surprising the people you meet there. This time I met Rick, a homicide detective from Louisiana, with his wife and brother, and I spent an interesting couple of hours with them.

Next day I headed back to Manuel Reef to catch up on a few jobs I wanted to accomplish before Ann arrived. I spent the best part of a day fitting decals. I had three of the name, two for the bow and one for the transom, two seahorses in the style of the Beneteau logo and several trim stripes. When finished the boat looked very smart. The only slight problem was positioning the stripes so that they looked level with the windows.

The marina had a hire car office and they did a special price for boat owners, so I hired one. The crew of Alida, Brian, Grant and Denzyl joined me for the ride round to Nanny Cay Marina for lunch. I don't usually order burgers (you never know what's in 'em) but as the others ordered them I went along with it and they weren't too bad.

Ann was greeted by a thunderstorm when she landed on May 23rd. I'd driven to the airport to meet her but the plane sat on the tarmac for quite a time and I wondered if the pilot was waiting for the rain to stop before disembarking passengers, but it was probably the ground crew holding things up for some reason.

We sailed over to Norman Island, and although it was crowded we found a vacant mooring buoy. It was a Sunday and several powerboats were zooming around. I often snorkel along the shoreline, but with the powerboats flying around it is too dangerous. Their wakes were causing the moored yachts to roll quite violently. They seemed to be enjoying every one else's discomfort, but they had all left by 4 pm.

I was still not happy with the mainsail track and spent the next afternoon pulling the sail up and letting it drop into the sail cover. I found that the boat needed to be dead into wind for it to work smoothly – common sense really.

We spent a few days sailing around the islands, and then at last it was time to lay the boat up for the hurricane season. This involves removing all the canvas awnings etc. and lashing the mainsail to the boom. The boat is then secured between two pontoons with a spider's web of warps, the end of the warps being secured to chains fixed to the pontoons.

The boats seem to survive using this method, although I think they would struggle if the island suffered a direct hit. However the Insurance co. are happy to accept this method.

We eventually flew back on 18th June. I consider this to be late and would have preferred to have left the boat in May to be clear of the dreaded 'H' season.

16th August

It has been quite an eventful year so far. I had a three-week break on the boat on my own and then came back for James's birthday. Ann and I then went out for another month on the boat, getting back the third week in June.

The business is doing very well. We had the best year on Cooney Marine for several years, although the Southampton Co. can't seem to make it.

Christian is shooting very well and recently won the Junior Skeet Doubles Championship. Two weeks ago he shot his first 100 straight!

I have at last changed my car, to a Jaguar XF which is a beautiful motor, very quick and luxurious. Also it has 4 doors. There is a seasonal downturn at the moment. A lot of our customers are closed for some of August, so it will be a light month.

10th September

This month is turning out very well for the business and I think we should have a good few months ahead. Last month I bought another suit of armour, a later design than the first one. I don't know whether it looks right in the hall but it will stay there for now.

12th September

This morning I went to the local creative writing group meeting. We meet once a month and the group is run by Ann's friend, also Ann, one of her golfing buddies. Each month we all write a short story of approx 1000 words, on a given subject. The first one was 'About a ball'. I did a story about the man that shot Nelson with a musket ball. The story I presented today was 'The Phone Call' and I did a cops and robbers theme. The next theme is 'The Secret' and I am looking forward to writing the story.

I have designed a shooting bag stand and have the prototype to try. It works very well and there could be a good market for it.

It is our 44th wedding anniversary on Friday and we are taking the family out to a restaurant to celebrate.

The accounts for last year are now finalised. We had a record year for turnover and the profit was 14%, which is where it should be. I don't know what this year will bring but it should be OK.

Last weekend was the first Kirby Hall shoot of the season. It was a good day out and everyone had reasonable shooting.

Monday 26th November

Well here I am back on the boat. I should have arrived two days ago. The plane took off from Gatwick on time on the 24th, but just as I was getting settled it was announced over the PA that there was an electrical fault and it had to return to Gatwick. The landing was a bit ropey and we then had to wait for the fault to be fixed, so by the time we arrived in Antigua I had missed my connection. Virgin didn't want to know and said their contract was to get me to Antigua. I went to the Liat desk and they informed me that there wasn't an available flight for two days. I booked into the Ocean Inn. I have stayed there before and it's convenient for the Tot club.

Last night I did the Tot and as it was so unexpected and unplanned I had one of the best nights possible. Everyone was so friendly and welcoming that it was almost embarrassing. I spent the evening chatting to Mike, Rose, Annie and many other members.

I have unpacked and started the fridge, but can't do much until morning. It is now pouring with rain, so all of the hatches are closed and it is a bit warm.

27th November

Had a good start to the day. I have now fitted the Bimini, sorted the warps and rigged the lazy jacks on the mainsail. If I have a good day tomorrow and rig the foresail I shall leave the dock on Thursday. I launched the dinghy and fitted the outboard engine. I struggled with the engine, which was a bit of a ball breaker, but it is now done.

30th November

Left berth at 0830 and sailed over to the Bight at Norman Island. Fridge playing up and I am struggling to keep it going. Spent a few days round the islands and on 5th December I decided to go into Nanny Cay and attempt to sort out the fridge problem. I berthed on A6 with no dramas, the marina guys were very helpful.

The bilge pump stopped working, I suspect a blocked filter but don't have a correct sized wrench. The Chandlery didn't have one either so I improvised using a pump handle and a rag. The filter was totally blocked, so I cleaned it off and the pump is now working.

I decided to head over to Norman Island. It was blowing about 30 knots and it took me three attempts to pick up the mooring. I then went to Grand Harbour, Peter Island.

9th December

I am in Grand Harbour, Peter Island and plan to go back to Manuel Reef tomorrow. I am looking forward to going home. I have not enjoyed this trip as much as I expected to. I've had problems with the refrigeration and worked very hard changing pumps etc.

Last night was the shooting club Christmas dinner, but I was not there of course. Christian was awarded Shooter of the Year and Skeet Doubles Champion. If he keeps his interest going he could be very good.

2013

11ᵗʰ January

The Southampton Boat show starts tomorrow. Ann and I plan on visiting and evaluating the marine equipment showcase, as we are showing several companies' products. It seems to work for us and Andy is very enthusiastic and it is thought that he would like to take it on himself. He is not happy and I think he may resign.

There are a lot of good things happening, and if only some of them come to fruition it will be a good year.

29ᵗʰ January

Driving down to Gatwick today and flying to Tortola tomorrow for 6 weeks.

Another gruelling 23-hour trip. I'm sure the employees at Antigua's VC Bird airport are determined to make travelling as unpleasant as possible, a little courtesy would go a long way. We arrived in Tortola minus bags, not unusual for Liat, as quite often bags arrive on a later flight when the aircraft is fully loaded. This makes a mockery of Tortola Customs as we are allowed to pick up the bags with no checks, several hours or a day later.

As soon as I step onto the boat all problems seem to disappear as a different set of problems rear their heads. Will the engine start? Has the boat suffered any damage while I've been away?

There is always maintenance to do, not a problem when chartering, also storing everything. *Amaranthos* was blessed with plenty of locker space and when leaving the boat for any length of time the dinghy fitted on the foredeck. It was fairly easy to lift it off the foredeck using a halyard. Woods Marine Services kept an eye on the boat at Manuel Reef and this was a very safe harbour, with the other occupants also keeping an eye.

I suspected the batteries were not taking a full charge from the alternator and tightened the drive belt. With the close proximity of the islands I like to have a good sail up to Virgin Gorda, and then from the Bitter End or Leverick bay, sail up to Anegada. The prevailing wind gives a run up to Anegada and then a broad reach to Grand Harbour, Jost Van Dyke.

6th February

Left Norman Island at **1000**, main up very squally reefed main, sailing to Virgin Gorda. Difficult to stay on the wind, and I sailed through the Dog Islands. The wind veered as we approached Moskito Island and I was able to sail up to mooring at Leverick Bay.

8th February

Motored over to Bitter End, having problems with house battery bank, may need to change. Discovered house batteries dead, decided to sail over to Nanny Cay to pick up replacements from their chandlery.

On berth A6 Nanny Cay Marina. Chandlery delivered 3 new batteries and I removed and replaced them one at a time. It was a struggle manoeuvring the dead batteries out due to their weight, and then getting the new ones in place and bolted down. It took several hours and it was a relief to get everything in place and bolted up. I then plugged into the shore power to bring the batteries up to full charge.

The vessel took 29.5 gallons of diesel on the fuelling berth as we left the marina to continue round the islands. We flew back 12th March.

19th March

Back after 6 weeks in the Caribbean. I would like to have stayed out there, but have Masonic commitments this month and next. Andy is now long gone and Cooney Fabrication is now being wound up. It's a shame to make the guys there redundant, but the company was costing too much to keep going.

The British Virgin Islands, although beautiful and a great area for boating, are very expensive. Most food items when available are twice the price you would pay in England, and there is very limited choice. I had to fit new batteries this trip and I will try and source a wind generator. The refrigeration needs attention and I will attempt to obtain spares in this country.

I'd measured up the stern of the boat to fit a wind generator. I liked the LE300, as having tried various brands over the years I found it the most efficient. I designed a pole in three sections for ease of transport, removed the blades from the wind generator and fitted it into one of Ann's golf bags. It was May before we took the spares and new equipment to the boat. The generator, pole and brackets all fitted in the golf bag and went straight through customs in Tortola without problem, even though there is no golf course in Tortola.

Prepared the boat for the Hurricane season lay up. I wonder how she would survive a storm – the storms seem to miss the islands most years.

CHAPTER 10

Finesse

✖

2013 started smoothly and we managed to keep our profit margins up. 2012 had been an excellent year, but of course that meant we now had to pay a fortune in tax.

August 14th 2013

The year has gone smoothly so far and we haven't missed Mr Sims. We have saved his salary and his expenses and are maintaining profit margins. The Southampton operation is now almost sorted out. We have a tenant for the factory, we've sold off most of the machinery and we won't be too out of pocket when it's finally sorted out.

This year we are having a large stand at the Southampton Boat Show. It was originally booked for the Showcase, which we are not doing, so we will put on a good show ourselves.

Christian has decided that he does not want to do shooting any more. He competed in some competitions this year but although he shot very well he has now totally lost interest. He seems to want to stay in bed most of the time watching TV or computer games. He is due to start work at the end of this month. That will be a shock to the system.

Last year I joined the local sub-aqua club. I have been training regularly at Corby swimming pool and also at Guildenburg diving centre. I also did a week in Estartit, Spain, diving in the Medes Islands. Last Friday I qualified as an ocean diver and I am looking forward to further training.

Ann and I are booked on a live-aboard diving trip September 2014 in the Red Sea. Ann doesn't dive but decided to come when she saw the 41ft superyacht that the diving club had booked.

Monday 11th November

Remembrance Day today, there were a lot of ceremonials at the weekend and a lot of emotional programmes on the TV.

I don't go into the office very often now. James seems to be handling things well, although I think we could do with more effort on marketing.

We are sourcing a new pipe bender, as the Nissin we have, although versatile, does have limitations on wall thickness and bend radius. James and I went for a demonstration of the latest Nissin pipe benders, which are now produced in Germany.

We went with Ivan, the representative of the agent selling the machines in the UK, taking the afternoon flight to Hamburg, then driving to the factory and staying in a hotel close by, turning up at the factory at 0900 for the demo. We got the impression that the company wasn't prepared for us. The bends they were producing were not satisfactory, which was annoying as we had sent them samples of our requirements. The engineer doing the demo said he could fix the problem by altering the mandrel, which he did by removing one of the ball sections.

We all stood around the machine expectantly as the machine commenced bending the sample, which appeared to be going ok when there was a loud report like a pistol shot as the clamp holding the tube shattered and dagger-shaped pieces of hard plastic plate flew in all directions, luckily not hitting anyone. The people doing the demo were very embarrassed and suggested that we went for a coffee while the machine was 're-set'.

We went for a coffee and Ivan was quite sheepish. We'd expected to do the deal and sign up for the machine, but this now seemed unlikely. After coffee we went back into the works to see if the machine was now operational. The covers had been removed and an engineer was on top of the machine sawing through the jammed tooling! I cheekily asked if they supplied a saw with each machine!

There was embarrassment all round. Our flight back to UK wasn't until 10pm, so we had to spend the rest of the day with an embarrassed Ivan. Since then we have looked at an Italian machine which didn't do the job either, but at least it didn't blow up.

Work seems to be holding up and this year should be quite good as long as nothing unforeseen happens. The Southampton Boat Show in September was successful. We had a large stand that was originally booked for the showcase. Andy Sims had a showcase stand near us, but it didn't seem very busy.

The diving club are coming here (Acre House) tonight for some training in our pool.

On Tuesday Ann and I are flying out to Tortola for a

sunshine break before Christmas. The figures for October were remarkably good, with a net profit of around 15%. The year so far has been a success, although I would like to see some new design products in the pipeline. The METS show has finished and our new davit was mentioned in the Dame awards.

Christian is working at Cooney's and is doing well. It's a pity he has given up shooting, he won most of the competitions he entered, but as soon as he got a car and a job he didn't want to do it anymore. I hope he will come back to it in the future, but time will tell.

I am enjoying the sub aqua training and may do some dives in Tortola.

On Saturday we purchased a tapestry for the hall, it is called 'Departure of the Knights'. The theme, against a background of dark and perilous forest, represents the departure of two Knights of the Round Table, Sir Gawain of Orkney and Sir Hector de Marys from the legends of King Arthur.
30th November

Back in Tortola for a sunshine break before Christmas. Early on in the trip the autopilot packed up, so we were hand steering for a time. The next drama was the engine refusing to start. The engine battery is a problem, I'd changed the house battery bank last time I was out. I tried jump leads and sometimes it worked and sometimes it didn't, so I changed the engine battery for one of the house batteries. This worked fine until I could pick up a new engine start battery.

Dave the electrician came on board to fix the autopilot and found the gauge to be US, so we decided to source new unit in the UK.

Most of the trip the wind was gusting up to 28 knots, but it was warm and nice to be away from UK winter chills.

Monday 16th December

Just returned from an 18-day trip to the Caribbean. The boat was in good shape and when Ann and I stepped on board I was reminded how nice a boat she is. She always looks her best when we have just arrived or are just leaving. We tried the new electric winch handle which we'd bought hoping to make lifting the dinghy on and off the foredeck easier. Lifting the outboard motor from the pushpit and onto the dinghy is difficult and awkward due to the weight of the engine.

The wind generator worked well, probably better than expected. Dave the electrician did a good job on the electrical installation and came on board to work on the refrigeration.

On the first Saturday we met up with Carl Walther and family, as their cruise ship had called into Tortola for a day. Their son Jack and his girlfriend Kate were with them and we spent a pleasant afternoon at Nanny Cay.

The autopilot packed up as we set off from the Marina on our way to Marina Cay. We hand-steered and arranged for Dave the electrician to have a look at it.

On arrival in Virgin Gorda the engine start battery was flat and I couldn't start the engine to charge batteries or run the fridge. I tried Jump leads from the house battery bank and these worked once and then gave up! I swapped the engine battery for one of the house batteries and the engine burst into life. We decided to return to Tortola and buy a new engine battery from Nanny Cay Chandlery.

2014
27th January

Christmas and New Year are now just a memory. It was

especially good this year as we had all of the grandchildren for Christmas Day. Next year Taylor and Casey will be with their dad.

At the London Boat Show I was able to obtain a new autopilot for only £200. The catalogue price was £350, but the unit is not being produced any more. Luckily one of my contacts was able to find a unit that was in stock.

I also bought an inflatable kayak at the show, as Ann and I thought it would give us something else to do round the islands. The package, which included, an inflator, life vests and various accessories. was fitted into Ann's trusty golf bag together with spares and parts for the boat.

Ann and I are due to fly out to Tortola at the end of the month, and as usual we have a lot of spares for the boat. We are undecided as to the best way to package them. The largest item is a new main hatch which I had made in Perspex. The original wooden hatch had de-laminated and looked untidy.

The business is doing well, but we are under constant pressure for cost downs. As usual when business picks up the cowboy element rears its ugly head and we get price pressure.

James is very good and doesn't seem to get stressed over things. The year is going well, with excellent profitability.

Ann and I decided to give one of our buy-to-let houses to Teri at Christmas. It should give her more income and perhaps be the start of her own portfolio.

I have designed and made a small crane for lifting the dinghy outboard, I hope it works! It is a very simple idea, but so are most clever inventions!

14th February

Valentine's Day today, we have been on the boat for 2 weeks and at the moment everything is working. The engine lift crane worked better than expected. The new Perspex hatch fitted perfectly and looks really good.

We have tried the kayak out a few times, and it is very stable once you are in but getting in and out is interesting. We are moored in Leverick Bay and it's very windy, which is good for the wind generator.

Once the kayak is afloat it is very stable. Ann sits in the front and I try to synchronise my paddling rhythm with her. We often we go for quite long periods before we have a clash of paddles! I try to steer and change direction and we like to explore areas that we would not usually visit, as with the kayak being so light it is easy to carry it ashore while we go for a wander. We stow it across the stern of the boat as it doesn't tow that well and tends to end up full of water, making it difficult to handle.

Although the BVIs are a most popular charter destination, secluded beaches and anchorages are there for the adventurous. The coral reefs can be navigated as long as care is taken and depths constantly checked.

16th March

After a few weeks round the islands, it was back to Manuel Reef to pack the boat up. We thought that perhaps it was time to change boats, as with all the improvements we had made to Amaranthos she was in remarkably good shape, far better than most of the Beneteau 393s around the islands. I fancied a catamaran, but Ann preferred a monohull. Catamarans do have advantages with their stability and roomy interiors, but with their large beam (width) they are more expensive to berth and handling in close quarters can be tricky.

3rd May

Last month I had a diving holiday in Ibiza with the diving club. It was a good week and I enjoyed it, but I found the diving to be very hard work. I have a new BCD (buoyancy control device) with integrated weight pockets but left the weight pockets behind, so I was then using a weight belt, which kept slipping. I am not used to the BCD and wearing two wet suits I found my breathing restricted and I was using a lot of air.

On the last dive I was diving with an Italian girl called Alexandra. When my air was low I signalled her and surfaced on her octopus (alternative air supply). It was an excellent week and I learned a lot. The Ibiza company were very efficient and competent.

Whilst in the Caribbean I'd decided to look at changing the boat. We looked at several and decided to try and buy an Oceanis 433. I contacted Moorings Brokerage and put Amaranthos on the market, and within a week they'd found a buyer. I made an offer on an Oceanis 433, but the survey was disappointing so we rejected the boat.

In 10 days Ann and I are flying out to Tortola to look at some more boats and will be staying at the Nanny Cay hotel.

The business is doing very well and James is investing a lot of money in new plant. A new tube bender is being delivered in a few days and the company will probably invest in a new water jet cutter later in the year.

Christian crashed his car last Saturday. Luckily he was uninjured and no one else was involved, but the car is a write off. He took a bend too fast, skidded and wrapped the car round a tree!

19ᵗʰ June

*Ann and I have been here for almost a week looking at boats.
The Nanny Cay Hotel is a bit run down. The boat that we
rejected due to the poor survey was in a sorry state, the floors
were badly damaged and in places had delaminated because
of water damage. It was a good decision to reject it. Another
Oceanis 433 also became available, but when we went to view
it the condition was worse. Ann was keen on a Jeanneau
42i and we almost made an offer, but then realised that the
draught was too deep to operate comfortably out of Manuel
Reef Marina, where we like to keep the boat.*

*We had arranged to remove some gear from Amaranthos
this week but the new owner dumped everything he didn't want
in the Marina Manager's office and disappeared with about
$1000 worth of my gear!*

I was beginning to despair of finding an Oceanis 433 in Tortola
in reasonable condition. I looked at one with another broker
but it had a different layout and was unsuitable. Others I
viewed in Tortola seemed in poor condition and needed a lot
of work to bring them up to a standard that I would consider
acceptable, and I doubted that "phase out" could bring them
up to scratch. The Moorings base in St Martin had two for
sale, so Ann and I decided to fly up there to view them.

20ᵗʰ June

*Today we flew up to St Martin to look at two more Oceanis
433s. They were both in very good condition, far better than the
vessels in Tortola although a year older. We made an offer on
the boat that we considered to be in the best condition. It was*

a long day, the flight was at 0700 so we had to leave the Hotel at 0530.

The Moorings base in St. Martin is a lot smaller than Tortola. The broker is a French woman called Gwen, a very efficient lady. The boats were on mooring buoys and she took us out to see them in an old hard dinghy. Both boats were in far better shape than the boats in Tortola and although a year older they had less engine hours and were not so knocked about. We made an offer on Finesse, the boat that appeared the better of the two.

24ᵗʰ June 2014

The new owner of Amaranthos has fallen out with Jim Woods at Manuel Reef Marina and has moved the boat to Virgin Gorda, where it has been hauled out. I don't know if he was hoping to get away with the rest of our gear but we are going over on the ferry Thursday morning with Giles the broker to hopefully retrieve it.

I heard this morning that the offer on Finesse had been accepted, which was good news. I would like Geoff Williams to do the survey. It's a bit complicated with the boat being in St Martin and it will work out expensive with travelling etc. but I trust Geoff to do a good job.

26ᵗʰ June

The ferry to Virgin Gorda was packed, Giles turned up at 0850 and the ferry left the dock on time at 0900. It took about 30 minutes to arrive in Spanish town and the boat yard was fairly close to the ferry dock.
Amaranthos looked in good shape out of the water and we

borrowed a ladder to climb aboard. The Bimini and canopy had been removed. Ann and I went into the boat to retrieve the charging plugs, mast climber, Kayak pressure gauge, paddles and log book while Giles fiddled with ropes and things. I removed the kayak from the aft locker and the dive bottle from the cockpit locker. Giles had brought a large bag into which we managed to fit everything except the dive bottle, which I carried on my shoulder, Giles carried the rest in his large bag. He has offered to store the gear until we bring the new boat to Tortola.

We landed at Gatwick on 29th June just 24 hours after setting out from Tortola, and had about seven hours to wait in Antigua so we decided to go to Dickenson Bay for the afternoon. The flight from Antigua was quite good. I managed to sleep for a few hours and was not too tired driving home.

I booked my flights for a few days for the survey of *Finesse*. I am going alone as there is no need for Ann to come, and I am travelling first class.

When I arrived home and checked my vegetable patch, the broccoli had bolted and the cauliflower looked peculiar, so I shredded the lot!

I had a pleasant week in St Martin overseeing the survey on *Finesse*. The brokerage people were very helpful and on the day of the survey I arrived on the boat at 0830. We were due to leave the marina and motor round to Bobby's 90-ton travel lift. The guy the marina supplied didn't really want to do it and during the hour it took to motor round he complained the whole time, but towards the end he became more friendly.

The surveyor, Geoff Williams, met us on the dock and Gwen, the broker, was there. After the hull was examined the boat was re-launched and Geoff came on board for engine trials. I expected him to stay on board for the trip back, but he asked to be returned to the dock and said he would drive back to the moorings base to finish the survey. I sailed the boat back with the crew member supplied by the moorings. The boat sailed well and we made good time returning early afternoon.

The survey was OK and as there appeared to be no big problems I decided to go ahead with the purchase. The only downside was the mainsail, which was in a poor state, but as I intended to replace it and the mainsail track I considered this to be irrelevant.

The rest of the week was a bit of an anti-climax and I spent the time going for drives. I soon mastered driving on the right. I spent the rest of the time lazing around the pool. The trip back was uneventful and it was nice flying first class.

There was a panic on at Cooney's. Sunseeker were finishing off their second 40-metre boat and we had a team down at Poole working all hours. The wages bill was horrendous, James was on holiday and we had a new water Jet cutting machine newly installed. We had already bought a new pipe bender. We had invested over half a million in new plant during the year.

Wednesday 22ⁿᵈ October

Off to St. Martin on Saturday to finalise the deal on the new boat. Last weekend the island was hit by Hurricane Gonzalo, but luckily, according to the brokers, our boat survived it OK.

Our main problem at present is that James's wife Louise, the company secretary, has walked out for no apparent reason. Her main job is payroll and although Debbie, the office manager, can do it unfortunately she is quite ill and may need time off. Ann and I are flying out in three days and will be away for a month. It never rains but it pours!

Ann is considering cancelling the trip. If she does and I go out alone I don't fancy taking an untried boat from St Martin to Tortola. I single-handed the last boat a few times on short trips but don't fancy doing 100 miles single handed in a boat that is untried and untested. The main priority is to sort out the business, so we may have to cancel completely!

In the end James insisted that we went. Debbie and Lyn offered to do extra hours to make up the shortfall and assured us that they could handle things.

We flew out via Paris, as the part of St Martin where the marina is situated is French. The Island is divided into a French sector and a Dutch sector, St. Maarten. Legend has it that 350 years ago the French and Dutch wanted to draw a border on the Island in a civilised manner. It was decided that a race should be held to determine how much land each nation should claim. The French competitor had to follow the coastline to the north, the Dutchman to the south, and once they circumnavigated the island and met up again a line would be drawn between the starting point and the meeting point to define the border. The French did better. French St Martin covers two thirds of the 37 square-mile island.

We stayed in an apartment for a few days rather than the Marina Hotel, and eventually the deal was done. We'd hired a car as we needed to buy an amount of new gear. The brokerage had an arrangement with Budget Marine to discount everything by 20%, which made an enormous difference when buying things like dinghies and outboard motors.

I decided that the first short trip in Finesse would be to Ile Fourche, as I had happy memories of the time we called in there when sailing around the Islands with Pat Patterson in Ocean Winds many years ago.

Friday 7th November

We spent the last night anchored off Ile Fourche, the first time I had been there since 1985 when I was with Pat Patterson on Ocean Winds and his crew Brenda, a young Canadian girl. We have now spent two nights in Finesse. It was a struggle with the brokers. I was under the impression that when they handed over a boat it should be fully equipped as if about to go out on charter. This was not the case with Finesse, as a lot of the gear was taken off, even items listed on the original survey. There were no flares, first aid kit, engine spares or tools, to name but a few items. One day I came on board and all the fire extinguishers had been removed! They were replaced and we were given three daylight smoke flares, but we never received a first aid kit and there were no cockpit cushions.

The gauges for the water tanks should have been repaired and calibrated and I was suspicious of the fuel tank, I insisted that a mechanic test the tank gauge and check the contents. I will be relieved to take the boat to Tortola.

Saturday 8th November

Last night it rained so much it filled the dinghy. It seems brighter today, but we will probably not leave until tomorrow night. We are going ashore soon to check out with Customs and buy any last-minute items for the trip to Tortola. It is only 90 miles or so but the boat has no radar reflector and I hope to buy one in Budget Marine. Although the fuel tank is full, the gauge only shows 3/4 of a tank.

Sunday 9th November

Tried to check out with Customs, but they closed at 12 and we arrived at 1300. Budget were also closed and are still closed today, although we were able to do Customs and immigration and check out.

The moorings had provided us with inadequate paperwork, so we had to check in and check out at the same time. It was a relief to obtain the clearance, as at one time it looked as though we would have to take a taxi to Marigot to sort things out. We are leaving tonight at dusk and should arrive Tortola eightish in the morning.

We weighed anchor and motored away from the Simpson Bay anchorage, but there wasn't a lot of wind, and what there was would be astern. I put out the jib and mainsail, looking forward to our first night at sea in Finesse. The wind was light to moderate with frequent squalls that seemed to be chasing us.

I did the 9-12 watch and Ann came on at 12. There was a ship that was always in a funny position. We altered course several times, but it was still there. I eventually turned in at 0110 and went straight to sleep.

Ann called me at 0400, having given me an extra hour in my bunk. The boat was making good progress, maintaining 6-7 knots, and by 0530 we were approaching the tip of Virgin Gorda. The plan was to transit the Necker passage between Virgin Gorda and Necker Island, enter Gorda sound and clear Customs and immigration at the office in Gun Creek.

I called Ann just after 0600. For the last hour I had been trying to slow the boat down and had taken down the mainsail and reduced engine revs. I wanted to do the Necker Passage in daylight. The customs office in Gun Creek were very helpful and after formalities we picked up a mooring in Leverick Bay to catch up on some sleep.

The boat performed very well and I am looking forward

to buying new sails and bringing her up to scratch. The basic boat is in good condition but a lot of the gear is knackered, the Bimini and spray dodger leak like a sieve.

22nd November

We spent a few days round the Islands enjoying the boat and learning her ways. Most things worked and we are generally pleased. We decided to go to Manuel Reef on Mon 17th, I'd decided to moor stern first and we did so without too much drama. Bob Phillips from Doyle Sails has measured up for a new Bimini and cockpit enclosure and we are having a new mainsail. The filthy rag that moorings had supplied with the boat is so awful that I was reluctant to put it up!

Tomorrow we fly down to St. Martin and then home, quite a successful month. I'm now looking forward to our trip in January.

31st December

New Year's Eve again, where has the year gone? Tonight Ann and I are going round to David and Penny's next door.

The problem at work is that Debbie is seriously ill and as Louise walked out and left us in the lurch Ann is having to work a lot more hours. I have booked to fly out to the Caribbean at the end of the month. Ann will follow as soon as she is confident that the finance office can cope without her.

The latter part of the year was a bit slow and work scarce. Our customers have been de-stocking and re scheduling orders. It should pick up in the New Year.

James is working very hard and we are hoping to keep the team together. Cash flow is good and there is a lot of money in the bank. With the new plant and the reorganisation of the factory, as soon as work picks up, production should increase significantly

2015

27th January

I am going to the boat on the 29th, but Ann is not coming for 4 weeks. I didn't want to go alone, but with the situation at the office Ann felt that she could not leave the new girl, Laura, for that length of time.

I intend fitting davits on the boat, they are made and are being shipped in the next few days.

According to the news, industry is doing fine with low unemployment etc. It is unusual for us to be slow when the rest of industry is booming.

I am off to the boat for 6 weeks. I wonder what I will find when I return!

Monday 2nd February

When I arrived the boat was in good shape. The new Bimini was fitted but not finished, the new sail cover and sail were also fitted but the name was not on the sail cover. I phoned Ann and everything seems fine although it is bitterly cold at home.

I asked Jim Woods, the marina manager, to recommend a fibreglass worker as the transom needs strengthening to be strong enough to mount the davits. The standard transom is too thin and flexible. It will be an awkward job as the gas locker will need to be dismantled, which I could do myself but I would prefer to get someone else to do it.

Two guys came on board to finish the Bimini this afternoon.

I left them to it and drove up to Sopers Hole to while away a few hours. I was able to get wi-fi there and caught up with my emails.

Thursday 5th February

I have been out nearly a week. The Bimini is a poor job and does not fit that well; the frame, which is the original modified to fit, is unsatisfactory. There are old screws in the end fittings and when I tried to speak to the fitters all I got was an unintelligible diatribe, although they could speak good English when it suited them. I don't know what to do. If I complain I am made to feel as though I am unreasonable and ungrateful. Poor service and bad quality seem to be the norm, and by complaining I am the bad guy.

Today I shall inflate the dinghy and put up the sail to check if the boom clears the Bimini.

I have been discussing the fitting of the davits with Ann, and she is of the opinion that $3000 is too much to pay for the transom work and I should do it myself. I don't mind some things, but fibre glassing has never been my strong point. I will probably get Jim Woods to organise it, and I would like it done as soon as possible.

Originally I was due to start the Job tomorrow, but it won't happen as I have not given Jim the OK. Ann thinks I should obtain another quote, but if it's cheaper will I be getting a worse job? I'll see Jim in the morning to discuss the job. The car goes back tomorrow, it's a nice little Kia with only one wing damaged (not by me!)

12ᵗʰ February

The davit job has turned into a nightmare and I don't think I have had as much stress over anything for a long time. Nothing has been started, so it's unlikely that anything will be done before Ann arrives.

George Shiells is arriving in Tortola tomorrow and her party are joining a Sunsail flotilla. Flotilla sailing is a good way to charter as you don't have the stress, worry and responsibility of bareboat charter. Flotillas are made up of several boats with a guide boat to stop you doing anything stupid. It is quite expensive, but with the costs shared among the crew, it's not too bad and works out cheaper than skippered charter. Flotillas appeal to all ability groups from the unqualified new skipper to the old hand.

Ann expects me to meet up with George's party around the islands. She is a good friend and I will make the effort, but I can't see any fibreglassing being done in the near future.

Today I serviced my toilet. I bought the spares from the marina chandlery, it now works fine and doesn't keep filling up.

There is a boatload of bellowing drunks just across the pontoon, German I think. "What shall we do with a drunken sailor" in German sounds quite different.

I rang George a couple of times to try and make contact, and she eventually rang back while I was on skype to Ann. I'd moved the boat to Norman Island thinking their flotilla may make this its first port of call. When she rang their boat was in Peter Island, but they were due to move to Marina Cay the next day.

16th February

*Sailed the boat from the Bight at Norman Island to Marina
Cay, it was a glorious sail and I loved how the boat performed.
I picked up a buoy and went ashore to buy some wine and
nibbles, intending to ask George and crew on board for a drink.*

*I was busy in the cockpit when a familiar woman's voice
said "Hello Kevin". I looked up and there was George waving
at me as they made their boat fast to the next buoy. I went over
and met Bob and Judith, George's sailing buddies, and then
we all had a drink and a chat. I invited them on board and
they asked if I would join them for dinner and they would pay,
as a return favour for all the boat show tickets I had given
them over the years.*

*They thought the next day would be a free day and were
going to a briefing at 1730 with the flotilla leader. I suggested
that we could all go to Diamond Cay the next day, as this was
not on the flotilla schedule. At their briefing the flotilla leader
changed the venue for the next day to Spanish Town, in the
Marina, so the day was not to be free after all.*

*I then decided to head back to Manuel Reef early and start
preparing the boat for the work to be done. After their briefing
they came on board for a drink and then we all went to the
Pussers restaurant for dinner. I enjoyed the company of Bob
and Judith and it was a super night.*

I'd moved the boat to Peter Island, as it was only about four
miles from there to Manuel Reef. I put fenders out, two on
the transom, two starboard side and five port side. I intended
to berth the boat stern to the dock, single handed. With the
cross wind this could be a tricky manoeuvre and I rang Jim,
the marina manager, to tell him I was coming in and would

require someone ashore to catch ropes etc. He told me not to rush as there was someone else on our berth and he needed to get them to move. I reduced speed as I approached the reef, moved the dinghy forward and put warps on the necessary cleats.

I rang Jim again and he told me the berth was clear. The buoys marking the channel through the reef were not easily visible due to the swell – the wind was a SE 4-5. I consider that southeast is the best possible wind direction for bringing a boat in, stern to, in this marina. Darren and a helper were on the dock ready. I brought the boat slowly down the line of berthed boats and then swung into wind, placing the stern on the dock and the boat about 45% knowing that the wind would gently push the boat straight as we reversed into the berth. Darren was shouting instructions, but I was fully aware of what I was doing and in no time at all the boat was safely berthed. Phew!

21st February

The fibreglassing on the stern is now well under way. There were two guys working on it this morning, and the boat is heavy with styrene fumes from the resin.

George rang this afternoon, they are moored in Cane Garden Bay. I spent the afternoon there yesterday. I'd been trying to contact her to find out where they were, but her phone is on the blink and she rang me on Judith's. It would be nice to meet up again but it largely depends on the work on our boat being completed.

Wednesday 25th February

The work on the transom is progressing well. There is going to

be over 4" thickness in the main load areas, it looks a bit over
he top but better that way than not strong enough.

Yesterday afternoon Judith rang and said they were again
in Cane Garden Bay, so I rang back and said I would drive
over and meet them in Myatt's restaurant. As I left Road Town
it started to rain. I got stuck behind a bus and going up the
steep hills the hire car I was driving kept slipping back because
of its bald tyres. It was a nightmare journey and I dreaded the
trip back to Road Town.

I met up with Bob, George, Judith and a German family,
Klaus, Susanna and their son Jonathan, who had a boat in
the same flotilla. We spent a pleasant evening at Myatts, but I
didn't drink as I had a nightmare trip back to Manuel Reef to
look forward to.

We said our goodbyes about 1030 and I set out back to Road
Town. The roads were now dry, so apart from the roller coaster
hills it was not too bad, until I took a wrong turn and ended
up running out of road. There was nowhere to turn around so
I had to reverse uphill for over 200 yards before I could find
a place to turn round. I eventually got back to the road and
flagged down a car to ask directions. I arrived back on board
about midnight.

Ann came out for a couple of weeks, by which time I'd
finished fitting the davits. We did a circuit of the islands. The
davits worked exceptionally well apart from the flexing of the
tubes when raising and lowering the dinghy. I decided to make
another pair of davits with a thicker wall tube which should
sort out the problem with the tubes flexing. I will ship them out
so I can fit them next time I am out.
It was difficult drilling the transom to get the backing plates to
line up, but all is well, it's a good installation.

25th May 2015

Yesterday Ann and I flew back from Tortola, having been out there for about three and a half weeks. We'd had some solar panels delivered – Doyle sails had fixed some Velcro to the Bimini to enable us to fit them. We hired a car and picked up the panels from the Fed X office in Road Town. There was a lot of import tax to pay but the panels themselves were very cheap. It took just over a day to install the panels and the electrics. I have always been sceptical about the value of solar panels, the thinking being that "when the lights go on, the solar panels go off". They did however save a lot of engine running hours for battery charging and I considered them a worthwhile addition, and as they are fixed to the Bimini with Velcro they are unobtrusive. A new propellor was delivered, which will be fitted in time for next season.

26th June

Last weekend was the Swanage diving weekend. I left at about 0800 Friday, hoping to get down to Swanage in time for an afternoon dive. I'd bought a new dry suit with the hope of doing some training in dry suit diving. On the way down my right eye seemed a bit prickly, as though it had some grit in it. I put this down to my contact lenses drying out in the air conditioning.

I didn't manage a dive on Friday but hoped to dive on Saturday morning, and we all arrived at the pier at 0630. The accommodation was very good. There were 12 of us and we hired two lodges, each with six beds. There was a hot tub with each lodge and Friday night was spent splashing around in these.

On Saturday morning, after parking the car and preparing the gear, we all went for breakfast at a small café near the pier.

My eye was becoming quite uncomfortable and regretfully I decided not to dive. I saw the others off In the boat and then two of the non-divers, Kelly and Sandra, marched me round to a pharmacy, where I bought some Chloramphenicol eye drops. The girls were going shopping, so I went back to the lodge and spent a miserable day feeling sorry for myself. By evening the eye was very painful and my vision was affected.

The crowd had booked a restaurant in Corfe for Saturday night, but I didn't feel like going out and had an early night.

The next morning Ron offered to give me a lift home and Kevin Church offered to drive my car back for me. Ann took me into the Corby walk-in centre and a doctor there ascertained that I had a lesion on the cornea and sent me to Northampton Eye Casualty, where the doctor there said there was an ulcer on the cornea and prescribed antibiotic eye drops, to be taken every hour. She also took some samples from the eye to be sent off for tests.

By Monday morning I had no sight in the right eye whatsoever, but by Tuesday it had started to improve. I am still not able to see perfectly and consequently had to cancel my shooting trip this weekend at Carlton Moor range. I'd planned to drive down Friday ready for a 9am start Saturday, staying at an inn Friday night.

22ⁿᵈ July

My eye is still not good. I can do most things, driving is not too bad, but the eye doctor has said scuba diving is out. I plan on diving anyway on Saturday, but I shall ensure as far as possible that my mask doesn't let any water in. The water at Guildenburg is quite murky and I dread to think what bugs it contains.

I tried rifle shooting last week, which was not too bad. I shall have another go next week and see if I can improve the grouping.

Last weekend, Dave Bosworth (Teri's first husband) was married, and we all went to the wedding. His new wife Julie is a charming girl and I hope they will be happy. Christian looked quite mature dressed up in his wedding suit. It was peculiar seeing Dave and all his family at the wedding, it reminded me of his first wedding, just with a different bride.

I now go into the office only once or twice a week to have a walk around and chat to James. Everything seems to be working OK. The profit percentage is a bit low, but cash flow is good and there is a healthy credit balance in the bank.

James is on holiday in Florida for a couple of weeks. He's left his boat on our drive to be picked up by the dealer for warranty work to be done.

Ann is playing golf several days a week, making the most of the summer weather. It's a nuisance that I'm not supposed to go diving due to my eye, although I am going to Portugal on 12th Sept for a few days' diving.

On the 8th August Ann and I hosted the diving club summer barbecue. It was a glorious day, possibly the best day of the year. I bought a gazebo to shelter the barbecue in the event of rain.

It started at about 3pm and about 20 people turned up, though I'd hoped for more. Teri and her friend Helen assisted with the catering. During the afternoon a lone Spitfire flew over and then proceeded to do an aerobatic display over the house. It was remarkable, the guests were enthralled. I suppose the pilot was just having a practice, but the guests were convinced that I had organised the display.

I started diving again on 9th August. With missing the

diving on the Swanage trip and the training on 25th July I have missed almost a whole season's diving. I have tried my new dry suit but need more practice to sort out the buoyancy.

Tomorrow Ann and I are off to York for the weekend.

In November Ann and I flew out to Tortola for our pre-Christmas break. I'd arranged for our new design davits to be sent out and eventually they arrived, and fitted perfectly. I'd been worried that somehow between design and manufacture something was bound to go wrong. As the new design required a thicker wall tube the bends had to be a different radius to the original, but luckily everything fitted. They look good and work exceptionally well. They are quite a bit heavier than the original pair and it was a struggle to fit them.

Problems with the masthead light and the engine fuel system were a thorn in my side, but I was hoping to obtain spare parts for the engine that would cure this problem.

Christmas was a happy time. We had Teri's kids and James and family on Christmas Day and Anne and Tony came for tea, although Tony was quite ill.

At New Year's Eve we had 11 including Ann and me – we didn't want a big party. I cooked a large piece of gammon and a joint of beef. I'd obtained fireworks for midnight – they were expensive as I bought five single-ignition barrages.

It poured with rain most of the day, so I placed the fireworks on a plastic sheet and covered them with another sheet. Our guests probably wondered what I was up to lurking in the garden setting it up. It was an impressive display for a few minutes though one barrage failed to go off – it must have got wet although I thought I'd covered everything and kept everything dry.

CHAPTER 11

Lightning strikes twice

❡

We were now looking forward to our next trip on 29th January. In November I heard that Fairline had gone into receivership, sad news when I thought of all the years we'd supplied them. For many years I had designed all of their deck gear and although we were not supplying them with much at the time I was sad to see them go to the wall. Luckily they didn't owe us anything.

2016
22nd April

Business is now booming. Last month was the highest turnover and profit month ever, and James is under a lot of pressure.

When we joined the boat in January the two jobs that should have been done had not been. This was annoying, and eventually we decided to move to a different marina.

Village Cay is in the centre of Tortola and is quieter than Manuel Reef but not so picturesque.

We are not going out to the boat until 10th June. I am not too happy about this but Laura, the finance lady, is getting married in May and it is Christian's 21st birthday on 8th June. I pointed out to Ann that this was the hurricane season, but she was adamant that the season started on 1st July. Next Wednesday, the 27th, I am going to Gozo scuba diving.

9th June

Gozo was a good trip, apart from the fact that several of the dive sites were inaccessible to me because of my dodgy knees. I also need more training with the dry suit.

Production is still good but has levelled off a bit. Last year's production and profit were far better than in previous years. James is putting in a lot of effort and we are also investing in a lot of expensive plant.

Yesterday was Christian's 21st and we did a small party for him at Acre House. He is having another party on Friday at his house, but we will be away, we fly tomorrow morning.

I have now finished my memoirs, apart from final editing. It will be interesting to see the finished book. I don't think I will sell many, but who knows? It will be quite a thick book, around 300 pages.

11th June

Flew out to the boat yesterday, all flights were on time and we arrived Tortola at 1915. I tried the engine and was amazed when it burst into life at the second attempt.

I'd decided to change the barbecue from gas to charcoal

(the gas kept blowing out) and I'd brought out a stainless tray which fitted perfectly and should need no modification. Everything on board seemed OK apart from the entire deck being covered in dust.

19th June

We are now at the Bitter End yacht club. We motored down from Leverick Bay this morning. Engine starting is still a problem and yesterday I changed the fuel filter and tightened up all the hose clips. I then tried to undo the top of the sea water strainer and managed to break the lid. On starting the engine I noticed that there was no water coming out of the exhaust pipe. Ann rang Parts and Power in Tortola and luckily they had the spares we needed, but as we were in Leverick Bay on Virgin Gorda and it was a Saturday it meant getting a taxi to Spanish Town, a ferry to Road Town Tortola and then another taxi to Parts and Power.

We arrived at Parts and Power at about 1230 and soon obtained the required parts before boarding the 1330 ferry back to Virgin Gorda. I decided we would have lunch at the Pussers bar and then spend the rest of the afternoon fitting the new parts. They don't seem to have made any difference to the starting, which was disappointing after so much effort.

I rang CRC, the Yanmar dealers in Spanish Town, and arranged for an engineer to visit the boat to try to fix the engine. The marina berth in Spanish town was very convenient with water and 220-volt power available. We arrived at about 1330 and paid our deposit of $200 to CRC – they will not do any work until a deposit has been paid..

The mechanic arrived at 08:45. He had a lollipop in his mouth with the stick protruding, a bit like Kojak from the 1980s cop show!

He spent about one and a half hours fiddling with the engine and then announced that the new pump I had fitted was not working and promptly left. The young woman in the office was super efficient and arranged for a new pump to be shipped out. By this time I was getting totally fed up so I took the pump off, fiddled with it and got it working. I put everything back together and ran the engine, but the starting was no better. I then cancelled the new pump and we left the marina, heading back to Leverick Bay on 22nd June.

I have just been on the internet and discovered that there is a problem with these engines.

24th July

It's Ann's birthday today, she is 70. We were rudely awakened by the alarm system, and in trying to re-set it I set off the fire alarm and a few minutes later two fire appliances arrived. I realised that the problem was caused by a power cut, and consequently the electric gates wouldn't open. Richard, our friend from down the village, turned up, he is a key holder and had been contacted by the alarm company. I soon sorted things out and Richard came in for a cup of tea.

We are going out for a family lunch today and tomorrow we are flying to Barcelona for a few days. I bought Ann some new golf clubs and a couple of Pandora charms for her present. On 29th August I had a new knee. The operation went well and the treatment since has been good. I came home yesterday and I am hoping that everything will be OK for when we go out to the boat in November.

6th September

I'm not getting so much pain now, the only problem I can see so far is bending the leg. I do the recommended exercises, but it seems to not want to bend.

13th October

The knee is almost better, I can walk, go up and downstairs and I'm getting about 120 degrees of bend. I am still taking painkillers when necessary but far less, and I hope to stop them altogether as soon as possible.

I now have a proof copy of my book, Pulpits and Plain Sailing. It looks pretty good, although there are a few things I will change – it seems every time I read it I find something. The official release date is 7th November but the PR company marketing the book has problems. I think that at the January boat show I should sell a few, although that was not the reason for writing it.

8th December

This year has been reasonable for business. James is under a lot of pressure as he has split from Louise, who has mental health problems. He is now living in Kettering with his two sons. They appear to be bearing up very well under the circumstances. Louise is living in their Islip house.

We are negotiating a big deal. If it goes ahead it should enable us to double our turnover and open another unit down in Poole, but there is a lot to do to make it happen.

We are now talking to Fairline again and there could be a lot of business to be had from there.

Ann doesn't like the book, I can understand why, so I have amended the text, removing most of the passages she didn't like.

17th December

Shooting at Kirby Hall today. I had a good day, shooting three cock birds and two hens. Carl asked me to sign a copy of my book which he has bought for his son Jack. Carl has read the book and thinks it very good. Most people that have read it think it's good. I have learned a lot writing this one and I can probably improve with the next one.

2017

2nd January

We have packed away the Christmas decorations and are looking forward to the New Year. We now have 'Heads of Terms' agreed by Poole, it's promising but our customer needs to behave themselves as we are investing around £500,000 to get the deal up and running.

Ann took Christian to buy another car last week. It broke down within a day or so, but hopefully it can be fixed.
Next week is the London Boat Show and I'll be down there for three days before flying to Tortola for a couple of months. My leg is OK and I can kneel, so I should be able to do the work on the engine.

16th March

We have arrived back in the UK after two months on the boat. In the first few days it needed to be re-commissioned, which was fairly hard work. The Bimini frames are ungainly and Ann took a knock on the head, so she wasn't very happy. The decks and hull had been cleaned and the boat looked almost new.

I decided to take the boat to Spanish Town on Virgin Gorda for the bottom to be cleaned and anti-fouled, and then we relaunched her and put her on a pontoon berth for a couple of days to finish off. The engine had problems in that it would stop shortly after starting – the cause was air getting into the fuel filter. I obtained some parts from Parts and Power in Tortola and after I fitted them it ran perfectly. The rest of the trip went well, although Ann seemed anxious most of the time. We are negotiating with Sunseeker, hoping to take over their fabrication division. James has found a large empty factory fairly close to the main Sunseeker site and the deal should be signed off within the next two weeks. We will be taking on their 22 employees and I can see all sorts of problems, as at the moment they have no incentive scheme and are inefficient. I'm hoping that we can tighten up their production and make it efficient, looking at the figures it should be profitable , but time will tell.

13th April

James has been down in Poole for a couple of days tying up the Sunseeker deal. They want to move on Tuesday, after the Easter break, and we all have our fingers crossed hoping it will go ahead.

Tomorrow is Good Friday and I am going diving at Gildenburgh Reservoir. It will be very busy.

Thursday 20th April

On Tuesday we completed the deal with Sunseeker. James and Chris are down in Poole supervising the move and trying to start production as soon as possible.

On Saturday I went diving at Gildenburgh. It was a fine day but the water was 7 degrees C, which was OK as I was wearing a drysuit. I had buoyancy problems, as I missed the drysuit training last August because I was having a new knee. Ann and I went to the accountants yesterday to discuss capital transfer tax. It seems a great pity to have to plan for death. After running a successful business and paying lots of tax, to hand over 40% of your assets to the Government seems so unfair, although It won't be our problem!

Monday 29th May

Today is a Bank Holiday, but it has been overcast all day and now it's raining. On Friday we returned from another trip to the boat. It is now in good shape. I replaced the bent gangway stanchions and with the davits the boat is better equipped than most of its type out there.

Ann is playing golf today, it's something she enjoys and she has lots of golf buddies. I could have gone diving at Stony Cove, but it would have been so crowded being a Bank Holiday and I decided against it.
I had three dives while I was away. It's so easy in the warm water with not having to wear a wetsuit or drysuit.

21st June

Ann has now announced that she does not want to visit the

boat or go sailing ever again. It didn't come as a shock, as she hasn't enjoyed the boat for a long time. She doesn't feel confident with the physical side and gets anxious under sail. She also suggested putting the boat with a charter fleet to cover the costs, or selling it. I don't want to do either, I would like to upgrade to a larger boat, possibly a catamaran .

I would like to take some crew out but the air fares to the BVI are so expensive. Perhaps Bob, Judith and George would like a trip out or some of the lads from the diving club.

Yesterday, Ian, Sandra and daughters Roxanne, Leanne, Rhiannon and Roxanne's friend Jaclyn together with Ann and Tony came over for a barbecue. It is several years since we have seen Ian and the girls as now they are living in Texas. It was the hottest day of the year and I set out seating for 19 in the garden. The youngsters all hit it off very well. Within minutes they were playing pool and singing along to the juke box. Some of the girls went for a swim, the pool was 30° (85F) and they had a great time. Afterwards they played football on the lawn – all of the girls are in football teams in the USA.

Cooney South in Poole appears to be doing well, turning out lots of product. James spends about two days there each week. Cooney International is also doing well.

3rd July 2017

Last Wednesday at the rifle range I was informed by a guy I knew, a former Fairline employee, that Sam Newington had died. I knew that Sam was ill and had suffered a stroke, but the news of his death was still a shock.

The funeral was on a Friday in June at Elton Church. As I entered the church I saw a few familiar faces – behind me were John Rudge, George Beedie and Basher. Ken Wappatt was there and Adam Greenwood, also Dave Wills, who must be very old now.

Sam was 82. His wife Briony, children and grandchildren were there. The funeral was a sombre affair and as I left the church it was pouring with rain. In the churchyard, some way from the church, around the grave was a forest of umbrellas. I didn't go to the committal as there seemed to be crowds there already, but stood and watched, listening to the haunting tones of The Last Post, played by an RAF musician from RAF Cranwell.

I didn't go to the pub after as I was suffering from stomach cramps and needed to visit a chemist before closing.

I first met Sam at Fairline around 1972, when we first started supplying them with stainless steel equipment. In 1974 he was very supportive when our factory burned down, and we had a good business relationship until he sold Fairline around 1996. I have a lot of good memories of Sam; he made a big contribution both to me and to Cooney Marine.

I had a phone call from Joan Thomas to inform me that her husband Glen had died suddenly. I had not seen Glen for years. It was Glen I first sailed with in his Sea Wych, the weekend that I launched my own Sea Wych. We were both building the kit boats and helping each other out, he with knowledge of small boats and me with supplies of stainless parts.

I sent Joan a letter including the first verse of my poem.

No one can know the way you feel
The loss of part of life so real,
The days will pass as dreams unfold
The longer pain at last will heal
As memories and stories be told.

The funeral was in Ipswich, and daughters Lyn and Sharon were there, Sharon having travelled from Ohio USA, where she now lives with her new partner. Lyn looked like a younger version of Joan, whereas I suppose Sharon was more like Glen.

At the lunch following the ceremony, Joan introduced me to Peter Morley, whom I had not seen since the 70s when we sailed at Wells. Peter came as crew when Glen, Keith Spain and I sailed the Kingfisher 30 Agape from Hayling Island to Wells. He had a photo of Agape on his phone and emailed me a copy, I still remembered him as a young man and wouldn't have recognised the distinguished looking man that he has become. He now has a wife and two grown-up daughters.

20th August

A lot has happened over the last few weeks. On 4th August we flew out to Guernsey for a few days, staying at the La Piette hotel on the sea front within easy walking distance of the marinas. As the taxi drove past the marina we saw 'Ragtime' Martin's boat – I knew he was going to be in Guernsey as he was doing a charter. After unpacking in the hotel, Ann and I walked down to the marina to see him. He was sitting in the cockpit having a rum and couldn't believe his eyes when we walked up to the boat. His charterers, two Americans, invited us to join them for dinner and we all went to an Italian restaurant on the sea front. We had an excellent meal and Freddy, one of the Americans, insisted on paying.

On the Monday we flew down to Alderney and stayed in the Adventurer's Rest, formally called the Chez. We spent a few days with Martin and Andre and on Thursday we went to see the 'Alderney Blowers' in the church and it was very good.

I now have crew for my Nov/Dec. trip to the boat, Colin, a fellow scuba diver, and his wife Catriona will probably be joining me.

Around the 6th November the British Virgin Islands and others were devastated by Hurricane Irma. Most of the boats in Village Cay were destroyed, including Finesse. I'd spent a lot of time and money bringing the boat up to a good standard including new sails, davits and loads of gear. I decided I probably wouldn't get another boat as Ann has lost interest, although I may charter one if I can find crew as I already had flights booked for November.

The Southampton Boat Show started on 15th September. Alex was down there with Rose and I am going on Monday. Ann was spending a few days in Norfolk, golfing.

3rd October

Autumn is now upon us, the temperature is dropping and summer is just a memory. It wasn't a bad summer weather wise, probably slightly better than average.

I haven't done much diving, although I am going to Egypt, the Red Sea, for a live-aboard dive trip on the 19th.

Tomorrow I am going into hospital for a minor operation. I am not looking forward to it, though I am only staying in for one night.

James is having a hard time on the costings for Cooney South. All of the prices were taken from our customers' figures. James has had several meetings with their financial people, he is a good negotiator and will hopefully come to a mutually beneficial agreement.

The Red Sea diving trip from the 20th to the 27th October was super. I was worried that it was a bit close to my operation, but the consultant said it would be OK. I'd decided to do only the dives I was comfortable with, not wanting to overdo it. The boat was a 32m live-aboard and I was sharing a cabin with Ian. The food was adequate and there was usually something I could eat. I did two dives on the first day, only one on day 2 but three dives on the next day.

I have now heard from the boat insurers, and they've appointed a surveyor.

On 30th October I was voted in as the diving club chairman.

The Charter was booked for the end of November. Colin and Catriona were joining me and had booked flights hoping to join me on *Finesse*, but when she was wrecked we'd decided to charter, hoping that Antigua wasn't too badly affected after the hurricane.

Four of the grandchildren have now passed their driving tests, leaving only Taylor. Casey now owns a BMW 1 series.

After the charter I will fly up to Tortola for a few days to try and sort out the boat insurance.

Monday 12th November

James is away at METS for a few days and then he will be down in Poole so I don't suppose he will be around much this week.

I am shooting more often now. I try to do clays one day a week and rifle shooting one day. My shooting has improved, last Saturday at Kirby Hall I had the most birds. Luck plays a big part, if the birds don't fly over it can be disappointing.
29th November

I picked up a new car from the Jaguar dealers the day before

I was due to fly out to Antigua. I'd only called into the dealers to buy a new battery for my smart key, but ended up changing the car!

I suggested that we all travel together, but as Colin and Cat were returning earlier it was more convenient for them to make their own way to Gatwick. I suggested that we could meet up for breakfast at the airport, but they were travelling with BA whereas I was flying with Virgin, one of us from North Terminal and the others from South. The Virgin flight took off a bit before BA, but they were both due to land around the same time in Antigua. As our flight were disembarking I saw the BA flight coming in to land and was relieved to see Colin and Cat an hour later in arrivals. The Horizon charters bus took us to Jolly Harbour where we boarded Soben, the catamaran that was to be our home for the next week.

The next morning we went ashore for breakfast and then to Horizon's office to fill in reams of paperwork. The couple running the operation seemed very efficient. We then went to the supermarket to buy provisions. We then had the "boat show", which is the briefing on the boat. We were told that when anchoring we should let out chain 5 times the depths of the water, eg, if the water is 10ft deep let out 50 ft. of chain. I asked "How is the chain marked?" "It isn't!" was the reply.

The Horizon people insist in taking the boat out of the berth and to the fuel dock to ensure that the tanks were full. We didn't get away until gone one thirty, heading for Falmouth. Colin worked out how to pull up the mainsail, but the sheeting was a bit peculiar and when we unrolled the Jib it was strange, but I suppose the fact that I am not used to catamarans had something to do with it.

We dropped anchor in Falmouth at about 5pm and went

ashore just after 6, hoping to find the dinghy dock in daylight. We ended up in the Trappas bar and having been told that we could check out online, Colin spent an hour doing it.

30ᵗʰ November

I thought we could now leave, but when I rang Horizon they told me we needed to go ashore and visit customs, immigration and port control. This seemed to take ages as we had to walk round to English Harbour. We didn't leave Falmouth until 10.30 and I was concerned that we wouldn't arrive at Deshais, Guadeloupe in daylight.

Colin put up the main and Cat unfurled the Jib and with both engines on we were making about 7.5 knots in about 11 knots of wind. I needed to keep the speed up to ensure a daylight arrival. When we had tweaked the sails they were setting reasonably well, although I was not happy with the set of the main.

We anchored in about 20ft. The anchorage was quite crowded with some of the other occupants glaring at us if they thought we were getting too close.

We cooked on board, or rather Catriona did. We'd picked up some steaks from the supermarket at Jolly Harbour and we had a very nice meal on board, drinking rather a lot.

1ˢᵗ December

Went ashore this morning to clear customs etc. The office is in a café called Le Pelican. We walked up and down looking for it and when eventually we found it we realised that we had already walked past it several times. Once there, it was fairly easy to put the details into their computer. We then went for a coffee in the bar where 'Death in Paradise' is filmed. It's a lot smaller than it seems on the TV.

We then decided to walk to the Botanical Gardens. It was a hard slog uphill but worth it, as there were lots of parrots, flamingos and exotic plants. On the road there is no proper pavement and the drivers are a bit kami kazi. On the way back I managed to fall across one of the deep gullies, badly grazing my foot. Catriona managed to fish my fallen sandal out of the gulley. The road was very steep and I was glad to return to the dock area. Did some shopping and returned to Soben about 1600. Engines on for battery charging 1620.

2nd December

Engines on and anchor up 0730. There was little wind, barely enough to fill the sails, but we managed to motor-sail all the way back to English Harbour and anchor in about 18ft in Freeman's Bay at about 1500. I decided to have a swim and shower and then go and check in with customs etc. We took all of the papers ashore but omitted the paper with the check-in password and were unable to check in, to the delight of the officials. By then it was 1620 and their office closes at 1700, so we decided to check in the next morning.

As time was getting on we went for a drink at a bar in Falmouth to await the opening of the Tot club. I signed Colin and Catriona into the club and it was most enjoyable as we had the Tot and met many other members. We went to the pizza restaurant, but I couldn't finish mine and nor could Colin & Cat, so we brought the leftovers back to the boat, something I have never done before, to make a meal tomorrow.

3rd December

Arrived at Customs at about 10am and apart from the slow

*and lethargic staff in the immigration depot we were sorted out
by 1115. We went for a coffee in the Copper & Lumber Hotel
and then went to a new supermarket called Covent Garden. I
managed to buy provisions for this evening. We went to the Tot
Club again and had a tot and then a Black Mass was declared
and Colin and Cat and I had another tot. Usually visitors
are not included, but as they were invited by Mike Rose, the
founder of the club, it was ok. We returned to the ship a bit
sloshed and Cat prepared the meal. It was funny sausages
called 'megaeus', but they tasted ok.*

4ᵗʰ December

*Left Freeman's Bay at about 1015 and motor-sailed around
to Deep Bay, anchoring in 10ft of water. The person anchored
behind us kept glaring at us and giving us dirty looks, but he
had no justification as our anchor was well dug in and with
the way vessels were lying we were no danger to anyone. In the
end he left, after shouting at us!*

*Colin & Cat went over to a beach and did some snorkelling.
The boat goes back to Horizon tomorrow, and we are moving
to an apartment.*

5ᵗʰ December

*Woke up at 0530, not looking forward to the trip back to Jolly.
The boat, although very manoeuvrable, has no port vision from
the helm, which is starboard side. There is a wheel port side
but the engine controls are starboard.*

*We were only about an hour from Jolly and upped anchor
at about 0930. The anchor, a CQR, has been holding very well
all trip, even though the chain wasn't marked and the scope*

was largely guesswork. The trip to Jolly was uneventful and we pottered down the buoyed channel looking for the fuel dock. Horizon take over as soon as you arrive at the fuel dock, and coming alongside was interesting with the offshore wind.

As soon as we had forward and aft warps ashore, I knew we had arrived, and a huge feeling of relief came over me. The debrief was short and to the point. We had nothing to report other to again mention that it is stupid to expect skippers to put the correct length of anchor chain out when it is not marked, also the fact that there was no anchor light. When the anchor light switch was on, it was the masthead tricolour that came on. I put the deck floodlight on so as not to be showing 'under way' navigation lights when at anchor and with the deck lit up it was visible all around, which I considered a reasonable compromise.

I rang the property company regarding the apartment where we will be staying for the next few days and they offered to give us a lift to the address. When Ann booked it we expected it to be close to the restaurants etc, but it was as far away as possible, quite close to the northern beach. We have a golf cart to run around in but it is so inconvenient!

We went to the same restaurant as the first night at Jolly. The golf cart only has front lights, so Catriona sat on the back seat with a torch.

6ᵗʰ December

Went to the dive shop to check our booking for tomorrow. I drove the golf cart and then we got the bus into St. John and visited Radcliffe and Heritage Quay.

7ᵗʰ December

After a breakfast of tea and toast, Colin and I jumped into the golf cart to drive down to the dock to find the dive boat. Another diver was waiting, a French Canadian woman who didn't seem very friendly. Eventually there were five divers, a dive leader and the skipper, who informed us that he came from Denmark. We then went to the Coco Beach Hotel to pick up another diver, making it six in total plus the dive leader, who was the wife of the boat skipper. The dive leader had a spear with which she hooked out lionfish and then killed them with her knife, then the sharks came and ate the lionfish.

I did 40 minutes on the first dive and 42 minutes on the second. I was using a lot of air, so I came up about five minutes before the rest of the group.

The diver from the Coco Beach was horribly seasick. The boat was rolling violently and it was interesting climbing aboard with the skipper barking instructions at us to take off our fins and hand them to him before attempting the boarding ladder!

I didn't do much else for the rest of the day – went down to the main beach, had a drink and watched the sunset. On the way back we called in at the new supermarket and bought provisions for tonight's dinner. It is quite new and has a great variety of different foods. We eventually bought steaks, which were quite large, and Colin volunteered to barbecue. Colin & Cat can both cook, but I don't want them to think I am leaving all of the chores to them, so I clear up and try and be as useful as possible.

8th December

Didn't do much today, decided to have a beach day and we went down to South Beach.

We all swam in the sea, which was very warm. The restaurant used to be poor but is now under new management and the food is quite good

We decided to go to Sandra's beach bar to watch the sun set. We had Dark & Stormy cocktails (rum and ginger beer), and then went for dinner at Mellinies restaurant. The food there is excellent.

9th December

Today is the last day. Colin and Catriona left at about 1600 and I am leaving tomorrow morning. I was hoping to get my dive log book stamped, but the office was closed all day.

I was sad to see my crew disappear down the road in the taxi, they had been excellent and we had all got on very well. This evening I met the villa owners, who had just arrived, and borrowed the golf cart to go to the supermarket. They are staying next door, which they also own. Now I have Tortola to look forward to and the dramas of a wrecked boat!

10th December

I arrived at the airport at about 0845. By the time I had cleared security it was about 0915 and I was told that my flight was on time and would be boarding at 1100. The air conditioning in the airport is set, in my opinion, far too cold and I should have kept a jumper in my hand luggage. There were very few people at the airport, possibly as it's a Sunday. The flight to Tortola is direct. It used to stop at St. Martin and St. Kitts, which made it tiresome, but direct it should take about an hour.

We arrived in Tortola, and as the plane came in to land, there were boats washed up on the beaches and quite a lot of hurricane damage evident. When I arrived at the Fort Burt Hotel, a very pleasant young woman on reception informed me that they didn't have a bar and the only place to get a drink was the Pussers Rum Bar, about a 20-minute walk away.

Although they were offering a dinner menu I thought to make sure of getting some food I would walk to the Pussers bar, and she was right, it took about 20 minutes. I ordered chicken breast and fries, which was adequate but not very hot. I can't understand how a restaurant can take half an hour to produce a meal and then serve it up cold. The walk back was dangerous as there was no proper footpath and the way the local drivers zoom around I decided to hire a car tomorrow. Although I was told the hotel had 95% occupancy I have yet to see any other guests.

11ᵗʰ December

No hire cars available, a bit disappointing – looks like another walk into town. I went to see Chris Juredin and he put me on to Simon Crook, the risk and loss coordinator for Caribbean Insurers Ltd. I briefly discussed the situation. He had copies of the photo of the sunk boat and was due to talk to loss adjusters this afternoon. He asked me to send him a copy of the quote to lift the boat, which I did.

I went to Bobby's supermarket and bought toothpaste and to an electrical shop to buy a new charger for the iPad and phone. I then called in at the Pussers to get some lunch. I ordered fish and chips. I waited ages and when it came the fish was undercooked and full of large bones. It certainly wasn't cod as advertised!

I spoke to Ann on the phone and she suggested that l try the Rite-Way supermarket just down the road. I walked down there, but it was boarded up, with doors hanging off and the shelves awry; it had probably been looted after the hurricane. On the way back to the hotel I called in at a bakery and bought their last beef pasty and some juice and water.

I didn't fancy eating at the hotel, the main reason being that I wasn't hungry. There was a guy in reception who was driving into town and he offered to drop me off at the Pussers Rum Bar. I thought I might fancy some wings or something later. He said they closed at 10 pm and he would pick me up and run me back to the hotel.

It was interesting in the bar. A table of piratical-looking characters sat near me. There was a mixture of beards, skimpy vests with heavily tattooed arms, the odd ponytail and a shaven head or two. I got the impression they were divers. Baseball caps worn the wrong way seemed to be the fashion, with lots of grunting, farting and swearing. I thought I might wander off to find another bar, but there didn't seem to be any open and with the inadequate street lighting, uneven paving with big holes and people lurking in the shadows, I decided to return to Pussers. The doctor has told me to drink a lot of liquid so tonight I am obeying orders. It just happens that the liquid is beer and rum.

Finesse on the dock in St Martin.

Finesse anchored in Filipsburg, St Maarten.

Finesse with new sail cover fitted.

New design davits on stern of *Finesse*, Jost Van Dyke astern.

Ann helming *Finesse,*

Finesse sailing,

Finesse at Manual Reef Marina, summer lay up, all canvas
removed and boat secured between two pontoons.

Finesse sunk during Hurricane Irma, dinghy still attached
floating next to the mast.

Devastation at Nanny Cay Tortola, several large
catamarans flipped over.

This catamaran apparently flew over and landed on Finesse, breaking
her away from the dock and damaging the hull, causing her to sink.

Colin and Catriona sailing on the chartered catamaran *Soben*, which we
chartered in Antigua after the loss of *Finesse*.

*As I sat outside Pussers waiting for my lift back to the hotel I
was hoping to not have to walk back. I was perfectly capable
but with the broken pavements and lack of street lights it was
dangerous.*

*As 10 o'clock approached and the crowd started to thin I
was expecting my lift to appear, but no such luck, he didn't
turn up, so I had to walk back. I was furious! I'd been sitting
in that bar for a couple of hours waiting.*

12ᵗʰ December

*The water was off this morning and so no shower. I went for
breakfast and waited until about 10.20. The good news is that
I now have a hire car.*

13ᵗʰ December

Went to Nanny Cay. The marina is destroyed, there are no pontoons and a lot of sunk vessels, and the whole area is a disaster zone. I drove round to Sea Cows Bay and it was the same, boats in extraordinary positions, enormous catamarans upside down. I think it will be at least a year before any offers are made. As long as I get a reasonable offer. who knows?

I decided to take the car back today rather than messing around tomorrow morning, as I fly back tomorrow, I think I have seen enough bashed-up boats to last me a lifetime, it's so depressing seeing so many people's dreams shattered. I'm glad I came, the hotel was a bit rough but they are doing their best under difficult circumstances and the week's charter was excellent.

CHAPTER 12

An accolade from the industry

✄

2018

Teri's 50th birthday was a bit peculiar. Her friend Sheila insisted on organising it, and Ann and I were not allowed to get too involved, which was good as we didn't really want to. If it went wrong it would not be our fault. Sheila came to see Ann and me to discuss arrangements. The first problem was finding the venue for the party. They'd looked at various rooms to hire, the village hall, a room at the local pub, but even a low-cost room, catering and drinks would put the cost up too much.

Eventually I suggested that they could use Acre House for the party, and this was enthusiastically accepted. Sheila said that "the girls", Teri's mates, would do everything, eg, decorating, providing food etc.

As the day approached it was difficult not to let slip that the party was to be at Acre House, although it was supposed to be a secret! I had ordered a barrel of beer and agreed to pay for the food. Sheila intended to hire a limo to pick up Teri and family from her house and go on a 'magical mystery tour' to fool her into thinking that the venue was somewhere different, if she suspected that it was our house.

Sheila had been collecting photos of Teri. We had some going back to when she was a baby, and in all she collected about 200. The idea was to suspend the photos from helium balloons on a ribbon. On the day before Sheila, Sam and Lisa came over to prepare the house. They had several canisters of helium and began the laborious task of inflating over 200 balloons. Lisa had made a balloon arch for the photographs with a gold lamé backdrop and two lamps to illuminate it, with a large Happy Birthday sign over the top. The drive was lined with little lanterns and the overall effect was magical.

Mel rang and told them not to inflate the balloons too soon, as they would start to deflate. Ann then volunteered to finish the inflating a couple of hours before the guests were due to arrive so that the balloons would still support the hanging photos. After about 20 balloons, tying the knots in the ends became a laborious task and with about another 100 to do it seemed never ending. Eventually it was done and I went upstairs to get ready. Ann was in the shower and I was dressing when the doorbell rang. I was wearing my dress shirt and bow tie and a pair of swimming shorts, I was wearing the shorts as I thought I might end up in the pool (having first removed my dinner suit). I ran downstairs to answer the door and it was Raymond and his partner, Teri's gay friends! Goodness knows what they thought with me standing there wearing a dress shirt, bow tie and a pair of shorts! I pointed them in the direction of the bar and then finished dressing. They were half an hour early, but most of the guests had arrived by seven o'clock.

By 1930 there was a satisfying buzz of conversation and the limo was due with Teri and family. It was a surprisingly mild evening for March and everyone stood outside chatting and laughing as we waited for the birthday girl.

Teri seemed speechless as she alighted from the limo, and as she entered the house with the many suspended photos she was awestruck and a little tearful. Everyone was laughing and wishing her well. On the island in the centre of the kitchen was an enormous cake that her friend Julie had produced, decorated with a huge '50' and lots of gold icing. The food was set out on top of the cooker, and I had put a board over the cooker covered in red cloth. The centre piece was an enormous ham surrounded by cheeses, a whole Stilton, Brie and various others together with breads of different types, plus a housebrick-sized slab of pâté, in all a magnificent spread. I thought it far too much for the number of people, but people tucked in with gusto and it soon started to disappear.

It was a mild evening for the time of the year and a lot of the guests were outside, where a bar was set up under the gazebo. Some were in the games room playing pool and the juke box was playing. Most of the guests had made an effort to dress up and some of the girls looked gorgeous.

The evening seemed to fly past and the guests started to drift away from about midnight, I think Ann and I turned in at about 0500, but I was up at 0730. I wanted to cook loads of bacon to make bacon rolls for breakfast, as we had about 10 people staying over and I wanted to be on top of the job! Grandsons Christian and Elliot had both brought their girlfriends, and James had also brought his new lady. Teri and her new beau Doug also stayed over. Everyone helped with the clearing up and the house was soon looking shipshape.

I'd decided that we would have lunch at the Woolpack and had booked a table for 12 people for 4pm, thinking that if some people had other commitments and didn't want to join us for lunch I could change the numbers before we arrived, however we actually did have 12. I thought the lunch was very good for a pub. The party was on 23rd March, her actual birthday being Sunday 24th.

On Tuesday 26th March I went with James to the Boating Business & Marine Trade Showcase held at Southampton Football Ground. Alex was already there, having arrived the day before to set up our small shell stand. Chris, who now worked for Cooney South, was there and Chris Elms, also from South, was there for the 'Meet The Buyer' meetings. Ian Walker also arrived during the afternoon. In the evening was the awards ceremony and dinner. At the entrance to the room where the dinner was being held the doorman had a metal detector, and on discovering that I had a small Swiss Army pocket knife he confiscated it! They said I could collect it on the way out. I was surprised – whether they thought I was going to run amok waving it about I don't know.

The dinner was exceptionally good and there were various awards presented during the course of the evening. The last to be presented was the Lifetime Achievement Award, and as the details were being read out I realised that it was me they were talking about! As I walked up to receive the award I had mixed emotions. It was 50 years ago I started the business and I had not expected to receive recognition.

It was a superb evening and we all returned to the hotel by taxi. I forgot to re claim my Swiss Army knife, which was a pain!

Tuesday 2nd April was my 75th birthday, but as Ann and I were flying to Spain early Wednesday morning we didn't plan on a lot of fuss. We had the kids and grandkids over and decided to get a chippy to save time. I had some nice presents. Ann bought me a DNA testing kit, I had various socks, chocolates and odds and ends but, surprise surprise, Teri bought me a new Swiss Army knife. It must have cost a lot, because it had lots more tools than the old one.

The flight to Spain was uneventful and the plane was on time. Peter and Sue met us. It was just over a year since we had visited them and as it was later in the year, I had hoped that the weather would be warmer. It was, but not shorts and T-shirts weather. We had a great time visiting many of the harbours on the Costa Blanca, some that we had visited over 30 years ago when we sailed the area in *Blue Amazon*, our Moody 37.

I miss the boat and sailing in the Caribbean, because although I am 75 I am still fit and not too confused. I am still scuba diving, but wonder how long I will continue, as with the weight of the gear I find it difficult. It's fine in the water, being weightless, but getting out is a struggle with my dodgy knees.

At the end of April several of the divers were organising a trip to the Red Sea again and I decided to go. The trip was with Blue O Two on the M/Y *Blue Fin* diving on the northern reefs and wrecks. I had been to the Red Sea twice before, and the diving is superb, with warm water and lots of marine life, and on the live-aboard we are looked after by the crew with help to kit up and assistance with everything. The food is edible and there's plenty of it.

I paid the deposit of £320. The trip departs on Friday 22nd November, feeling that at last I had something to look forward to after losing the boat last September.

I also booked myself on a sailing trip from Martinique to Grenada in January on a 60ft. ketch. I had done this trip many times on my own boats over the years and was really looking forward to it.

On the trip to Egypt I would be flying with the other divers cattle class, but for the Caribbean trip I had booked a premium economy return to Grenada and an overnight stay there with an island hopper trip up to Martinique the next day. This worked out more expensive than the flights suggested by Rubicon, but a lot more convenient. They were suggesting flights from Paris to Martinique and all sorts of options, some via Canada or Miami, which seemed a roundabout way of travelling Just to save a few pounds!

On 26th May the next instalment of £320 was due for the Egypt diving trip, but I decided to hold off paying until after I had taken my Fitness to Dive medical, booked for 5th May. I always go to the Midland Dive Chamber in Rugby for this. When you're over 70 the BSAC insists on a medical every 12 months and without the medical certificate one cannot officially dive. The medical is exhaustive with stepping exercises whilst connected to heart monitors and rigorous other tests. I passed the examination and the doctor said I was extremely fit for my age, also a lot fitter than men much younger!

I then paid the second instalment towards the Red Sea trip. I had already paid a deposit and for the flights for the Caribbean trip.

Our 50th wedding anniversary was on the 14th September. I gave Ann a fairly plain card, but wrote a short poem in it that went down very well. As it was our golden anniversary I also gave her a very nice gold chain. I was concerned that she perhaps wouldn't like it, but she seemed thrilled with it. It was a heavy chain and quite expensive, but 50 years is an achievement in this day and age.

We had a party organised for 60 people at our house on the 15th. I had been quite worried about it, but Ann had insisted that she was organising it. Stanley Street Food were doing the catering. We'd seen them at a gig where Philip (nephew) was playing and they seemed so professional that we decided to get prices and consider using them. But it seemed that everything I suggested regarding the party was out of bounds and Ann was in charge!

As the evening approached I was allowed some input. Whereas Ann had ordered from the hire company three tables and 24 chairs I changed it to four tables and 32 chairs, because although the house is large, I was worried that 60 people was more than it could comfortably hold. I had bought a stronger gazebo, as the last one had blown to bits in the freak winds.

The first couple to arrive were Colin and Catriona, which was a surprise as they had enquired about the start time. The meet and greet went fairly well. Casey (granddaughter) and her friend Kitty went around with a tray of fizz and some very nice canapés. We had "Jinder" (our very talented nephew) for the entertainment, and to begin Teri and James did a couple of numbers which went down very well, then Jinder entertained us for the rest of the evening.

I noticed that with the music everyone seemed to be jigging about in their seats. Sheila, one of Teri's friends, asked me to dance, and when we got up that started everyone off, so soon the floor was full of people dancing around

All too soon the evening was over and people started leaving at around 11 O'clock, with some stragglers drifting off after about 0100. The party was a great success and was a fitting celebration of our anniversary. Ann did most of the organisation and I think most people enjoyed themselves.

17th September 2018

*Today I drove down for the Southampton Boat Show. James
and Alex were already there, as it had started on the 14th. The
weather was warm but a bit chilly in the evenings. I arrived
at about 1400, parked the car and just as I arrived at the hotel
I saw Alex. He told me that James had just arrived and was
taking his case up to his room and was then coming down to
go to the show.*

*Rose, our hostess, was on the stand and she made us coffee.
Apparently it was a much busier day than yesterday.*

*Other stands that I visited were optimistic and seemed to
be doing OK. I met Alex and Jenny from the R & D stand and
we decided to go on a trip on the Princess Caroline, a former
ferry that was used for corporate entertainment. Dinner was
reasonable; several people complained, but I thought it was
OK under the circumstances. The next item on the agenda was
a talk which seemed to go on for ever. The microphone didn't
work, so it was difficult to hear what the speaker was saying,
and as he droned on and on. As we were on a ship pottering
about in Southampton Water, there was no escape!*

*I enjoyed talking to people. One couple were buying a
Discovery 55 and planned to go off sailing. I knew the D55
having worked on hull no 1 when it was in build at Sea Ranger.
The wife seemed worried about doing long passages under sail.
I told them that I had done several Atlantic crossings and she
asked how many crew I recommended for an ocean crossing.
When I told her it was usually just Ann and me she seemed
shocked, but her husband was delighted.*

*I was there for four days and the time flew. Our stand looked
impressive, and often we had an audience looking at our pipe-*

bending video. We went to Ennio's restaurant and although it was all right, I didn't think it was as good as previous years.

On 19th October Ann and I flew out to Thailand for what was predominantly a golf holiday. Of the 12 people on the trip there were three other non-golfers, and I planned to pal up with them. Rebecca, who was the wife of Jim, and their friends Tilden and Rachel were the non-golfers and we would meet at breakfast and decide on what to do each day. Mostly it was to sunbathe and swim in the hotel pool. I often went for walks around Wha-Hin where we were staying, and when the golfers returned we would all meet up for the evening.

Some of the men had Thai girlfriends. The girls like white men, as they treat them kindly and of course give them money. In the bars there were a lot of bar girls, and it was disturbing to see little girls around six years old selling roses to the tourists at all hours, sometimes into the early hours of the morning. Apparently it's a tradition that the children work to support their parents! One of our group suggested that the parents should be out selling flowers and not the kids, until someone said "would you buy flowers from an old woman, rather than a pretty little girl?"

A group of us went snorkelling. The boat was a 60ft. powerboat with two enormous outboard engines and it was nice being out on the water. I had my own snorkel and mask and hoped that I could hire some fins, but there were none available. We anchored in the lee of a small Island, where the water wasn't that clear and not very deep. Sea urchins were in abundance and I kept well clear. A few small shoals of tiddlers swam about and there was the odd larger fish around. Some of the crew fished off the boat and caught some large fish that looked similar to bass.

After the snorkelling we anchored off a small Island for

lunch. A fire was started, some of the girls used their fans to make it flare up and it was soon burning merrily and the crew were cooking the fish they had caught, suspended over the flames with twigs cut from the trees.

On the last night we all went to the Condoms and Cabbages restaurant. The story goes that the local people worked in the cabbage fields and ate loads of cabbage, which made them very randy, so they were producing loads of children that they could not support. Someone had the bright idea of educating the people about birth control and supplying them with condoms. All profits from the restaurant go to provide condoms for the people. The restaurant is decorated with a condom theme with life sized figures made from condoms and all sorts of artwork also made from them. Upon leaving everyone is given packets of condoms!

The flight home wasn't too bad. I prefer to fly business class or at least premium, but Ann was adamant that we should fly cattle class. The flight takes about 12 hours. I did manage to sleep and we were in Dave's car, so I didn't have to drive home.

On Wednesday 28th November at the rifle range there were about eight people shooting when suddenly the local hunt came galloping across. We all stepped back from our weapons and they were checked to be empty by the RCO. Red flags were flying - very dangerous.

CHAPTER 13

Gran Canaria and Split

❖

As 2019 began we decided we needed some winter sun, but we couldn't decide where to go. Previously I have always had the boat to look forward to and being a 'tourist' didn't excite me. We decided to visit Gran Canaria, as we'd been there a few times in our boats. It is where the ARC starts from and we have many fond memories of the island.

We flew out on 28ᵗʰ January. The flight was on time and we had an uneventful trip, arriving at the Hotel in Mogán late afternoon. The hotel was on the marina and our room overlooked the moored yachts. It was almost 'role reversal' – we would look down upon the moored yachts and the people in them and those people wandering by, but only fairly recently we would have been the crew looking out at the tourists!

2019
Wednesday 31ˢᵗ January

We took the bus to Las Palmas and visited the Marina, from where we set off on our two ARC trips. It brought back a lot of happy memories; it was 17 years ago when we left in Blue Genie.

On Thursday we decided to go to Arguineguín on the ferry. It took about an hour and 30 minutes, the ferry stopping at several places on the way. In '99 we spent a few days in this area with Martin in Ragtime and Dennis in Shilling.

I am surprised at the low prices of the public transport here. We visited most of the tourist areas either by ferry or bus and the low cost and efficiency of the services was remarkable.

Monday 4th February

We took the bus to Mas Palomas. This is probably the most concentrated of the tourist hotspots with massive developments of apartments and miles of sand dunes and beaches.

Wednesday 6th February

Took the Ferry to Anfi, a nice place to visit, and although there were loads of apartments, the public areas were well laid out. The town seemed more upmarket than Puerto Rico.

In the hotel the catering was quite good, the only problem being the buffets, with a vast array of different foods that didn't keep the food very hot. Maybe it's a British thing, but I like my food piping hot and Ann does too. There were a few ways to get round this problem, the chef doing the eggs in the morning cooked them while you waited so it was a case of get the toast ready and then get the chef to put the freshly cooked omelette or fried eggs straight onto the toast and then collect the bacon and other bits and pieces. Similarly at dinner, the chef would cook steaks or chops, so if you collected these first and then the potatoes or anything else required it wasn't too bad.

Most days during the trip we would catch a bus or a ferry to one or other of the resorts as we are not ones to sit on a beach every day sunbathing, although we did this on one of the days.

I also did a couple of dives with Gran Canaria Divers, one a drift dive at 18m on a reef and the other on a couple of wrecks that had been sunk specially for divers at 17m. The dive centre was very well organised and the gear for hire was in first-class condition. We went out in a large Inflatable for the first dive and then came back in to pick up two more divers for the wreck dive.

The rest of the trip went very well and I was sad to leave. The return flight was on time. The worst part of the trip was the drive home from Stansted. The journey that normally took an hour took three hours due to extensive road works at Huntington!

I have been shooting fairly often. I am now a member of the Kibworth target shooting club and I shoot .22 rimfire there. I have fitted a new scope to my .22 rifle and I am getting good results, I shoot my full-bore rifles at Barnwell Range, I have not been deerstalking for some while as my knees are a problem.

I have a diving trip booked for November for the Red Sea, northern reefs and wrecks. I have dived in the Red Sea twice before.

My neighbour David, who a couple of years ago I had introduced to rifle shooting, was now an avid air rifle marksman and he invited me to the range to try air rifle shooting. On the way to the range we stopped at a garage and David bought a large tin of biscuits. He often did this as a "present" for the instructors. He had arranged for the head coach to set up a firing point and for me to try out several rifles. I ended up with one of David's rifles on the 70-yard range and did OK.

One of the instructors, Laura, had a strong Spanish accent and it turned out that she was from Colombia, South America. She was very friendly and said she was interested in sailing, so when David told her I was an experienced yachtsman she just wanted to talk about yachts and sailing. The three of us went up to the café for a coffee and a snack and she told me she had a small sailing cruiser on Rutland Water and as yet had never sailed it. As it was on a reservoir the boat had no engine or overboard discharges. Electric outboards were allowed but were quite expensive.

I agreed to meet up with her and go for a sail. The boat was on a mooring and although she had a dinghy it had no outboard motor. That wasn't a problem, I could row, and thought probably so could she, the main problem would be sailing the boat off the mooring and picking the mooring up afterwards, a skill that I had not practised since my yacht master training days.

We agreed to meet at the sailing club. I pulled up to the car park barrier and pressed the button. A Dalek-sounding voice finally agreed to let me in and as I drove into the car park I saw Laura's car and we were soon chattering away, or Laura was, as she tends to speak very quickly and is sometimes difficult to understand. Her dinghy had two small wheels on the transom, which made it fairly easy to drag around, and we were soon rowing out to the Pegasus 800 in the late morning sunshine.

I checked the rig and it seemed OK except for the Jib, which could never work the way it was set up. I lashed the Jib sheets onto the clew and promised Laura that I would find her a shackle for the next time.

I had explained how I wanted to sail off the mooring, the mainsail was hoisted and the boat was lying to wind with one mooring warp holding us onto the buoy. I said to Laura "when I say cast off, let go of the mooring". She said "OK", and I waited for the wind to be the right side to enable us to sail off. I shouted "Cast off!" but nothing happened, and we soon drifted so that the wind was the wrong side. I told her to hang on and then explained that when I say "cast off" I mean now! She said the rope had got stuck. We got ready again and I shouted "cast off" and soon we were gently sailing past the other moorings. We unrolled the Jib and after a few adjustments to the sheets we had the boat sailing on a beam reach down the lake.

The sails and rig were in good condition. The Jib sheet winches, although small, were adequate for the rig, but I managed to drop one of the winch handles over the side. Laura looked at me and said, "don't worry, I have another". I felt so guilty and promised to get her a replacement.

We sailed up and down the lake. Laura wanted to practise tacking, so we did that, and soon it was time to return to the moorings and pick up under sail. The jib was rolled up and we crept up to the mooring with the wind on the beam, came into wind and Laura picked up the mooring. The mainsail was stowed and we then climbed into the dinghy to row ashore.

We were putting the dinghy ashore when Laura realised she had left her car keys on the boat. The prospect of rowing back out to it did not appeal, but she needed her keys, so back we went. Laura said she would row, but I hadn't realised that she had never done it before. It took quite a while to reach the boat, so I rowed back!

I went to the shooting ground the next day and left a shackle for her Jib and a couple of boat show tickets with Rob, the chief instructor. He said he would give them to her the next time she was there.

I spent four days at the Southampton Boat Show, and it was most enjoyable. While there I picked up a new winch handle to replace the one I'd lost overboard from Laura's boat. She didn't come to the show and the next time I saw her was at the shooting ground, where we arranged another sail on her boat.

It was another fine day when I met Laura at the sailing club. When I gave her the replacement winch handle she seemed surprised and pleased. I then rowed us out to the boat. I'd brought a flask of coffee and some biscuits for lunch, and Laura had also brought some things. We sailed off the buoy and had an enjoyable sail round the lake. Laura took the helm and we tacked and gybed and did a few boat handling manoeuvres before returning to the mooring for lunch.

Laura told me a little about her life. She'd spent some time in Canada and spoke French as well as her native Spanish and of course English. It was early afternoon when we went ashore. We didn't arrange to meet up again but agreed that we might bump into each other and go for a coffee at the shooting ground sometime.

The next time I saw her was on the training range at Kibworth, where she was training an Egyptian lady to shoot.

Trip to Split, June 2019

The trip to Gatwick was uneventful apart from the usual inconvenience of security, taking off belts, shoes and then going through the X-ray machine – my titanium knee has a lot to answer for!

On arrival we couldn't find the tourist rep and had to

go to the enquiries desk, but were soon in the minibus with our 10 fellow sailors. The accommodation on the boat was adequate with a lot of mahogany panelling, a bit reminiscent of our Halberg Rassy. An ensuite heads made the apartment complete.

As soon as we were on board and had been given our customary glass of fizz the boat cast off, and we had a short trip round to the Split waterfront. It seemed to take ages to moor up, but we went ashore for a short exploratory walk into town. Back on board we had a seafood pasta for dinner and then went ashore again to find a coffee shop.

The other crew members were a nice bunch. I think Ann and I were the oldest.

3rd June

Breakfast was excellent, loads of fruit, cereals, yoghurt, followed by eggs and bacon. I managed to drop my egg onto the deck, but picked it up quickly and put it back on my plate. The yoke was very nice!

There is no wind and a calm sea, I don't think there will be much sailing done today.

Arrived at the bay on Hvar island and went for a swim. Water not too cold, although not much visibility and didn't see any fish, couldn't find a snorkel suitable for my mask.

Lunch was a minced fishy thing that I found inedible, followed by squid with polenta, which wasn't much better. The crème brûlée that followed was very nice. I am now looking forward to going ashore tonight for a steak. The weather is nicely hot with a cooling breeze.

4th June

Breakfast similar to yesterday and then we set off and anchored in a bay for a swim and snorkel while some of the guests had a go in the canoes and paddle boards. We then set off for Hvar city, where we will anchor off and possibly go ashore by water taxi.

It's windy at the moment and there is no sign of sails being deployed. The two mainsails are fixed to the awnings and I suspect they are never used. Yesterday they unrolled the jib but it strained a shackle and was rolled up quickly. Then they unrolled the staysail, but I suspect that the sails are only for show!

We are all going ashore at 1830 and plan to return at 2000.

We all went ashore in the water taxi and wandered off in different directions. It was an ancient town with ancient architecture, but we were fully aware of the tourist trade with cafés and restaurants everywhere. We bumped into several of our cruising buddies and ended up in a restaurant not too far from the taxi dock. The meal was very good and the service reasonable. It was about 9:35 by the time we paid the bill and made our way to the water taxi. We wandered along the dock looking at the stainless fittings on the luxury power yachts tying stern to the dock to see if there were any Cooney products on the boats!

The water taxi ride back to the ship was uneventful and Ann and I retired to our cabin.

5th June

The rumbling of the engine starting woke us up at about 0645. Apparently we are headed for Korkula. Breakfast was inside today and the weather is windy and overcast. I managed to get my egg to the plate without dropping it on the deck.

It was about a 5-hour trip to Korkula and on arrival we anchored off in a bay about 20 minutes from the town. Several went for a swim and played with canoes. Kevin (the other one) and Paul's partner Sam swam over to a slide and a trampoline anchored off the beach.

It was then up anchor and motor round to the town where we moored stern to. The vessel we were going alongside didn't like the way our anchor was set so we had to re-lay it, though it looked fine to me. We were sorted by about 1500.

Lunch was superb. The starter was a shrimp gnocchi followed by fillets of fish accompanied by a potato and chard side, which tasted a bit like bubble and squeak with salad. Some of the crowd went off for an island tour with visits to local wineries with cheese, but Ann and I stayed on board till about 1730. We then went ashore and walked around the marina, looking at the picturesque town and stopping for a drink. We bought some pastries, being unable to face an evening meal after such a good lunch. Back on board about 1915 to catch up with the others and hear their stories.

6th June

We were under way at 0800 this morning whilst we all had breakfast. We anchored off for a swim, but I didn't as the water was too cold. We then upped anchor and motored to Makarska. Lunch was the best food I have had for a long time. It was tomato soup followed by fillet steak on a bed of potato and stir fry vegetables, followed by a very alcoholic liqueur. We were moored stern to the beautiful waterfront.

It was suggested that we all went white water rafting this

afternoon, and I reluctantly agreed. We were picked up from the boat at approx 3:15 and then had a 40-minute mini-bus ride to the village of Slime, where we donned lifejackets and helmets and picked up our paddles. Boarding the inflatable was interesting. Some of the team decided to have a dip before boarding, but luckily all of our team were in the same boat.

We set off and negotiated a few simple rapids and I was beginning to think "this is a bit tame", but then the rapids got more interesting and at one time we were all collapsed in the bottom of the boat. The other boats doing the same trip from time to time came close only to be splashed, everyone getting soaked.

It was about 10 kilometres down river and everyone had a great time, but we were all exhausted by the time the trip finished.

In the evening Ann and I wandered into Makarska and found a restaurant, though we weren't very hungry after the enormous lunch.

7th June
Itinerary for today:
Breakfast 8am
Departure 9am
Anchor in Bay 11am
Lunch 1pm
Depart 4pm
Arrive Pucisca (island Brac) 5 pm.

The itinerary says it all really. After breakfast we anchored up and motored to a bay, arriving at about 10:45. Most of the team went for a swim or a snorkel, while Sam and Kevin took canoes for a trip round the bay. Ann and I did not swim but sat in the *sun reading. Lunch was an octopus dish plus salad, followed by pork cubes in mashed potatoes with mushrooms. The pork was 2" square cubes, and there was loads of it, everyone had their fill. It was followed by a strawberry trifle.*

The trip to Puscia was uneventful, the captain mooring the boat stern to with his customary skill.

Tomorrow is our last full day. The week has gone so quickly. The other guests mixed in very well and some would like to keep in contact. This rarely happens, because as soon as people return to normality their memories fade.

8ᵗʰ June

Left the dock at about 9am. After breakfast at about 11am we anchored in a bay on a small island, where some of the guests went for a swim and Sam went off in a canoe. On seeing some plastic items washed up on the shore she went to pick them up for disposal and found one of Jacqueline's swimsuits that had fallen off the drying line. Several guests swam, but it clouded over and the wind got up.

Lunch was truffles with pasta and cheese to start, and I couldn't eat it, but it was followed by monkfish with fried potatoes, which was edible.

*We left the bay at about 5pm and went into Stomorska for the evening. We are apparently leaving at **0600** tomorrow morning.*

Went ashore and met up with Kevin and Jennifer. We had a few beers and I had pork skewers, while Ann had a salad and some of my fries. As we got back on board it started raining. Soon it was a full-blown thunderstorm and the sky was lit up by lightning. It was as though the deck was being pressure-washed by a giant. The boat's awnings were unable to provide shelter, so we went below. In the cabin I had to close the portholes to stop torrents of water flooding the cabin.

9ᵗʰ June

It was breakfast at 0630 and then cast off at 0700 for the short trip back to Stomorska to board taxis for the airport. When we said goodbye to the captain and crew, the other guests suggested that each couple should give the crew 40 euros as a tip. Ann and I thought this a bit mean so we put 50 into the total, which was to be shared among the crew, giving them 480+ euros between them. The local currency is the kunar and we were left with a few hundred, so I decided to give the waiter/steward that had been so attentive and helpful 400 kunar, which worked out at about £50.

The airport was very overcrowded and it was difficult to find a seat anywhere, however the flight was on time and two hours after take-off we landed at Gatwick. We said our goodbye's to the rest of the crowd – sad that we probably won't see them again.

The trip was successful and it was nice to be on a "small" boat and not have to make any decisions regarding the running of the ship. Although a sailing ship, the Gulet motored everywhere, only flying a jib twice during the whole week

We were fortunate in the mix of people on the trip. We were 12 very different people, but we all mixed ok and there were no tensions. All in all a very successful trip.

CHAPTER 14

Bursting a blood vessel

✖

In the early afternoon of Tuesday 11th June, I suddenly had a dreadful pain in the middle of my back. I was unable to stand and Ann, not having seen me in this state before, rang 111. I suspected that it wasn't a heart attack. The operator spoke to me and between groans I told him that I had a stabbing pain in the middle of my back. He asked if there was a lot of blood! I told him that it was a stabbing pain, I'd not been stabbed. I gave the phone back to Ann and the operator told her to take me to the GP's surgery and they would contact them and warn them of my imminent arrival and said I could see Dr Cotterell at 530.

I was in terrific pain and had difficulty getting into Ann's car, though it is only a short drive to the surgery. I was doubled up with pain and sat in the waiting room waiting for the doctor to see me. He took my blood pressure, which was over 200, examined my stomach and asked loads of questions. He gave me morphine and Diazepam, and as this started to take effect he examined me. Eventually he suspected a type B dissection of the aorta, a leak of blood close to the heart. They called 999 to summon an ambulance, which came in record time, and I was rushed to Northampton General Hospital with blue lights and hooters blaring for a CT scan. By this time the pain relief was working and I didn't feel too bad. Ann picked up Teri and followed in her own car.

The paramedics were first class, constantly checking my vital signs all the way to Northampton. I wasn't allowed to move. I was wheeled straight into the radiology department and in no time was obeying the Dalek instructions from the CT scanner. They then decided to send me to the vascular department at Glenfield Hospital in Leicester. The same paramedics stayed with me all the way to Leicester.

On arrival at Glenfield I had another scan and was put into the high dependency unit and connected to wires which were stuck all over my torso. I was put on a course of pills to lower blood pressure. I was surprised they didn't operate, but as it was a type B dissection, not type A, it was decided to keep me under observation. On Wednesday I had another CT scan. I expected them to operate to repair the tear in the aorta but they decided to keep me under observation!

For the next few days, nothing much happened. I was not sleeping very well. Then the nurse informed me that the person in the next room had passed away and the family were due to visit. She offered me earplugs because of the noise of crying and wailing that was sure to ensue. I accepted the earplugs and was glad that I had. The pitiful cries of the bereaved relatives were awful.

Next I had a mental patient who was shouting and swearing loudly. The nurse once again offered me earplugs, which I took but didn't use,

Sunday 17th was Father's Day and I was pleasantly surprised that all the family visited. As I looked up at them all gathered round the bed, I suddenly thought, why are they all here? Do they know something I don't?!

Monday 17th June

The consultant came to see me and said that if my BP stayed low I would be allowed home. The room I am in is about 3m square and I have been confined to it for almost a week. I cannot leave the room as I am connected to various monitors.

The nurses and all of the people I have dealt with are so kind, so helpful, but today I have been informed that I should no longer dive or swim, also flying may be a problem. This is a pain – I am now effectively an invalid!

Wednesday 19th June

I was hoping to go home today, but overnight my blood pressure had gone up to 136/54 and the doctor said he wanted to see it below 120. I am looking forward to going home and accepting my new lifestyle.

Whilst here I have received visitors every day. Today Ann came, expecting to take me home, and was disappointed when she had to leave without me. Anne and Tony also came. Visitors take the edge off the boredom.

I am now back on a higher dose of BP meds, so I hope that everything is within limits so I can go home!

Thursday 20th June

By the time everything was sorted out it was about 4pm. After a last talk to Prof. Squires, the consultant, I left the room that had been my home for the last 9 days. On the way out I said goodbye to the nurses and staff who had looked after me. I was given a copy of the discharge letter that was being sent to Dr Cotterell at Nene Valley surgery.

It was a beautiful summer day and it was such a relief to be in a car and on the way home. Ann was also relieved to be getting me back!

I think the hospital would have liked to keep me under observation for a few more days, because now if I had a problem I could no longer summon help at the press of a button!

The lawn had looked very scraggy when I left, but now it looked quite succulent and the new plants seemed well established. I was very tired, it was great to be back home and I looked forward to sleeping in my own bed.

On Friday morning I took the 4 pills that had been prescribed and was concerned that my BP still seemed high. It seemed to settle down as the morning wore on and I wondered about the accuracy of the two monitors I possessed, so Ann ordered a new state of the art digital device, but although it may accurately record the pressure it won't control it.

Saturday July 20th

I have now been home for a month and I am booked in for a CT scan on 31st July. It is boring as I was advised not to drive, so I can't go anywhere without a chauffeur. I am doing very little as I'm not allowed to lift anything, although I have done a few jobs in the garden to try and stop it drying out and attacked a few weeds. When I have the scan I will then have to wait up to two weeks for the results. I'm hoping that some treatment or procedure will be offered to enable me to resume an active lifestyle. I have cancelled my Red Sea diving trip and a holiday to Italy with Ann, and also a sailing trip to the Caribbean on a 60ft ketch.

I get very tired and tend to fall asleep within minutes of sitting down. If I have a more active day my blood pressure rises. I was told to keep the systolic around 120 or lower, but it often rises above that figure if I am more active.

My worry is that the consultant may recommend that I carry on as I am. I want to be able to drive and go on holiday again, also to go into the office to see everyone once or twice a week. It would be awful if I had to mope around like this for the foreseeable future, not able to do anything.

Teri is good and offers me lifts when she can, and I have been doing trips to garden centres with her. She has taken me out to lunch a few times. I have been accompanying Ann to the golf driving range, I watch her and make a few hopefully helpful comments, although I know very little about golf. I have designed a bracket to stand next to my .22 rimfire rifle, It's a semi-auto and ejects the spent shells out sideways, and they sometimes become a nuisance to the next shooter. If a hot cartridge went down the back of someone's neck they wouldn't be very pleased. This is only a problem if my stand is not the end one, as they would then just bounce off the end wall.

It would be nice to go to the rifle range, but handling the rifles would be too much weight for me at the moment. The .22 may be OK and I may take a trip to the air rifle range next week and have a go with my air pistols. That would be a nice break from the everyday monotony.

It is Ann's birthday on the 24th July, she will be 73. I had a trip out to Rushden Lakes shopping complex with Teri and bought Ann a necklace, not terribly expensive but quite nice.

Teri bought a pair of matching earrings. Teri loves birthdays and likes to buy several presents, some Jokey, and this time she had bought a Paint Yourself Gnome!

On the 24th I woke up at about 0700 and decided to make Ann a cup of tea, which I took up to the bedroom and then gave her the card and presents. In addition to the necklace I gave her a bottle of Chanel No. 5, her favourite perfume. She seemed pleased and happy, but with me not being able to drive, I was unable to do much more.

For dinner Ann suggested that we get fish & chips for everyone, as it would be a lot easier than doing a barbecue. It was a successful evening. Ann was pleased with her presents, the paintable gnome caused a laugh, and she liked the earrings that Teri had bought to go with the necklace. James gave her a trip to the Open golf tournament, which was a nice surprise. On Saturday we did a barbecue for the family. We had 13 people including Anne (sister) and Tony. It poured with rain, so we decided to eat in the dining room. I cooked the steaks on the barbecue and the other food was cooked in the kitchen. At about 930 the pool was full of shrieking laughter and lots of splashing and fun being had by most of the guests.

30th July

The weather over the last few days has been typical English summer weather, days of hot sun followed by days of thunderstorms, just as I remember as a boy, but the global warming catastrophists are prophesying doom and disaster every time there are a few hot days.

Tomorrow I am booked in for another CT angiogram on my aorta, and I was hoping for a meeting with the specialist to discuss my future, whether I need any more treatment etc, but apparently he is on holiday and I won't get to see him for two more weeks! I am managing my blood pressure OK and not driving or exerting myself, but two more weeks!

I haven't picked up a rifle for two months or done any exercise. I may do a trip to the rifle range on Saturday. Ann played golf today and came home very damp.

Friday 9th August

This morning I rang Leicester Royal Infirmary hoping to speak to Lesley, Mr Mike McCarthy's secretary. She was very helpful and explained that he was on holiday for the next two weeks but they had received the CT scan and would be fixing up an appointment for me to see him on 4th October, which is 8 weeks after the scan. I explained that at the moment my life was on hold and I was not driving, had cancelled holidays, was not lifting etc and she said she would get another vascular surgeon to give me a ring. I thought that would be the last I would hear from the hospital, but two minutes later a Mr Serami (I think that's how you spell it) rang and I had a good conversation with him, the main points being as follows:

– *The importance of keeping blood pressure low.*

– *Local driving probably OK.*

– *Holidays, nothing strenuous. I told him I had cancelled my scuba diving trip and my Caribbean sailing trip. He said walking was ok but not hill walking, and bungee jumping was definitely out!*

– *Heavy lifting out.*

– *Gardening with caution.*

– *Occasional drink to relax and lower BP.*

   –   *Nothing confrontational that would increase blood pressure.*

We had a general chat, and I think common sense is the main message. It's disappointing that I'm not going to have a face-to-face with a surgeon for two months to discuss the possibility of surgery, but the conversation I'd had with Mr Serami at least gave me a bit more freedom. Whether this is to be my future for the rest of my life, who knows?

Saturday 10th August

The Tadsac summer barbecue, hosted by Angela and James, both divers. The weather forecast was for heavy rain and gales, but luckily the rain didn't materialise although it was very windy and cool for a summer's day. It was a nice occasion, and the new members that came enjoyed a friendly atmosphere. Ann and I left at about 10 o'clock, but the party went on until about 0200 on the Sunday we'd decided to have lunch out, but after a shopping trip to Rushden Lakes decided against it.

Wednesday 15th August

Writing group. This year I have managed to produce a story most months. The theme for this month was "The Birthday", but there were only five of us at the meeting, most of the others being on holiday. My story was well received as usual, and we had a new member, Trish. She wasn't very confident and asked David to read her story, which was OK. I remember that when I first started I used to dread reading my story to the group in case it wasn't good enough!

Thursday morning was the photo shoot for the article in Business Times celebrating Cooney Marine's 50th anniversary.

I've not seen the text, it was written by Kieran and OK'd by James. I would have liked some input and just hope it will be satisfactory.

Saturday 17th August

We have the carpet cleaners in at Acre House, and they are making a bloody awful noise. Ann is playing golf. This morning I went to Barnwell rifle range for the first time since 11th June. when I became Ill. I found that the biggest problem for me was putting the targets up. The range is 100 metres long and it seemed an awful long way to walk quickly. Most of the other shooters are younger and I felt myself lagging behind. This wasn't really a problem, but I used to be as quick as the fastest.

28th August

I took Alan to Kibworth clay ground. I was using my Beretta semi auto and Alan my o/u. It was the first time I had been clay shooting since the illness. My Beretta weighs about 9lb, and I'm considering buying a lighter gun, as they are available at around 6lb. Alan did very well considering he had not shot for many years. I looked at a lightweight Winchester in the gun shop.

The new factory and offices project seems to be taking ages to sort out. The architect was supposed to apply for planning Feb/Mar and it should have all been sorted by about May, but we have overrun that date and the project seems no nearer. The council planning officer has asked for clarification on a few points, but is receiving no answers from the architect. This is unacceptable as I had hoped the building work would have been started by now.

The summer is now officially over, although the weather is still forecast to be pleasant a little while longer. I shall try and shoot more often and perhaps have some tuition to sharpen me up!

September 2ⁿᵈ

Ann and I went over to Simpson Bros. gun shop, where they had in stock a Caesar Guerini ultralight 12-bore I was interested in. I took my Beretta, hoping to do a part exchange deal. The C/G was a beautiful gun, it looked brand new and had done no work at all, the only problem was that when they inspected my Beretta it had a cracked stock and fore end, which made it worth a lot less than I had hoped. In the end I bought the C/G for £1180 and decided to make a trip to the clay ground to try it out.

Thursday 5ᵗʰ I took the new gun to Kibworth Shooting ground to try it out. The recoil was more noticeable than with the Beretta, but it pointed well. The only problem was that the safety catch came on each time I reloaded. This needed getting used to but I had some success on the targets.

I met a couple of the guys from the rimfire club. As I've been ill I haven't been that often for the last three months, but I intend to go more often now I am recovering (I hope).

The building project has moved on. We now have a surveyor who will hopefully complete the planning application, enabling us to start the project.

On Friday Ann had an important golf match that she didn't want to miss. I was about to get into the truck to go over to Kibworth to have another go with the new gun when the phone rang – it was James. Would I pick him up from his house in Northampton and take him to the doctors, as he was feeling ill and giddy and didn't think he was able to drive. He had an appointment at 11:15 with the surgery in Thrapston, as he had not moved to a Northampton surgery when he had moved house.

It was about 10:15 and I realised that it would be almost impossible to drive to Northampton and then back to Thrapston in the available time. I left straight away, but although I had a good run I didn't arrive at James's till about 10:50. When I picked him up he was very unsteady on his feet and I helped him into the truck. He rang the surgery and was able to postpone his appointment until 1130.

The nurse diagnosed an ear infection and gave him a sick note for 7 days and a course of antibiotics. She obviously didn't realise that when it's your business you can't afford to take time off! I then took James to the chemist to pick up his pills and then to Acre House, where he turned in. After a sleep he said he was feeling a bit better but felt hungry, so I cooked him steak and kidney pie, broccoli and cauliflower, which he hungrily polished off!

That evening was the Cooney Marine 50-year anniversary dinner and I was worried that James perhaps wouldn't make it, but luckily he recovered sufficiently to attend.

The dinner went off OK and James was able to make it. The Chinese restaurant was full besides the Cooney party and the staff seemed efficient. There were several speeches and some of the lads came and said what a wonderful place Cooney's was to work. I had a prepared speech that went down well.

The next morning I went to Kibworth to have another go with the C/G and Ann took James back to Northampton.

The writing group was at Cindy's house. Sheena, our usual host, and David, who sometimes hosts the meetings, were both away. Cindy lives near Teri and their houses are similar. My story "Through the Gate" was OK, but not one of my best. The next month's theme is even more bizarre and I can't rustle up any enthusiasm.

A busy week – Ann flew off to Portugal on Thursday 12th, the Southampton Boat show opened on the 13th and it was our 51st wedding anniversary on the 14th. I went down to Southampton on the 16th for the show. Ann was due back on the 17th and on the 18th it was the Cooney 50th anniversary drinks party, I managed to persuade her to come to the show, I had a double room at the Dolphin and James was coming down that morning.

The 3pm drinks reception was pleasant. The two Chrises from Cooney South and Keiron and Ian from international were there. Alex and Rose had organised the drinks and nibbles and it was a pleasant afternoon. We then want to Ennio's restaurant for dinne;, there were 10 of us, James's girlfriend Laura was there and it was a pleasant evening until the bill arrived. We'd been overcharged for a bottle of wine and 8 pints of beer, as well as the deposit paid to secure the table!

I stayed on until Friday, I found that standing for several hours a day was quite exhausting and my knees were protesting!

As Ann and I had not had time to celebrate our wedding anniversary we decided to do it on Sunday 22nd. Teri, Doug, Taylor and Casey came to dinner, and it was a happy occasion with the usual family banter.

As October approached I was looking forward to the new game shooting season, I had taken the Caesar Guerini out a few times and was getting used to it. I took Alan a couple of times, he likes the Beretta auto and had some success with it. I have claimed on the gun insurance for repairs to the Beretta. It seems a quite slow process, although I am in no hurry.

On the 4th October I had a meeting with Mark McCarthy, the consultant at Glenfield Hospital. I had had the last CT scan 8 weeks ago. I wrote to the insurance company re cancelled holidays, whether I could fly, drugs, progress etc.

On 19th October we had the first shoot at Kirby Hall, and seeing the shooting group was a happy occasion. On the first drive, I once again seemed to have one of the furthest pegs and the walk was tiring. I need to walk slower now and I was lagging behind the others. I had a super shot at a hen bird. I thought it might have been first bird of the day but it wasn't. It was a great shot though!

On the next drive after elevenses, once again my peg was one of the furthest away and I was unable to walk quick enough, so I decided to pack up and call it a day. This was a shame, as it was one of the most productive first days ever.

Friday was the Heritage Preceptory installation, and I had to install my successor into the chair. It was a good night, the ceremony went well and the only problem I had was inaccurate prompts, I knew the ceremony, having done it before. Knights Templar is my favourite Masonic order and this was my second time in the Chair.

I had invited James and Laura to the St. Crispin ladies' night on Saturday. I think Laura was a bit in awe of the occasion with all of the singing. It was a great night, and I even managed to get Ann on the dance floor to do the Gay Gordons and a Barn Dance!

November was uneventful. As we moved into December and preparations for Christmas, the weather was very cold. On 7th Dec it was the diving club Christmas dinner, which was pleasant enough, and on the 11th we had the writing group Christmas party. We all contributed to the food, I did pigs in blankets and Jean provided a cake, and there was a curry and rice dish and various other titbits. I look forward to the monthly meetings listening to the different stories. Some are very good, others are mediocre, mine included. I find it difficult to find inspiration for the chosen topic, although I have managed ten stories in 2019, only missing two months.

On 20th December we had the Cooney Marine Christmas party. There were 45 of us in the Thai Garden restaurant, and the food there is good. Ann, James, Austin and I arrived at 7pm. A lot of the lads had been in a pub since early evening and were plastered before arriving at the restaurant, but on the whole it was a good evening.

It was good to see most of the family over Christmas. I had to miss shooting on 28th December, as I was still suffering from a heavy cold.

On New Year's Eve, for the first time ever, we decided not to go out or have a party. We played pool and had a few games on the pinball machine, and after dinner we watched TV. The London fireworks were impressive as usual despite the usual inane interviews with spectators, but the New Year dawned with Ann and me in sober reflection. I wonder what 2020 will bring.

2020

22nd January 2020

This shooting season I have only been about three times. I had a chest infection that would not go away. The last shoot is on Saturday , in three days' time. I am looking forward to it and I hope the weather is not too bad. I am shooting OK with the Caesar Guerini.

Saturday 25ᵗʰ January

The shooting was OK. I managed to last the whole day and had some good sport. There is an extra shoot this year on 1st Feb. to celebrate Brexit, but I decided not to go.

11 pm on 31ˢᵗ January was when the UK officially left the EU. I expected a lot of celebrations, as it was a significant event in the history of the country, but the news coverage was subdued and the media seemed almost resentful of the fact that we were leaving. The massive party in Parliament Square, supported by hundreds of thousands of people who were joyful that the country is throwing off the shackles of the European Union, was poorly reported. Most of the news media appeared to be playing down the importance of the event and the Government was very low key.

Ann and I watched the proceedings on TV, expecting it to be reported as a joyous occasion almost like the end of the Falklands war with Mrs Thatcher's 'Rejoice, Rejoice' speech. I suppose the reason for the low key approach is that the Government don't want to upset the Remainers! Although I can understand this sentiment, the only way leaving the EU is going to succeed is by grabbing it with both hands and making it work.

I am looking forward to the January Figures. December was as usual a poor month with the holiday taking up almost a week of production time and Christmas bonuses to pay out. Customers generally are slow paying and we have to 'put them on stop' each month to get our money out of them.

February 15ᵗʰ

Ann and I flew out to Tenerife. The UK weather was dreadful with floods everywhere. The climate change doom mongers were saying we're all going to die and that carbon emissions are to blame for the unusual weather, although there was no evidence that this was the case. I remember in the early 1950s Bedford was flooded and in the 80s floods were everywhere with Thrapston High Street under water. It seems now that every time there is slightly unusual weather the catastrophists start whining about climate change. A few weeks ago there was a programme on the TV warning that the country was drying up and we're going to run out of water. It has rained every day since and it seems the country may sink!

Luckily our flight was on time, the storm didn't arrive until later in the day and by the time it struck we were basking in sunshine in the Canaries.

The weather in Los Christianos was like a good English summer, hot during the day with a cooling breeze, and it was comfortable to wear a cardigan during the evening. The hotel, H10 the "Big Sur", was similar to the one we stayed in last year in Gran Canaria. With buffet breakfast, and dinner it was possible to gorge oneself silly if required and some guests did just that.

I do miss the boat – I am not really cut out to be a tourist. The marina here seems to have a mixed bag of oldish boats, not very exciting. I would like to spend a lot more time in the sun, but a boat is not really practical. An apartment perhaps? We've done a couple of trips, one around Tenerife and one to La Gomera, which we have done before, and we have a boat trip to look forward to tomorrow hopefully to see dolphins and pilot whales.

February 17*th*

The pilot whales decided not to put in an appearance, although we did see a few dolphins. We were only about 1 or 2 miles offshore. It was nice to be at sea, if only for a couple of hours, and it was something to do to pass the time.

I have thought of buying an apartment, but I don't think Ann would be agreeable. There are some good deals being offered by the charter companies on yachts that pay an income and you have a few weeks' sailing with no costs other than flights and living expenses but I don't think I could persuade Ann to go for it.

I think I need to spend much more time away in the winter, but can't see a way forward at the present time

When it was time to come home, we wondered what was in store for us. A lot of flights had been cancelled due to sandstorms that have struck Gran Canaria and other islands. Tenerife didn't suffer too badly, although the airport was closed for a day and a lot of flights were cancelled. The bus was on time to take us to the airport, but when we arrived hundreds of people were milling around, many from the previous day's cancellations. We were told to go to the back of the queue, which stretched from one end of he airport to the other. It was hardly moving, but the Jet 2 staff were no help and appeared to be wandering around in a daze.

When we finally arrived at the check-in desk we were told to get through security as soon as possible, as the flight was due to leave. There were hundreds of people trying to get through security, and it was chaos, I think we were the last two people on the plane, which took off about two hours late. We were lucky, the other H2 hotel was on lockdown due to a coronavirus outbreak!

5th March

James is negotiating with a developer on extending the

Kettering factory. We originally had plans drawn up around 2006 and received planning permission, but now we have had to apply for planning and building regs approval over again and the planners are being difficult. We have planning, with just a few items to finalise, but it has been a very expensive exercise. I would like it to go ahead as soon as possible, but we now have the coronavirus panic causing uncertainty. The media are loving it, with doom-laden projections every day in the press, and I think that for a few months it will affect finance, I just hope our large customers aren't too badly affected. Our production is starting to take off again after a year or so of stability.

As Ann and I are over 70 and I have health issues, we are expected to avoid other people. Teri has done shopping for us and we saw James yesterday, it was Mother's Day and a pity we couldn't have a family get-together. We need to keep 2m or 7ft away from people. James stayed in the garden and we spoke to him through the French doors. Nobody knocks on the door, parcels are left in the front porch. It was a beautiful spring day today and to spend time in the garden made a nice interlude. I am exercising every other day.

The pool boiler is not working, an engineer is coming tomorrow, I hope. I have not been swimming, the water is too cold, so I hope it is fixed tomorrow.

23rd March

The Prime Minister is going to announce to the nation more restrictions regarding the covid 19 virus. Schools were shut today and also lot of restaurants and leisure centres, and people are being urged to work from home if possible.

24th March

Last night the Prime Minister announced more measures to try and stop the spread of the virus, including shutting all restaurants, pubs and places of entertainment and telling people to travel on public transport only if absolutely necessary. The only problem is that the London Mayor has reduced services and the remaining tube trains and buses are jam packed, making social distancing impossible. Although there will be financial help for those laid off, anyone self-employed or on zero hour contracts won't benefit. If they don't work they have no income.

I think our two companies will continue to work, but I wonder if our customers can continue. Today is Teri's birthday and we won't be seeing her as we are advised to keep away from everyone in case they infect us!

On the TV news there are pictures of hundreds of people queueing at supermarkets and panic-buying toilet rolls and essential items that they don't really need. I think it will settle down as soon as people realise that there are no food shortages and the empty shelves are only the result of panic buying.

Due to the coronavirus panic, Cooney Marine closed down at lunchtime. Local authorities sent everyone a text telling them to go home and James had a meeting with supervisors and managers where it was decided to shut both companies down for the time being. This is the first time in 51years that this has happened. The government have agreed to pay employees 80% of their salary/wages up to a maximum of £2,500 per month. this should help with employees, we have an excellent team and I wouldn't want to break it up. As far as suppliers are concerned, we are fairly up to date. The problem will be customers not paying us, although we are OK and with reasonable credit balances at the Bank.

25ᵗʰ March

The government have announced that the 'lockdown' will be enforced by the police. It's a bit boring but with the swimming pool, a large garden and a large house we are fortunate, and we have a good stock of a lot of necessities. America looks a lot worse off than UK with many more deaths. Italy seems to be the worst-affected European country. It's frustrating not being able to visit the supermarket, because when we were sailing one of the pleasures of coming home was the well-stocked supermarkets. One problem is some shops profiteering and taking advantage of the situation. I consider the Prime Minister to be doing a good job under the circumstances.

27ᵗʰ March

It was announced today that the Prime Minister has been diagnosed with the virus, He stated that he would run the country by telephone and video links, and he has asked the USA for ventilators. I think the USA are probably as short of essential equipment as the UK. Matt Hancock, the Health Secretary, and Chris Whitty, Chief Medical Officer, have also been diagnosed with the virus. I am concerned that Teri and James are vulnerable as they are more active, doing shopping etc, but they are sensible and taking practical precautions.

Karen, one of our neighbours, contacted us to say that her daughter is now working at Tesco, she starts at 0400 and works making up orders for delivery before the store opens. She could do shopping for us and deliver it in the afternoon. This was great for us as we felt guilty asking Teri or James to shop for us, putting them at risk.

It's been reported that over 500 people have died in the last

24 hours. There is no end in sight, and a vaccine will not be available for months. It is my birthday tomorrow, April 2nd. Shame I can't have the kids over, but we will have a party when restrictions are lifted.

I ordered a pack of seed potatoes and I dug one of the raised beds, if the spuds arrive I shall plant them straight away. I'm not really supposed to do digging in my condition but I feel very fit at the moment and I work out about twice a week.

Teri came over with Casey the morning of 2nd and stayed out in front of the house. They sang Happy Birthday and gave me a little cake, birthday cards and a present of a Jumper and some aftershave. It was sad that we couldn't have hugs all round, but nice to see them.

In the afternoon James and Laura came over and sat in the garden as Ann and I stayed in the house.

8th April

Today was the writing group meeting. We couldn't meet up because of 'social distancing' regulations but Terry suggested that we had a Zoom meeting with our iPads or PCs, and it went very well. There were seven of us and we all read our stories. As usual some were better than others, but I think Terry's was his best effort so far. I did a true story about the time we chartered a catamaran in the Caribbean with Alan and Karen, when one hull developed a leak and we had to beach it. I changed the names and the story went down very well. I enjoyed the meeting, but sadly Trish, Denis, Jean and Doris weren't able to join us. We plan on doing the same next month if the restrictions haven't been lifted.

I have planted some old seeds that I found in the greenhouse. They were several years old, so they may not germinate. I also *planted some potatoes, but they were not chitting before I planted them so I am not too hopeful.*

Boris Johnson was discharged from hospital on Easter Sunday, and I was relieved, because with the lockdown and industry at a standstill and the dreaded Brexit to finish off we need him back and firing on all cylinders.

The lockdown drags on. Ann and I are in our 4th.week. As we are over 70 we are both considered to be 'high risk' and are confining ourselves to the house. Shopping is not a problem, because Acorn Close, the small housing estate next to us, have a WhatsApp group which they have included us in to help with shopping. Teri is also shopping for us and collecting prescription items from the pharmacy. I have been sorting a few things out in the garden. Ann had a fall as she was pruning some bushes and has a nasty injury on her leg, so cannot help much at the moment although she did pressure-wash the putting green. We rarely use the green. It was a nice idea but it gets covered in moss and looks a mess most of the time.

Each evening there is a report by three Government ministers into the progress of the pandemic, followed by questions from various journalists. Most of the time it seems the questions are posed to show how clever the questioners are rather than to provide viewers with answers! This is tiresome, and then we have the BBC news and we have to go through the same rhetoric again. There is now a new Leader of the Opposition, Sir Keir Starmer, and they are now joining in with negativity and nonsense.

The lockdown is now carrying on for another three weeks. If it is lifted then I will be relieved, although until a vaccine is available it will still be unwise to socialise in large numbers.

I am anxious to get the furloughed employees back to work. Although the Government have stated that they will reimburse companies, the wages for *100* employees will soon decimate our company's finances. I wonder how our customers are faring – some were struggling with their cash flow before this disaster. Ann has now been to the surgery with her leg injury. They are very strict, no one is allowed in. You have to wait outside, knock on the window and wait until someone beckons you in a side door. The nurse dressed the wound and prescribed some antibiotics, which Teri picked up from the chemist and dropped in later.

25ᵗʰ April

The business is still shut down. The government furlough scheme started on Monday and apparently our claim was entered. We had plans to extend the factory and offices and were hoping to do it without resorting to a loan from the bank, but now those plans are shelved. I hope the planning will not run out and we don't have to apply afresh. This will cost a lot and it is so disappointing when everything was due to start in March and be completed this year.

On Saturday Teri organised a Zoom quiz. It worked very well with everyone staying in their respective homes. We could see five teams on the bottom of our iPad screen, it was a good laugh and went on for over two hours. I started the evening off by reading one of my writing club stories which went down very well. We rarely see Christian and Amber or Elliot and Austin, James's sons, although Austin works three days a week at Cooney's.

I am attempting to grow some vegetables, and I've bought some plug plants for beans and peas and planted a bed of potatoes. I don't think there will be a supply problem during *this pandemic as the government seem to be pretty well organised despite the negative press printing scare stories at every opportunity.*

The "lockdown" has now lasted about 4½ weeks and now people are tending to flout the rules somewhat. The weather has been unseasonably hot and parks are becoming full of people relaxing, mostly trying to observe social distancing.

At Cooney's the end of April is the end of the financial year and we have "unfurloughed" some of the staff to do stock taking. We've also had Ros. our health & safety lady in the office to work out social distancing measures for when we re-open. We also need a skeleton staff to complete urgent parts for Princess, who intend to re-start production imminently.

They plan to hit the ground running with a two-shift system to complete boats for the summer. We are discussing payment requirements, and everyone is trying to keep things moving. We should have the first of the government furlough payments in today.

In order to comply with the distancing measures we may also need to operate a shift system in order to keep the team together.

Sunseeker plan to resume production in mid May, so Cooney South are still closed. I am hoping that by the end of May things will be almost back to normal.
It seems from the media reports that as we progress from the lockdown the trade unions are determined to screw things up as much as possible. They are already making demands regarding working conditions to try and justify their existence!

8th May

Today is the 75th anniversary of VE Day. Most of the celebrations were muted by the fact that we are in lockdown.

Street parties that had been planned went ahead with people trying to maintain social distancing, and a lot were cancelled. Teri and family planned a party and put up bunting. There was a programme on TV showing the end of the war celebrations with patriotic songs and interviews with a few of the remaining survivors, all now in their late nineties and some over 100 years old.

The Queen gave a very good inspirational speech at 9 pm, which was the exact time when her father, King George VI, announced the end of the war, and she compared the war with the current pandemic crisis. Then there was a singalong led by Katherine Jenkins and Dame Vera Lynn, now aged 101. It was strange, a lonely Ann and me singing along in front of the TV when we should have been at a party.

A WhatsApp message came from Karen of the Acorn Close group inviting us to their street party. Ann declined, but I went over and had a glass of fizz and a chat with neighbours I rarely saw. We observed social distancing and It was a pleasant time and nice to escape the lockdown, if only for an hour or so. They are a nice crowd, mostly a lot younger than us, and had offered help with shopping etc. if required.

Saturday 9th May

Tomorrow, Sunday, Boris is expected to announce a relaxation of the lockdown measures. James has already re-opened the factory, they had 16 in last Monday and will be calling in more men to meet customers' requirements. I am hoping that we are now coming to the end of the restrictions and we can get back on with our lives. It's not been too bad for us. We are owed an enormous amount by customers and I am hoping that they all survive this crisis and don't default, because if they do then *we will have real problems. Before the crisis we had money in the bank to finance the new factory and office. I just hope we get paid!*

Thursday 14th May

Ann played golf today, the first time for 7 weeks. There has been an easing of lockdown rules. I drove to a garden centre but when I saw the queues I turned around and came home.

Monday 18th May

It's Anne, my sister's birthday, so we did an internet card as we're still supposed to be in lockdown, although it's easing and there is more freedom of movement.

The government seem to be losing some credibility regarding their approach to the crisis generally. Every move is dissected by the negative media, with opposition politicians gleefully highlighting any decisions that may not be popular.

They are now introducing a 14-day quarantine for all travellers entering the UK from abroad, a measure that should probably have been introduced 6 weeks or so ago, so it seems to be shutting the door after the horse has bolted. To introduce this measure now after thousands of travellers have passed through and the lockdown is now being eased appears futile.

The latest scandal now being hushed up is boatloads of illegal immigrants being escorted into our territorial waters by the French Navy, enabling them to be 'rescued' by the RNLI and UK Border Force. There is actual film and photographic evidence of this happening. Several hundred illegals are arriving every week, but the press are not allowed to report it! Tens of thousands of them are being housed in hotels around the country. The government seem impotent and unable to do anything to stop the tide of humanity invading our shores.

The rifle clubs and shooting grounds that I'm a member of are now opening in a restricted manner, trying to maintain social distancing, but I shall not be going just yet.

Some pubs and restaurants are trying to re-open, and I can see things are starting to get back to normal despite the various trade unions trying to stop people returning to work and cause the Government as much disruption as possible. A lot of people are now on the furlough scheme, so they're enjoying being paid to sit at home and are in no hurry to go back to work. The problem with any such scheme is that it is wide open to abuse.

Cooney's are starting to return to work with over half of the workforce back already, Cooney South are still not back yet as their main customer, Sunseeker, are not starting back for about another week.

Saturday 23rd May

Another quiz night, the fifth the family have done, and tonight I have another story to read, they seem to like them. I now have over 50 short stories, so I am not likely to run out before lockdown ends.

Wednesday 10th June

Tomorrow is the anniversary of my being taken ill with the aortic dissection. I seem in good health and I am trying to keep as fit as possible.

Last weekend was the funeral of George Floyd, a black man who died whilst being restrained by US police. There were enormous protests by the Black Lives Matter movement in the USA and also in the UK. The protests here got out of hand, with police attacked, statues vandalised and looting. The police did nothing and stood by as the anarchist mob rioted with impunity. Over 50 police were injured, some seriously, including a mounted woman police officer knocked off her horse. Several statues of historical figures were vandalised, including Sir Winston Churchill, and in Bristol a statue of Edward Colston was dragged from its plinth and dumped in the docks. There were also calls to remove the statues of Cecil Rhodes, Sir Francis Drake, Lord Nelson and several other historical figures. I cannot understand why the government is allowing this to happen. These left-wing anarchists jumping on the racist protest bandwagon are a disgrace and should be sorted out.

Ann is now playing golf three times a week. I have not started shooting yet, but I am going for walks, swimming, and exercising.

25ʰ June

It has been announced by the Government that a large part of lockdown is to be lifted, and pubs and some restaurants will reopen on July 24ᵗʰ, although some restrictions will remain. Gyms will stay closed and sporting events can take place providing there are no spectators. Several football matches have taken place, the teams all 'taking the knee' before kick off, and all wearing the Black Lives Matter logo on their shirts. I can't understand why intelligent people are bowing to this racist left-wing anarchist movement. Last weekend three white men were murdered by a Muslim terrorist knifeman and several others were injured. There have been no expressions of outrage in the media and anyone wearing a White Lives Matter T-shirt is branded racist – it is so one-sided. A banner bearing the White Lives Matter message was towed across Burnley football stadium by a light aircraft, just after the teams had knelt for

BLM. the people that organised it have all been sacked from their jobs and everyone involved branded racist!. This is so unfair.

I sat in on a Zoom meeting with Cooney South. So far they have about 9 people un-furloughed and are working hard to survive, as Sunseeker are not back yet and they owe us a fortune.

Chris Sleet, who now lives down there, told me that the beaches are absolutely choc a bloc with people, and they are far busier than normal weekends or holidays with all of the people still furloughed. When the pubs open on 4th July it will be mayhem for a few days, until the novelty wears off!

Saturday July 4th

It wasn't too bad, at least not around our village. Looking at news reports it looks as though a lot of people did let their hair down in town centres and holiday resorts. Most pubs tried to uphold social distancing, but when people are drunk they lose their inhibitions. I hope it does not cause another outbreak. It has been reported that in Leicester there are 1000 small companies that have been operating continuously making fashion garments with no precautions whatsoever. The employees are being paid £3.50 per hour, which is about half the minimum wage. Leicester has a high number of new cases of the virus and the city has been ordered to stay in lockdown for two more weeks. Most of the ethnics will ignore the ruling and then wonder why there is a higher percentage of BAME people with the virus!

6th July

I took my car in for a service, as in November I will have had it for three years, but due to the dreaded virus the Jaguar garage were not offering loan cars, so as they needed my car for most of the day Ann followed me there. Steve Hunt, the salesman I have dealt with for the last 25 years, ended up persuading me to change the car! He offered me a superb deal on a black XE with every extra imaginable, but I didn't like the colour. Another XE in French racing blue caught my eye, they were calling it the Reims edition and I was hooked! I wanted to transfer my personal number to the car, which took a few days for the paperwork to be processed.

The photo that Ann took of the two cars side by side with identical number plates was an opportunity not to be missed on the 15th July when we swapped over.

On Friday 24th it is Ann's birthday and on Saturday we are doing a barbecue. During the lockdown it was frowned upon to have social events, but as restrictions are easing we've decided to have a family party, to celebrate the birthdays that have been missed.

The overcast and threatening sky didn't bode well for the Saturday barbecue. We set out the tables outside, trying to observe social distancing. I'd bought sausages and burgers from the local butcher and Teri was bringing chicken kebabs. Everyone was due to arrive at about 5, although Teri and Doug arrived earlier to help set things up. The rain when it came was a steady downpour, so we moved everything inside. We had three seating areas to keep people apart. Then the sun broke through and it stopped raining, so we all then moved outside. Everyone was chattering and laughing and it was a happy time. Grandson Elliot and his girlfriend Mez didn't arrive until about 730, but that completed the party of 13.

James and I are considering whether to now start the factory *extension that we cancelled when lockdown was imposed on us. We have approx 80% of employees unfurloughed in Kettering and in Poole they are nearing 50% as Sunseeker resumes production.*

CHAPTER 15

Picking myself up, again

❤️

Production figures for **2020** were as to be expected. January and February produced a healthy profit, but March and April were loss months, which was no surprise as we were shut down due to the epidemic. A small profit was shown in May as we started to resume production and in June the profit was unbelievably good as we approached full production.

Cooney South figures were disappointing, but understandably so due to the fact that Sunseeker did not resume production until mid-July.

The management of South were working hard to pull in business from other sources and were having some success. They were doing some fabrication for the NHS and some super yacht parts for which our competitor was unable meet quality standards, so I was hoping they would show a profit in August. The government furlough scheme was a lifesaver for many companies, ours included, enabling us to keep our production teams intact. By mid-August we were able to unfurlough most of our employees in both companies.

2nd September

Ann and I visited Cooney South, who were now almost in full production, having pulled in a lot of fabrication work from a supplier to the NHS. It was made up of tables and stands but in large quantities. The factory had been laid out differently from the last time I'd visited and there seemed a buzz about the place. The employees I spoke to were thankful of the support that Cooney Marine had given them by keeping them in a job. Chris Sleet and Chris Elms have the company working efficiently and I hope profitably. We called in to see Ron and Kate and in the evening went out with the Cooney team.

The weather was miserable, overcast and cold, although we did go for a walk around Sandbanks. We stayed in the Harbour Heights hotel and it wasn't too bad, though due to the coronavirus precautions they were not making up the rooms and masks had to be worn in all of the public areas.

On the 3rd we took Ron and Kate out to dinner in the Lakeside fish restaurant, which was excellent. On the 4th we went to Bournemouth beach and in the car park a woman came over and accused me of damaging her new car with my car door. There was a tiny mark but it was almost too small to see and there wasn't a mark on my car. I gave her my name and phone number, but whether I will hear anything remains to be seen.

The service in the Cliff restaurant, which we chose for our last night, was exceptional and the food also was excellent. I wanted a place within walking distance of the Harbour

Heights, which was on a hill. Most of the restaurants were downhill, but the route to the Cliff was fairly level.

On 13th September we drove down to Hayling Island for a five-day break and to spend our 52nd wedding anniversary on the coast. The Langstone Quays hotel was very nice, the room excellent and we looked forward to a relaxing few days.

After unpacking we went for a walk around the Marina. A Moody 34 caught our eye, it looked very clean and the price, £30,000, looked reasonable, but even so I was surprised that Ann seemed so interested. As we wandered on and looked over at the boats afloat on the marina, a Beneteau 43 was on the end pontoon, the same as *Finesse*, our boat lost in Tortola. I felt quite emotional seeing what had been my lost dream. I seem not to have anything to look forward to now. Another boat is unlikely as Ann has lost interest and my health is not up to it.

Just before the dreaded lockdown we had been planning a factory and office extension, and in February we were about to start the project, but fears of impending doom and the lockdown persuaded us to put the project on hold, although there was enough money in the cash flow to finance the project.

With the easing of restrictions and almost in full production I considered that we could commence a slimmed-down development, so we told the developer to go ahead on the factory but to hold fire on the office until normality prevails.

On 18th September James and I gave the go ahead to start the factory and we should have contractors on site around mid October. James prepared a press release for the yachting press and local media. This should send the message to our customers and competitors that Cooney Marine is doing OK.

20ᵗʰ September

Just as I thought everything was returning to some form of normality, the Government have now decided that a new raft of restrictions is necessary. The daily totals of Covid infections are rising and there are fears of massive amounts of people being hospitalised. The problem seems to be that people are now ignoring the government guidelines and not social distancing, especially now pubs and restaurants are re-opening.

23ʳᵈ September

I'm hoping that there won't be another general lockdown. Businesses generally are suffering, but as long as we can keep the factories open and make a profit things should recover.

I am still exercising and swimming a couple of times a week and my fitness is reasonable. Walking I find difficult if it is uphill or on very rough ground. The first game shoot is due at the end of October and I am looking forward to it, but I need to practise. I have done some rifle shooting over the last couple of months, but no clay shooting.

Ann was due to go away on a short golfing trip on Monday 28ᵗʰ – she goes away two or three times a year with the golf club. She was travelling to Hereford with Dave and Sue, the friends we went to Thailand with last year, and I planned to catch up with my writing for a few days. I used to go on weekend diving trips from time to time but since becoming ill I have not been fit enough. Most of the trips have been cancelled due to coronavirus restrictions anyway.

While she was away I planned to treat myself with a small lamb joint and a couple of glasses of Châteauneuf du Pape.

What I hadn't planned to do was to fall in the bedroom and smash my head against the chaise longue. I realised I was bleeding profusely all over the bedroom carpet, and staggered into the bathroom to try and clean myself up. I managed to stop the bleeding by holding a pad over my damaged forehead and fell asleep for a few hours. Then I rang Teri and explained what had happened. She came over, saw the state I was in and immediately rang the surgery. During this pandemic surgeries are closed, but it is possible to speak to a nurse for advice. I spoke to Karen, who advised me to go to the Corby urgent care centre. Teri drove me there straight away, but they said they could not handle the Injuries and that I needed a CT scan to check for broken ribs etc, also a brain scan as I may have passed out and they were worried about concussion!

Teri then drove me to Kettering A&E and after asking me the same questions over and over they admitted me. This was about 1145. A doctor came to see me and he explained that I was to have a full body scan and the head wound would be cleaned out, glued together and then steri-strips would be applied and the wound dressed. I was told that the scans would then be sent to Glenfield Hospital for comparison with previous scans.

The scans were done, and every now and then a nurse would come and look at the head wound, shake her head and say that she was coming to sort it out in a few minutes. The doctors also said they were waiting for Glenfield to come back to them after inspecting the CT scan.

A nurse then came to say that they were still waiting for Glenfield to come back to them and I might have to stay overnight. She said she was going to do the head wound 'in a few minutes'. I was then told she had gone off duty and another nurse would be in charge!

At 1145pm a different doctor came to see me and announced that they had now spoken to Glenfield and everything was ok, in fact there was some improvement with the aorta dissection and I could go home – they would call me a taxi. I asked about the head wound, and he said I would be escorted to the entrance and a nurse would put on a dressing.

The nurse that took me to the entrance stopped en route and put a large plaster over my head wound. It was such a relief to be out of there, as staying overnight would have been a nightmare!

I'd told Teri not to tell Ann about the drama, as I didn't want to put a damper on her trip away, but I asked her to warn Ann on the Wednesday what to expect, as I looked as though I'd been fighting!

On the Wednesday Teri and my granddaughter Casey came over to attempt to clean the bedroom carpet, I'd expected it to need replacing, but they did a remarkable Job.

On Friday 9th October I was due for a CT scan at Glenfield Hospital., I still felt ill after my fall, with aching ribs and bruising down my right side, so Ann took me. It was all very efficient. Ann had to stay in a waiting area due to Covid, but everything went smoothly and on time. It seemed a lot less hassle than pre-Covid times apart from being six months late! *The long-awaited factory extension has now started. James negotiated the contract price down very well and it is a glimmer of good news among all of the bad. It looks like the pandemic is spreading at an alarming rate once again and there is talk of another lockdown, although I'm sure Industry will be allowed to carry on.*

Tuesday 13th October

I see that the company has made the front page of Boating

Business with a large picture of James and me with Peter Hubbard, the contractor tasked with building the factory extension. Most of the front page was taken up with a picture of James, Peter Hubbard and yours truly. I think it will send a positive message to the marine industry that Cooneys' are doing OK.

Friday 23rd October

While driving down to the factory for a meeting I hit a pothole in Henson Way that flattened my front and rear nearside tyres. I managed to reach the factory and on inspection found both tyres U/S and impossible to re-inflate. There was visible damage on the tyre wall and I had to have the vehicle taken to a tyre place for two new tyres to be fitted. This was annoying and very inconvenient, Ann had to take me home to pick up the truck while this work was done, as I had an appointment for a Covid test at the Woodlands hospital at 4 pm. I eventually picked up the car with two new tyres after parting with £507. I'm hoping to claim damages from Kettering Borough Council.

Wednesday 28th October

Had contractors in at home to clean floors in kitchen/sunroom and downstairs cloakroom. We are having the cloakroom refitted with new loo, wall units and redecoration with feature wallpaper, and I'm hoping to have it finished by Christmas. It has not been started yet, these things usually take longer than planned.

The pandemic seems to be getting worse by the day and various areas of the country are being placed in lockdown. This is bad news for the economy, and all sorts of different pressure groups are demanding government handouts. It's all very well but someone has to pay for this. The government has supported Industry with the generous furlough scheme and it is now becoming evident that over a billion pounds has been fraudulently claimed. I think the government were naive to introduce such a generous scheme so early in the pandemic. If there's a way to commit fraud there is always a section of the population that will take advantage.

The pound appears to be holding its own against other currencies, which I suppose have their own problems, but it can't go on forever with the government doling money out so freely.

It was stated in yesterday's news briefings that a vaccine could be available by Christmas and that the government has purchased millions of doses. It needs to become available as soon as possible. All the time they are dragging their feet and discussing it people are becoming infected and dying!

5th November

We will certainly remember this 5th November, because the government has placed the country in lockdown again! The difference this time is that manufacturing businesses can remain open. There are numerous conspiracy theories and a lot of nonsense is being bandied about by the media. Boris is doing his best with the information his advisers are giving him.

The US election seems to put Joe Biden as the clear winner of the US presidency and a lot of anti-Trump Brits are celebrating. What they don't realise is that Biden is a left-wing socialist and is anti-Brexit and an IRA sympathiser and no friend of Britain. It will be interesting to see how things develop over the next few months. It was reported in the US media that the firework displays on or around 5ᵗʰ November were to celebrate Biden's election win! They have probably never heard of Guy Fawkes.

Boris Johnson has now announced that there will be a massive increase in renewable energy. Thousands of wind turbines will be erected on land and in the seas around our coast and the number of solar parks is to be increased in an effort to reduce or even do away with power generation by fossil fuels. I think this must be the influence of his fiancée, who would like to see the world through green-coloured spectacles. Apparently the fossil fuel companies are backing this policy. Renewables in use at the moment are wind or solar, both unreliable, and wind turbines only work less than 30% of the time, many of them 10% or less. Solar parks in the UK only work approx 5 hours a day in the summer and only 1 hour per day in the winter unless covered in snow, when they don't work at all! Due to their unreliability, renewables need 100% back up by other sources, ie fossil-fuelled power stations. The only power that is totally emission free, safe and cheap is nuclear power, but the greens are totally against this and this is why the fossil fuel companies support them.

The new factory extension is now well under way and the first stage payment is becoming due, though James has a few issues with the bill.

The government is in disarray. and two of Boris's top advisers have walked out. I am now concerned that as two of his main Brexit advisers have left, he may give in to Europe's demands.

The steelwork for the new factory extension is being erected this week if all goes according to plan, and it should soon start to look like a building.

It's a relief that November is drawing to a close. Another month in lockdown and then we go into the tier system, which looks like it may be as bad or worse than lockdown. I think 2020 will have a special place in history as the year like no other, the year when a virus brought the country to a standstill, wrecked the economy and saw a lot of normal people acting like spoilt children. Christmas will not be as normal with restrictions on numbers of people allowed to mix. I don't think everyone will comply, Ann and I are undecided, both of us being in a high risk group.

We are having a pond constructed in the garden, so we have mud everywhere, although it will look good when finished. It's made a dreadful mess of the lawn with the workmen traipsing up and down with barrowloads of earth.

Monday 21st December

What a year this has been. Christmas has now been cancelled and the French have stopped all transport and visiting from the UK because of a new strain of Covid. I feel sorry for the truck drivers stuck in massive tailbacks with no facilities for hygiene, toilets or catering. There are prophecies of doom and disaster from so-called scientists and the government is being blamed for everything, including the weather.

On the bright side our two companies are doing remarkably well and I am looking forward to the new year and whatever Brexit we end up with. I am optimistic for the future and looking for the opportunities the difficulties will bring.

The French have closed the border and Dover has 10,000 lorries gridlocked for miles around, the reason given being fears of a new strain of Covid. It looks as if literally thousands of drivers will be stuck in their vehicles over Christmas with no facilities.

This appears to be due to a massive overreaction by the French president. It is thought that this is a ploy by France to make the UK give ground in the Brexit negotiations. My thoughts are that this situation may well harden the UK position and be a dress rehearsal for a no deal scenario.

Thursday 24th December

With self-congratulatory smiles and a Churchillian-style speech, the Prime Minister has announced that a deal had been agreed between the EU and the UK. He claimed that at last we were free of Europe's stranglehold, and could go out into the wide world to win trade deals anywhere. Parliament would be recalled to debate the bill between Christmas and new year.

Christmas was a subdued affair, the new Covid regulations forbidding parties of more than three families. Ann and I went to Teri's and we were within the "rules", but it wasn't like a normal Christmas. Normally we have all the family around on Boxing Day and do dinner for about 14, but to stay within the rules we just had James, Laura and the boys. It was a happy occasion but we missed seeing everyone.

New Year's Eve, 29th December

The Brexit divorce bill is now all signed up and we are leaving. The biggest problem is that the UK have agreed to still pay billions into the EU on a sliding scale until 2064, and this is a considerable amount, as the net cost to the UK is somewhere in the region of £33 billion!

There are no New Year parties, apart from a few Covid deniers and protesters. Gordon next door had planned for fireworks but cancelled at the last minute. We just watched TV and at midnight there was a display in London, but it was political and heavily PC themed. There were even drones showing a BLM closed fist salute. Most people turned it off in disgust.

The Covid vaccine roll-out started in December and in our area most over 80s have had their first Jab, with another promised 21 days later. It was trumpeted in the news that now the Oxford vaccine is available two million people a week will be vaccinated by the end of January. Now they have announced that there are supply problems, so people will now not receive their second jab, but instead more people will get the first jab to make the vaccine go round! The vaccine suppliers are claiming that they have adequate stocks for the 2 million jabs a week to go ahead, but it seems that the inefficient, over-unionised, NHS can't get their act together.

2021
4ᵗʰ January

The country is now being plunged into more severe lockdowns. The new strain of the dreaded Covid is supposed to be more severe than the existing virus, although the current vaccine is supposed to work just as well. The task now is to vaccinate as many people as possible, so vaccination centres should be working 24 hours a day 7 days a week. In the news one elderly person was seen being injected with the vaccine amid much fanfare and self-congratulation by the medics involved. It would be nice to see someone in charge of the vaccine roll-out making it happen instead of making excuses why it isn't.

The factory should re-open tomorrow, I hope it goes ahead, we have the orders and our customers are desperate for supplies, but with the threat of another lockdown it could all come crashing down again.

The Prime Minister has said that he will make an announcement at 8pm regarding the current situation. We are now in lockdown again, even golf courses and shooting grounds are closed. This lockdown seems to be similar, if not worse, than the last one. Luckily the factory can remain open, so as long as our customers keep producing boats we will be ok. We have two building projects on the go at the moment. One that should have been started yesterday is now not starting until Friday. This is an extension to the machine shop to enable us to move the stores into the extension and leave more room for extra machines.

16th January

I had my Covid vaccination today, and it was well organised, Ann drove me down to the surgery and we were directed to a car park and then I walked down to the vaccination centre, I went straight in, had the jab and was directed to a seating area in a tent, where I had to wait for 15 minutes to ensure that there was no adverse reaction. I was back in the car within half an hour. All in all it was a slick operation. The government is trying to ramp up the vaccination program and have stated that they want all over 70s done by the end of February. There is some opposition to the scheme and apparently a lot of doctors are refusing to work more than four days a week, but the nurses and paramedics are working 12 hours a day.

23rd January

Ann had her first Covid vaccination today. Whereas I had the Pfizer vaccine, she had the Astra Zeneca. I think they both give the same level of immunity, but I am concerned at the 12-week wait for the next dose. There is controversy in the press, as some of the vaccination centres are jabbing people with the left-over vaccine instead of throwing it away. The NHS is saying this is wrong, people in the age group must be vaccinated and any excess thrown away! This to me seems madness when the Government wants to vaccinate as many people as possible to achieve immunity and seems to sum up the bureaucratic NHS. They would rather throw away left-over vaccine than see it used to immunise as many people as possible.

The new factory building is well on the way to completion. Yesterday the floors were being poured and the contractors were working through the night to get it finished. Completion date is March some time, but with the progress they are making I think it could be earlier.

The lockdown drags on. Luckily our two companies are working flat out. Money is difficult to get out of customers, but we keep the cash flow going by a regime of supply when paid which works well.

Sunday 24ᵗʰ January

It snowed most of the day and on Monday morning the driveway had a 4" (100mm) carpet of snow. Our Tesco delivery never turned up. We had a message to say that it was delayed, it was due between 5pm and 6pm. We waited up until 1130 but it didn't arrive, so Ann looked online and it said it had been delivered! Ann rang the helpline and was told that they had cancelled the delivery but we would receive a refund. The next available delivery was 2 weeks hence.

3ʳᵈ February

The UK have now vaccinated around 10 million people and

we're on target to have jabbed all of the most vulnerable by the middle of February. The EU have only vaccinated about 1.5 million people, and have not ordered sufficient vaccine. They are now trying to stop vaccine that has been ordered and paid for being exported from Belgium, even to the degree of closing the border with Northern Ireland. The UK government has assured us that everyone in the UK should have been offered the vaccine by August, the only fly in the ointment being Scotland where their incompetent First Minister is causing problems and their vaccination levels are far behind the rest of the UK.

Although there is a lot of self-congratulation regarding the UK roll out, I am puzzled by the fact that the surgery where Ann and I were jabbed is not doing any at the moment. One gets he impression that the vaccination centres are working 24 hours a day to get on top of the problem.

Today is grandson Taylor's 18*th* birthday, but with all of the lockdown regulations we cannot have a party as such. Teri is doing a cake and bringing some pizzas over and we'll give him his present, a large cheque. After the Covid nightmare everyone is looking forward to the time when we can all meet up without fear of catching the disease or being arrested!

25th February

The month drags on, or should I say the year drags on. There has now been an announcement by the Prime Minister regarding the easing of the current lockdown, but it will be May before there is any return to normality with pubs, restaurants and sporting venues back to normal. I don't think we will be going on our rail trip to Lake Garda in June as with Europe's shambolic vaccine roll-out, Italy will still be considered unsafe.

There is some light at the end of the tunnel. The factory extension at Telford Way is progressing and the moving-in date fast approaching. We plan to extend our large fabrication facility into the new build with a design office one end. It has not been decided which department will move up to the large mezzanine. The new space should coincide with an increase in business caused by a competitor deciding to give up on boat work and our two main customers ramping up production.

The government managed to achieve the target of 15 million people vaccinated by the middle of the month, a remarkable achievement, and because of this success, Boris was able ease some of the restrictions going forward. But it would now appear that the vaccination programme has slowed down, with only half the number of people being jabbed each day. A large proportion of the BAME community are reluctant to accept the jab, which is surprising as this section of the population has a large number of Covid sufferers.

Pubs will be allowed to re-open and serve people outside on 12th April and fully open on 17th May. I fear that many pubs may go out of business, especially those without a garden.

25th March

I had my second jab today – I was slightly surprised as there has been a lot in the press regarding the shambolic vaccine roll-out in Europe and over there they have now brought in laws forbidding European countries to export vaccine supplies. This is largely due to resentment of the UK, which has successfully vaccinated over half the adult population and is on course to have vaccinated everyone by June. The EU have vaccinated less than 10% of their population and seeing the UK figures each day of over 500,000 jabs and over 30 million people vaccinated makes them green with envy and determined to punish the UK for their success.

Tomorrow, Friday 26th, is the handover of the new factory extension. I thought that perhaps they would ask a local celebrity to the handover with a press release for the various business publications, but I think it will be a low key affair.

The extra space will enable us to double our capacity for producing large fabrications and re-site the products department design office.

All our customers are busy, but with the Covid travel regulations, marinas are becoming overcrowded and I worry that the boat builders may soon have to slow down with nowhere to dock their finished boats. This will be a big problem with Europe now going into a third lockdown and with their vaccine shambles it could be months before they are back to any semblance of normality. The sad thing is that it is reported that they have millions of doses in stock but seem unable to get them from their refrigerators and into the arms of their people. The weather is a touch milder and yesterday I was able to plant my first batch of potatoes. I miss my trips to the Caribbean, the winters here seem to last for ever and the summers are gone in the blink of an eye.

2nd April

It's my birthday today, 77 years old. I had a card from my sister Anne, and my wife Ann gave me a card and a couple of presents before she went off to pay golf. James came over with Laura, his partner. Due to the Covid restrictions we are allowed to have only six people together in the garden, but eventually most of the family came over and we had a most pleasant afternoon. Christian brought me some fish for the new pond. I had hoped that someone would buy some fish, although it was probably difficult to know what to choose.

The pond has been a success. We now have 12 fish, and as soon as I am more confident that they will survive I will buy some more. The surrounding grass is now growing. It's a bit patchy, but it is still early in the year and cold as we await some spring sunshine.

10th April

Yesterday the media were full of the sad news of the passing of the Duke of Edinburgh. He was 99 and had been ill for some time. There were tributes from around the world for a man who has been the support for the Queen and an example to us all for the last 70 years.

Teri and Doug have today been trying to heron-proof the pond. Ann ordered some floating net sections to be placed around the edge, and these are supposed to stop herons from wading into the pond to take the fish. There is a heronry a couple of miles away and apparently the birds treat people's ponds as their local take-away! We've had one lurking round the pond and I've chased it off a couple of times. The first time it appeared I thought how nice it looked, strutting around as if it owned the place. Ann borrowed a plastic heron from her friend at the golf club, but the real one soon got used to the imposter and simply ignored it.

13th April

A pair of ducks have taken up residence. They sit around on the lawn in the sun or splash around in the pond, totally ignoring me as I potter around the garden.

Last Christmas James bought me a trail camera. I had a pole made up so that I could set up the camera to record the wildlife around the pond. It has a motion detector that triggers still pictures, short video clips and Infra red to capture goings-on during the night. There is a lot of heron activity mainly in the morning or evening as they stalk around the pond looking hungrily at the heron guard, it seems to be working so far! Sometimes we get a large crow waddling round and a Red Kite sometimes pops in for a bath.

The extension on the machine shop is taking shape. It was decided to build an area on the end of the building to house the stores, enabling the area of the machine shop previously used for this purpose to house a large VMC (vertical machining centre) and make room for a new CNC lathe. When all our plans materialise we will probably be the most high-tech company in the marine industry, especially when we increase our oval tube manufacturing capacity. Oval tube guard rails are now becoming popular on the larger power yachts and super-yachts, and we are the leaders in this field with our oval tube manipulating capacity. We are now obtaining plant for manufacturing oval tube to highly accurate dimensions.

With the new factory extension and the extended machine shop, we need to recruit more people. The biggest problem is polishing, because the polishers are earning a lot on piecework and are reluctant to assist in training anyone else because it might water down their earning power.

The year-end figures show that last year we had record turnover in both companies. Surprisingly, quite often when general industry struggles, we do well!

The heron guard appears to be working. The herons still stalk around, but so far the floating plastic sections are doing their job. The grass round the pond perimeter is now growing and the pond is beginning to look very attractive as the planting becomes established.

I removed the plastic heron and returned it to Suzy, Ann's friend. I don't think it made any difference to the herons, which just ignored it!

11th May

I couldn't believe my eyes on checking the trail camera. It showed the heron stalking around the pond, then suddenly taking off and diving in. It emerged with a struggling fish in its beak and then flew onto the pond edge and proceeded to eat the poor thing. This behaviour was totally unexpected, as everything I'd read about herons' eating habits stated that they wade into the pond edges, where they take fish using their long necks. Nowhere does it report that the birds actually dive into the water to take fish. This is more like the way a pelican would hunt. So the so-called heron guard doesn't work as advertised!

31st May

I over-ordered and had a lot of sections of heron guard over, so I was able to cover all of the surface, hoping this would give protection. This seemed to work for a couple of days, but then another fish was seen to be taken, one of the larger ones. The bird stood brazenly eating it in front of the camera, and I realised that the only way to stop them was to completely cover the pond with a net. Various net systems are available for ponds and we bought some nets, but they all seemed difficult to rig up without sagging into the water and looking a mess. Ann eventually found one on line that had adjustable poles, a bit like a tent. I had my doubts, but we have now fitted it and I'm hoping it will keep the hungry "vultures" out.

May was a bitterly cold month and we looked forward to flaming June. I'd decided to have a lift fitted in the house. I was hoping to have one fitted when the house was built, but costs were escalating and the house cost far more than our original estimates and at the time a lift was the last thing we needed. We had several estimates from different companies and although not the cheapest had decided to go for a Stiltz lift. The original plan was for it to be fitted in the hall downstairs ascending into the first floor airing cupboard.

I contacted the architect who designed the house and he brought over a drawing of the first floor, which is a solid concrete beam and block construction, but he thought this area would not be suitable due to the position of the steel beams.

When the Stiltz surveyor attended it was decided to site the lift in the front lounge so that it would rise up to the hall on the first floor. We first started looking at lifts in February with the order being placed in March, and the actual construction is due at the end of July. I hope it goes ahead. It seems difficult to speak to anyone at Stiltz and they often give the impression that different departments have no idea what has been agreed about who is doing what.

June 21st was supposed to be Freedom Day with the lifting of the coronavirus restrictions, but it didn't happen as there was a new variant of the disease. Pubs and restaurants were allowed to open, but with restrictions; social distancing had to be observed and masks had to be worn except when eating or drinking.

The lift that I'd ordered months ago was eventually completed around the middle of August without too much disruption, although it looks ugly and the room will need some re-decoration

28ᵗʰ September 2021

We have had the sad news that Ron, Ann's brother, passed away last night. He had been very ill for a long time and for the previous few months had suffered awfully. Kate, his wife, has been caring for him, with not a lot of help from the NHS.

It was Ron who in 1972 introduced me to John Sadler, who was building the Sea Wych sloop in workshops in Grendon Underwood. Meeting Sadler was the start of my manufacturing stainless steel marine products

Travel restrictions are being eased, although every day in the press there are horror stories of travellers being subjected to some indignity or seemingly unnecessary inconvenience. To escape the British weather is almost a dream, but the thought of queueing for hours in overcrowded airports makes the dream seem more like a nightmare.

Without a boat and the freedom that this enables, the options for foreign adventure are limited. An apartment somewhere warm would be an option, where we would not have to worry about the weather and be warm all the time.

A boat is a good option for a 'place' in the sun. A vessel of around 38-40 feet (15m) with fore and aft accommodation could be purchased for the fraction of the price of an apartment, and the berthing or marina fees would probably cost no more than an apartment service and maintenance charges. There would also be the advantage of being able to change to a different marina, or even a different country, if circumstances changed.

Although vessels in the Caribbean are often half the cost of craft in Europe or the UK and are VAT free or exempt,

I think there could still be a case for buying in the UK and shipping the boat to the favoured destination. One advantage is knowing the market and being able to ensure that engines and equipment are all serviced and in tip-top condition, and of course for sailing vessels there is the ARC, which departs each November from Grand Canaria, often 200+ boats heading for paradise!

The ARC is the culmination of many sailors' dreams and is the largest Trans Ocean sailing event in the world. The organisers ensure high levels of safety with seminars dealing with all aspects of shipboard living for the 2700-mile trip from Gran Canaria to the Caribbean.

The trade wind route gives the opportunity for days of exciting downwind sailing and a chance to experience life at sea for an extended period.

For most people deep-sea sailing is just a dream, as it was for me all those years ago in '99 with Dennis Knight and our "55" club.

Berthing a boat across the Channel has the advantage of warmer weather and cheaper marina costs, but this is a summer option – it can be very cold in winter even on the Costa Brava, and the travelling involved is inconvenient for weekend sailing.

Cooney Marine International is going from strength to strength, especially the capacity for manufacturing oval tubular products. We are investing heavily in plant for manipulating larger ovals, which we can now produce – at the moment there is not another stainless steel manipulator that can produce quality Items in the larger sizes.

The deal is done – contract signed for building a 10,000 sq, ft, Factory extension at our Telford Way site.

The Caribbean is for me the ultimate sailing destination. In the season there is always a good wind and it's warm all of the time. The weather never seems too bad when you're in shorts and T-shirt. Various options are available, Flotilla sailing is a good way to start, Flotillas offer informal, relaxed cruising with a lead crew to guide you to the various bays and harbours, and if required a skipper can be provided.

Bareboat charter is another good way to experience an unfamiliar area, and monohulls, catamarans and power boats are available. Many people in small boats have a fear of being out of sight of land, whereas I consider being at sea is in many ways safer, as there are far more dangers around the coast than out at sea.

Looking to the future, with dreams of dolphins and flying fish.

As this book comes to a close in late 2021, I wonder what adventures lie in store. It would seem that flying and travel generally will soon be back to normal. I hope to soon revisit the places which hold so many memories and who knows, perhaps, rekindle my enthusiasm for another boat. Perhaps this time it will be third time lucky after having boats hit by Hurricane Ivan in 2004 and Irma in 2017, during which Finesse was a total loss.

If I acquired another boat, sailing a trade wind passage with twin headsails set heading for the endless horizon and hopes of an exciting landfall, accompanied by dolphins diving in the bow wave and flying fish skimming the wave tops, may no longer be just a dream.

D X 52 Y N D Z D M 4K.